ITALY AND AUSTRALIA:
An Asymmetrical Relationship

ITALY AND AUSTRALIA:
An Asymmetrical Relationship

Edited by
Gianfranco Cresciani and Bruno Mascitelli

Connor Court Publishing
Ballarat

Published in 2014 by Connor Court Publishing Pty Ltd
Copyright © Gianfranco Cresciani and Bruno Mascitelli 2014

ALL RIGHTS RESERVED. This book contains material protected under International and Federal Copyright Laws and Treaties. Any unauthorised reprint or use of this material is prohibited. No part of this book may be reproduced or transmitted in any form or by any means, electronic or mechanical, including photocopying, recording, or by any information storage and retrieval system without express written permission from the publisher.

PO Box 224W
Ballarat VIC 3350
sales@connorcourt.com
www.connorcourt.com

ISBN: 9781925138023 (pbk.)

Cover design by Ian James

Printed in Australia

CONTENTS

Acknowledgements	iii
Abbreviations and glossary	v
Tables and Figures	viii
Preface (Richard Bosworth)	ix
1. Italy and Australia. Different Origins – Different Strategies (Bruno Mascitelli)	1
2. Italo-Australian Cultural Relations after the Second World War: The Case of the Frederick May Foundation for Italian Studies (Gianfranco Cresciani)	39
3. The Anglo-Italian Treaty. Australia's Imperial Obligations to Italian Migrants, 1883-1940 (Catherine Dewhirst)	81
4. Australian-Italian Relations in World War I. The Italian Consul-General and the Australian government (Karen Agutter)	115
5. Mussolini's Australian Campaign of 1935-1936 (Gerardo Papalia)	145
6. Australia-Italy: A not so "Special" Trade Relationship (Bruno Mascitelli)	177
7. Exploitation, emigration and anarchism: The Case of Isidoro Alessandro Bertazzon (Gianfranco Cresciani)	211
Conclusion	285
Biographical Notes	289
Index	291

Acknowledgements

The editors of this book aim to set straight some aspects of the Italian-Australian relationship. The aim to clarify the relationsip between these two countries is in part because relationships evolve, as they have, between Italy and Australia, and in part because they have been inadequately documented and analysed. We are mindful that in both cases we have only scratched the surface and hopefully with this book, other similar projects will follow.

The idea of such a book owes much to a pleasant late afternoon lunch at an Italian restaurant in a Sydney beachside suburb in September 2012 between the editors and two inspirational individuals who provided invaluable ideas and enthusiasm for this book to see the light of day. These two individuals, Rory Steele and Paolo Totaro, in their own way have contributed partially to these stories and history of Italian-Australian relations. We are also honoured that Professor Richard Bosworth, who is one of the prominent voices on Italian-Australian relations not only provided the preface to this book but also took the trouble to review each chapter and give significant feedback for its improvement. These recommended changes were undertaken and readers can now read a complement of chapters on different aspects of the Italian-Australian relationship.

We are clearly indebted to the authors for being succinct, precise and timely in their writings and we believe that readers will be impressed by the quality and scholarly output of these chapters. Without doubt we have certainly missed areas worthy of further research and study. While we must apologise for this from the outset, the scope of the book was very specific and all projects have their limitations and restrictions. We also have to thank Connor Court Publishing who did not blink an eyelid once they heard the theme of the book and the authors involved. It was their stamp of approval that is appreciated.

While we, as editors, have sought to ensure the correctness and fairness of the commentary by the authors, the ultimate responsibility for the content presented in each chapter is that of the authors.

The Editors, December 2013

Abbreviations and glossary

ABC	Australian Broadcasting Corporation
AIF	Australian Imperial Forces
ALP	Australian Labor Party
ANZAC	Australian and New Zealand Army Corps
ASIO	Australian Security Intelligence Organisation
CALD	Culturally and linguistically diverse communities
CGIE	General Council of Italians Abroad
CIB	Criminal Investigation Branch
COASIT	Comitato di Assistenza Italiano (Italian Committee of Assistance)
COMITES	Committees of Italians Abroad.
CPC	Casellario Politico Centrale (Central Political Records Information System).
DC	Christian Democratic Party
DFAT	Department of Foreign Affairs and Trade
DIAC	Department of Immigration and Citizenship
DILGEA	Department of Immigration, Local Government and Ethnic Affairs
DIMA	Department of Immigration and Multicultural Affairs
DLP	Democratic Labor Party
EEC	European Economic Community
FDI	Foreign Direct Investment

FILEF	Federation of Italian Workers and their Families
FOI	Freedom of Information
ICE	Istituto per il Commercio con l'Estero (Italian Trade Agency)
ius sanguinis	meaning the right to claim one country's citizenship through ties of blood with a citizen of that country.
ius soli	meaning the right to claim one country's citizenship in virtue of the birth rights in the given country's national territory.
IWW	Industrial Workers of the World
MAE	Ministry of Foreign Affairs (Italy)
MESCI	Monash University European Studies Centre Italy
NAA	National Archives of Australia
NATO	North Atlantic Treaty Organisation
NBN	National Broadband Network
OVRA	Opera Volontaria Repressione Antifascismo (Voluntary Organisation for the Repression of Anti-Fascism)
PCI	Partito Comunista Italiano (Italian Communist Party)
POW	Prisoner of War
SME	Small and Medium Enterprises
SISA	Società Italiana di Studi Australiani (Italian Society of Australian Studies)
UK	United Kingdom

UN	United Nations
US	United States of America
USCIS	United States Citizenship and Immigration Services
USSR	Union of Soviet Socialist Republics

Tables and Figures

Tables

Table 1.1 Australian-Italian ambassadors serving in Rome and Canberra (1949 onwards)

Table 6.1 Australian trade with Italy, 1950–2012 (in $A 000's)

Table 6.2 Italy trade with Australian States, 2007-2008

Table 6.3 Australian trade with selected countries, 1950/51-2004/05 (in 000's)

Table 6.4 Milan Consulate General (Trade post) – 1968 onwards

Table 6.5 Italian Exports to Australia in 2012 – Top six products

Table 6.6 Australian Exports to Italy in 2012 – Top six products

Table 6.7 Stock of Foreign Direct Investment in Australia by Country, 2011

Figures

Figure 6.1 SME international country export ratio comparison: 1999

Preface

R.J.B. Bosworth

What exile could be more intellectually gilded than mine, safe in the arms of Jesus College, Oxford? And who could be more grateful that I, who have devoted my life to being a historian of modern Europe, will live out the years of the sere and the yellow leaf away from the Australia that nurtured me, gave me an undergraduate education and then allowed me for four decades to teach its own splendid undergraduates, while occasionally escaping on research forays to Europe? That was an Australia that was, however. For, in very many aspects, Australia in 2013 is further away from Europe than it was when I first studied modern Europe in the wonderful course taught by the refugee from Nazism, Ernest Bramsted, at Sydney University in 1962.

No doubt the plane trip now takes twenty-four hours or less when once it took much more. No doubt, in a globalised world (shorthand for neoliberal hegemony in the "end of history"), every serious country pursues per force the same economic line. No doubt, modern technology allows the news from Rome or Berlin or Bucharest or Bukhara to float across my computer screen at a simple command. It might even be conceded by some that the Australian population is in large part still "European", as are its culture and major institutions, at least in their first formation. Although the way the Senate is elected or the domination of the media by Mr. Murdoch and his epigones might raise doubts, Australia remains a parliamentary democracy, following the Westminster system, British law, speaking English as the "national" language, and possessed of bankers and businessmen whose world views are not so distinct from their European colleagues.

Yet there are also many factors that have distanced Australia and Australians from Europe. Since first prompted by Hawke and Keating (the latter ironically pushed by a perverse Irish version of Australian nationalism), successive Australian governments have accepted the rules of neoliberalism with greater alacrity than have most Western European countries. The latest reckoning of the percentage of its GDP spent on the state is 34.3 against the figures in France or Sweden which stand above 50 per cent, while even "Thatcherised" Britain has a projected total of 44.4 per cent for 2013-4. Australia may not quite yet be a mixture of Texas and Dakota in its social policies and attitudes, as I sometimes jokingly claim it is. But it does move in that direction. Presumably that is what Rupert Murdoch was celebrating when, in his recent Lowy lecture, he gloried in the defeat of "elitism" across the nation.

Presumably, his fans in emigrant communities in Australia might read that pronouncement joyfully. After all, back in the pre-neoliberal era of Whitlam and Fraser, the term multiculturalism seemed to promise that, from then on, "Anglo-Celtic" [sic] Australia would give greater space to those who had arrived speaking different languages from English and bearing different cultures and histories. Might Australia be another "rainbow nation"? The answer two generations later seems, however, to be "No". A cultural accompaniment of neoliberalism has been Australian nationalism – the annexation by nationalists of indigenous history allows them to claim 60 000 years of an Australian past, a tally which makes shallow the "3000 year" histories of Rome or the Japanese imperial system, while the British monarchy, commenced with Egbert, King of the West Saxons from 769, is a neophyte indeed. But the most powerful cultural underpinning of the Murdochised order, whether in Australia or elsewhere, is populism. In the first post-Second World War generations, democracy meant a commitment to equality or anyway equalising policies of some kind and, with an assumption, that such a process would allow everyone to read Shakespeare or Wittgenstein or the latest eminent historian with pleasure and profit. Now, instead, sport and TV and computer games offer entertainment first and foremost and news, too, is best digested as "infotainment".

From the 1970s, emigrant groups in Australia did begin to sponsor their own "community" histories, with the Italians prominent in this process given their numbers and the emergence of some community 'leaders', notably in Victoria and N.S.W., ready to pay for historical work. The results were mixed. In mainstream Australia, "ethnic history" carried the curse that it necessarily deployed a language or languages other than English and "Australian historians" were almost universally equipped only with English. They remained, and remain, bemused by "foreign sounding names". Moreover, the paymasters of ethnic history were not often merely generous but pushed their historians to write a past that was Whiggish in philosophy – migrant communities started small, ideally in the First Fleet, but grew and grew – and detached from what might be dangerous politics, except those that could be utilised to assert a migrant "victimhood". Thus the internment of Italians in Second World War Australia was automatically recorded as a mindless and ignorant persecution by the old Australian bureaucracy. However, the nature of immigrant Fascism was rarely probed and there was no attempt to imagine what Italians in Australia might have done had the Axis won the great conflict. Easier still was a concentration on the family and lifestyle past, where, say, the Australian consumption from the 1960s of spaghetti, prosciutto crudo, olive oil and chianti was ascribed to happy migrant effect (in fact, it owed at least as much to Australian tourist trips to Europe, as well as to global fashion spreading from the USA).

Over the next decades, as far as Italians in Australia are concerned, the efforts to find them a niche in an Australian national story were further vitiated by, first, the end of Italian immigration in any mass sense from the late 1960s and, secondly, by the assault on Italians' reputation everywhere (except among themselves) resulting from the career of Silvio Berlusconi. *Il Cavaliere*, as the Italian press always calls him, seemed to non-Italians the epitome of a spiv and lounge lizard, ancient stereotypes that had long afflicted the Italian image abroad. Although "conservative" and "anti-communist", he seemed too busy keeping himself out of gaol to push through the "reforms" that neoliberalism expects. Not for nothing did *The Economist*, major global organ of the theoretics of neoliberalism with a human face, become perhaps his most open and intransigent critic. Despite Berlusconi possessing many fans in immigrant Australia, his recurrent scandals and the scarcely surprising poor national economic performance of the country under his leadership seemed to confirm that, on some world hierarchy of significance Italians did not really 'matter'. They were a holiday people and only that. How could they compete in Australians' limited concentration with the peoples of Asia who were making the new century 'theirs'?

My perhaps provocative commentary can act as background to the essays assembled in this volume edited by my old friend and first student, Gianfranco Cresciani, and by Bruno Mascitelli of Swinburne University in Melbourne. All the essays are in some sense focused on what some contemporaries might think is "old fashioned political history"; there is no mention of emotions, food or dance. The editors themselves contribute about half the contents, with Mascitelli offering the broader pieces on the grand themes of Italian-Australian diplomatic and economic relations. Cresciani concentrates instead on rescuing the career of Isidoro Alessandro Bertazzon, a pre-1914 "subversive" from the Veneto with a global range who washed up in 1920s Australia and died there in 1940, while bravely trying to keep his Anti-Fascist ideals and comradeship alive. Cresciani's other chapter is a mixture of history and autobiography as he recounts the rise and fall of the Frederick May Foundation for Italian studies at Sydney University, an organisation that, for a period, favoured elite cultural ties between

Italy and Australia more successfully than other organisations had done before or have done since.

The other chapters are monographic in character. Catherine Dewhirst provides a sober account of Australia's official obligations to immigrants under the terms of a treaty signed between imperial Britain and Italy in 1883, an arrangement that lasted until the outbreak of war in June 1940. Karen Agutter alerts Australians to the career of Consul-General Emilio Eles, an activist, idiosyncratic and amusing diplomat with a vivid career during the First World War, both in regard to the Australian political world and the infant Italo-Australian "community". Gerardo Papalia examines the efforts by Mussolini's dictatorship to wean Australia from too automatic following of British policy during the bloody Italian invasion of Ethiopia in 1935-6 and notes in passing the zeal with which diplomats posted in Australia collected "secret" details of the country's military and naval weakness. Such half "plans" might be recorded when rhetoric about internment after 1940 grows too sentimental.

The themes are significant. The research is serious. Archives have been probed and detail from them is made available that was not public before. Australia and Italy may be quite a long way apart in 2013 and the gap between them may be increasing. Nonetheless they share quite a bit of history. Important aspects of it are recovered in this collection of essays. It is as much a part of Australian history as is more familiar tales about "resistance" on the frontier, the growth of mining or the spread of "Meals on Wheels" across the nation.

Oxford, November 2013

1
Italy and Australia:
Different Origins – Different Strategies

Bruno Mascitelli

Introduction

Italy and Australia both achieved modern statehood through distinct endeavours in the second half of the 19th century. Italy was unified in 1871 while Australia achieved nationhood through an act of the British Parliament bringing the six colonies into a federation in 1901. As these two nations entered the 20th century they had little in common and would, over time, find themselves on different sides of geo-political indicators. They were in the first place geographically on opposite sides and in opposite hemispheres of the world. They pursued different political trajectories as will be seen on more than one occasion, especially in moments of crisis and war, and found themselves on opposite sides during the Second World War. It took this global conflict – and especially its aftermath – to bring them together in the middle of the 20th century, first as adversaries and then as partners.

While researching for this book chapter, it became obvious that the term "Italy", in conjunction with Australia in historic, political and economic narratives, was a pretty rare occurrence. Countless authoritative accounts of Australian political and foreign policy discourses throughout the 20th century simply never mentioned Italy as a subject of relevance. Not locating references to Italy provided a feeling that this nation was partial to Australia's development. The nation Italy was simply not on Australia's official or unofficial radar screen. Was this a matter to be surprised about? It should not have been, though in some circles illusions about some special relationship between these two countries are still heard. On the other hand what was present in Australian literature, in contrast, was the sad chapter on Italian internment during the Second World War and more positively the presence, role and legacy of "Italian immigration" to Australia in the second half of the 20th century.

Nor was it different from the Italian perspective. Was there an acknowledgement or presence of Australia in Italy's foreign relations? The answer is no. As one former retired Italian Ambassador indicated the mainstay of Italian foreign policy in the post war period:

> post-war Italian foreign policy increased as Italian politics polarized around two mass parties, the Christian Democrats and the Communists, taking their cues respectively from Washington (and the Vatican) and from Moscow (Lenzi 2011: 1).

Uppermost in Italy's priorities post-1945 was its economic and political rebuilding after the fascist experience and its positioning in the Cold War, that created a new European scenario. There was little space for consideration of small nations like Australia that did not figure in the European landscape. This of course changed when Australia became a recipient of Italian migrants and this new country now took on an importance it previously did not have. This accidental relationship defined by migration is in large part the message of this chapter and the theme of this book overall.

Without the historic coming together of Italy and Australia over the migration program, discussion of these two countries, as friends and allies, or strategically connected, in the one breath seems distinctly out of place. This relationship has been on the whole one of reciprocity and engagement. A southern European nation with a significant

European legacy versus a European populated nation with a long, rich indigenous history within the Asia Pacific region. These two nations have been defined by their separate alliances interested in distinctly separate issues. In certain moments and especially in world crises these two nations have found themselves arguing very different causes and rubbing shoulders with different interests and global friends.

Australia, as a former colony of Britain prior to 1900, was in no position to have an independent foreign policy and so its tenuous connections to Italy were either through Britain or in other random ways. While there are references to the presence of Italians at the first European landing in Australia, these were accidental and casual occurrences that have acquired a folklore quality rather than any significant development of connections with Italy and Italians. There was an "Italian" convict in the First Fleet, and two "Italian" sailors were on the *Endeavour* when Flinders circumnavigated Australia. Garibaldi in his memoirs recalled vividly the brief time he spent on an island in Bass Strait in 1852. Two years later Raffaello Carboni, who played a prominent role in the Eureka Stockade, would also be highlighted because of his "Italian" origin. In 1881 a ship brought two hundred Italian survivors from a failed project in New Guinea to New South Wales where they settled in "New Italy" near Lismore (Metcalf, 2011:118). Italy's first Consul General (Pasquale Corte) to Australia arrived in Melbourne and the Melbourne branch of the Italian cultural entity Dante Alighieri was established in Melbourne in 1896 (Mayne 1997:19).

Australia's new found post-colonial direction initially required it to continue to hold onto the apron strings of its colonial master. After the Second World War these needs changed along with the way the world looked. Entering into play for Australia would be the need to secure its borders, build its labour power, find security arrangements, and adhere to a Cold War framework in its geographical region. Historian E. M. Andrews provides a personalised description of this shifting

Australian strategy through the eyes of loyal allies and in the words of former Australian Prime Minister Robert Menzies. He states:

> ... 'great and powerful friends' who will form the backbone of, and incidentally provide most of the money for, our defence. The most dramatic change in this policy has been the ally concerned – from Britain in the 1930s to America in the post-war era. But the basic policy remains the same (Andrews 1978:122).

The nations, which fell into the category Menzies defines, would not include Italy. Italy was a nation of contrasting interests and perspectives. Besides being located in Europe, the post-war period was also defined by Italy's participation in the concept of a European community and an entirely different set of allies, concerns and trajectories which made it position itself in a different orbit than that of Australia. Where there was a meeting of needs, minds and events, they were fortuitous rather than reflecting any parallel development of these two nations. But changing Australian economic and social needs required a new and vast migration program in 1947, which would change the dynamics of this relationship. The two countries now had common destinies in relation to migration – Australia needed people to help build its country whilst Italy encouraged its impoverished rural population to emigrate to this distant and foreign land. A relationship was born.

The purpose of this chapter is to examine the factors which, in contrast to their history and strategic interests, brought these two distant nations together, if only for a short period. This chapter seeks to critically appraise this relationship, explore where it came together and where it drifted apart. Most importantly, this study seeks to place the relationship in a clearer critical perspective, seeking to set apart the emotive connections and game changer of the past like immigration and address what are the scenarios that make up this relationship.

In the second millennium, the game changer that had defined the relationship between these two countries is no longer present. These two nations have a low level but solid engagement – a product primarily of the immigration connection – and not as some wish to believe some inane love for each other. The story, whatever the relationship is, needs to be told and defined. It is a story that will be told primarily from the Australian standpoint. While an attempt will always be made to be empathetic from the other side, the need to understand and define the relationship is stronger from the Australian side. Many in the Italian-Australian community hold onto these nostalgic connections and at times inflate their presence and importance. This includes accusing governments in both Italy and Australia of underestimating and not pursuing the relationship. This sentiment reflects some sense of feeling abandoned and forgotten, which is understandable. The message of this chapter is to acknowledge what was an unlikely and accidental relationship that defined Australia, more so than Italy, and the surprise that it ever lasted as long as it did. We are not wishing to state that the relationship has come to an end, but the immigration relationship and its immediate aftermath maintained a dialogue, interconnection and engagement that has drifted into history. From the Australian perspective it is but one of many relationships which Australia has with diverse nations of the world.

Background to an unlikely connection

In 1881, according to the census, there were fewer than 2,000 Italians living in Australia, many lured by the search for gold. In the 1890s more came, for employment opportunities in mining in Western Australia and in sugar cane operations in Queensland. In 1911 there were only 6,719 residents who had been born in Italy. In 1933 there were 26,756 Italy born immigrants and by 1947 their number had reached 33,600.

New arrivals in Australia increasingly came up against prejudice at both societal and government levels. The union movement feared the economic impact of immigrants as it was concerned about the lowering of wages of their members. The dominant Anglo-Celtic culture saw the newcomers as "swarthy" and liable to form enclaves. In America, allegations were made, claiming that Italians, along with Greeks and Hungarians, "had become a greater pest in the United States than the colored races" and in Australia for decades there was frequent questioning of whether or not Italians qualified under the White Australia policy.

Italy's national unification in 1861 (the 150th anniversary was recently celebrated with pomp) was a defining event. After centuries of foreign domination, fragmented and locally defined powerbases throughout the peninsula, Italy acquired national unity and statehood. As uneven as it was, and weak in parts such as the Italian south, it was the culmination of decades of struggle for national consciousness. But as observed by one scholar, it lacked, "a genuine mass movement for unification, and ... the peninsula's enduring regionalism ... [they were] citizens of 'Italies but not Italy'" (Mayne, 1997:7).

As Bosworth eloquently noted:

> Italy has always conducted two foreign policies. One that was of the government ensconced in the Farnesina and its predecessor palaces; the other was that of the people, the emigrants who moved all over Europe, the Americas and Oceania. The participants in this alternative and subaltern foreign policy took to their new worlds the cultures of *paese* and *parrocchia* rather than *palazzo* (Pesman 2000:270).

On the other side of the world was Australia, a nation in waiting and only decades away from the essential ingredients for self-government. As opposed to Italy, Australia in 1901 acquired nationhood without a fight and through an act of the British Parliament. From the British perspective:

> Canada, Australia and New Zealand were largely self-governing, and their parliaments were more representative of the people

than was the British parliament. Foreign policy, however, was one domain where they were not independent. Nonetheless the mother of parliaments on the banks of the Thames had digested the lesson of why the American colonies had broken loose in the 18th century, and so it permitted Canada, Australia and New Zealand sometimes to ignore or defy Britain's foreign policy on a topic vital to them. They increasingly paid for their own armies and navies, though in times of war they would accept Britain's leadership (Blainey 2005:7).

Despite formal independence, Australia, as Blainey reminds us, did not have an "independent" foreign policy and was on the whole loyal to British interests for decades to come.

The First World War and the continuance of divergent paths

When a Serbian nationalist assassinated the heir to the Austro-Hungarian throne in Sarajevo on 28 June 1914, the crisis quickly escalated into a full blown European war, to become known as the Great War and later as the First World War (Stone 2009). Both Australia, under the direction of the First Australian Imperial Forces (AIF) in 1914, and Italy in 1915 would find themselves in a war on the same side, equally subjected to heavy casualties and losses. Not surprisingly, because of their recent acquisition of nationhood, this war also contributed to their national cohesion and identity. For Italy it was the first significant battle (besides the Libyan war in 1911) in which Italians from different regions fought under the single banner of the Italian flag. Young Sicilians fought alongside young soldiers from Lombardia or the Veneto and new loyalties were created for this new nation. Though Italy entered the war in 1915, its casualties and the Caporetto defeat became, like the ANZAC events in Gallipoli, symbols of national rallying and identity. During the period of the First World War, Australia's relations with Britain were close and warm and Australia remained committed to its war effort. One Prime Minister after the other, Joseph Cook, Andrew Fisher and Billy Hughes, all pledged loyalty to God, King and Country.

At the end of the First World War both countries pursued radically different paths. Australia continued its nation building while Italy went through protracted social turmoil between workers and employer organisations both in the cities and in the countryside. This period of intense internal social and class conflict in Italy following the war is often referred to as the *'Biennio Rosso'* – or the Two Red Years. This social turmoil ultimately produced rising inflation, exacerbated by the increasing levels of unemployment and poverty, which arguably contributed to the demise of the liberal state and the ascent of Mussolini to power in Italy (Bosworth 2007). Mussolini's National Fascist Party began to take to the streets overpowering the militancy of the trade unions and imposing fascist terror on its political opponents, especially the Socialist Party. By 1922 Mussolini had effectively consolidated his role in power and government and by 1926 had eliminated all opposition to fascist rule. In taking such a course, Italy had embarked on a collision course with Australian political values and alliances.

Italian fascism and the Australian response

The fascist victory in Italy solicited varied responses in Australia. In some quarters the new fascist government attracted an odd mixture of admiration and in others loathing. In the early period, Italian consuls in Australia began to raise pressure on Australian authorities to seek out and arrest the Italian enemies of fascism located in Australia. Australia refused to act on what was considered to be an internal Italian dispute, though this consular interference would be resisted once Italy began infringing League of Nations directives in the 1930s. Italy joined the Anti-Comintern pact with Germany and Japan, but initially this created no particular concern to Australia, as there seemed to be few immediate consequences (Booker 1976:32). This attitude changed once Australia took part in the embargo against Italy, though it never resulted in open hostility despite Italy's invasion of Abyssinia and the League of Nations boycott (Mayne 1997).

The imposition of tighter US immigration restrictions in the early 1920s caused some 25,000 Italians to turn to Australia during that decade. By the mid-1930s approximately 40,000 Italians were living in Australia and another 10,000 Italians immigrated to Australia immediately preceding the Second World War, producing 90,000 first and second generation Italians living in Australia (Mayne 1997:52). During this inter-war period Italians became the largest European nationality in Australia, the majority of them living in Victoria.

The Second World War and the diverging paths of Italy and Australia

The onset of the Second World War was a moment of crisis for Australia-Italy relations. After remaining undecided about participation in the war, and fearing on missing out on territorial gains, on 10 June 1940 Mussolini declared war on France and Britain. With Italy declaring war against Britain, it was tantamount to declaring war against Australia. The paths of Italy and Australia would diverge until the collapse of Italian fascism in July 1943, leading to the infamous 8 September 1943 declaration, when Italy changed its support in favour of the Allies and declared war against Germany.

Italy's entry into World War Two on 10 June 1940 "though not unexpected, still caught some people by surprise. Until then, Italy was considered to be a faraway, second-rate country of no direct relevance to Australia" (Cresciani 2003:98). Though Italy was of "no direct relevance" to Australia, matters between the two countries changed entirely. Diplomatic relations were promptly broken off. When Prime Minister Menzies heard of the Italian declaration of war against Britain he angrily noted he was tempted to "sing a hymn of hate" adding that while Germany was unscrupulous, it had never "sunk to quite the depth to which Italy has sunk today" (*The Age* 1940:5). Fascist Italy, which had already substantially severed trade ties and banned emigration, was now on a war footing with Australia.

As Menzies stated, "Britain is at war therefore Australia is at war" (Booker 1976:29). Menzies asked London to inform Germany that as part of the Commonwealth of Nations, Australia's war participation was imminent. Matters deteriorated when Japan also entered the war in December 1941. For the first time Australia began to express concern about a possible British defeat and being exposed to possible Japanese southern expansion after Japan captured Chinese Shanghai and Nanking. Events, as they unfolded, saw Australian fears materialise when conflict in the Pacific became closer and more dangerous than anticipated.

With changing fortunes in 1941, Menzies's successor, John Curtin, felt obliged to address Australia's changing strategic direction when he stated "Australia looks to America, free of any pangs as to our traditional links or kinship with the United Kingdom" (Curtin 1941). Things had changed. Japan's entry into the war, the proximity of its troops to Australian territory and the recognition that only the United States could provide for Australia's national security needs, brought about this strategic realignment. It was not a simple swap of patrons. Australia remained committed to the idea of a British Commonwealth, and indeed was influential in the decade ahead in helping shape that post-imperial set-up. Australia's successes between 1939 and 1945, both military and diplomatic, ensured that its voice was heard in the new and radically altered world of the late 1940s.

Internees and Italian prisoners in Australia

Immediately upon the news of Italy declaring war in 1940, the Australian government issued directives to monitor and arrest potential supporters of the Italian State (as well as the German and

Japanese ones). A growing concern over national security and possible acts of espionage and uprising prompted the Australian government to implement the National Security Act which empowered authorities to essentially detain any person for reasons of national security (O'Brien 2007). Australia began to round up some 4,700 Italian born and Italian heritage residents of Australia who were interned in camps across the country. Of this number, 1,191 Italians were naturalised, and were made up of farmers, hairdressers, housewives, fishermen, tailors and butchers (O'Brien 2007). There was a climate where Australian public opinion readily accepted that Italians might pose a security threat but this action was driven by government as well as public opinion. The hurt was great as the internees were overwhelmingly innocent and many had become Australian citizens. In Queensland there was also evidence that internment was motivated, to an extent, by economic envy, while on the Western Australian goldfields widespread internment allegedly was undertaken to prevent the supposed recurrence of riots led by Italians in 1919 and 1934. Many Italians had to change residence, businesses were closed, and in farming communities the internship created additional sacrifices for women as the majority of the detainees were male (Cresciani 2003). Although some leaders were interned, like Prince Alfonso Del Drago, president of the Italian Ex-Servicemen's Association and a Sydney Fascist Branch member (Cresciani 2003), many argue that Italians were interned for no reason other than their country of origin (Cresciani 1980).

In urban centres, organisations such as the Dante Alighieri in Melbourne were forced to suspend their activities the moment Italy declared war. According to Dante Alighieri sources:

> The Society was deemed by Australian intelligence authorities to be the chief publicist for Fascist Italy in Victoria. In an internal memorandum, one intelligence officer noted that it had long been "a well-known fact ... that the Dante Society was the main channel for distribution of propaganda ..." (Mayne 1997:46).

While Australia was rounding up Italians, representatives of the Italian government, especially staff in Italian consulates in Australia, hurried to destroy documents and memos before the inevitable closure of Italian missions by Australian intelligence officers.

Internment had dire consequences for many Italians and their families. People who were not interned faced restrictions on travel, work, land purchase and possession of certain items like cars, petrol, cameras and radios (O'Brien 1988). Scholars such as Pascoe (1987:46) and Rando (2005:19) have declared that the experience in Australia of Italian internment was: "… on balance, a pointless exercise, instigated by irrational fears. They perceived internment as not only unjustifiable but also rightly unjust" (Rando 2005:19).

Australia clashed with Italian forces in North Africa ending in an Allied victory, with nearly 20,000 Italian prisoners of war spending years in confinement in Australia as a result. More than half of them were employed on farms for token wages, a situation that continued until 1946 despite the fact that three years earlier Italy had surrendered and thereafter posed no threat to the allies. The availability of cheap labour must have been a motive for the delay in releasing the Italian prisoners, but the official excuse was that it was impossible to obtain ships to repatriate the Italians. For the most part the POWs were treated leniently, and some returned subsequently to live permanently in Australia.

Something positive did nevertheless come out of these wartime experiences. Those who employed internees and prisoners of war – who on the whole enjoyed a friendly and egalitarian treatment – found them hard-working and generally good-natured and these views spread and helped overcome earlier prejudices. This laid the basis, in terms of public opinion and in government, for the subsequent acceptance of mass Italian immigration to Australia.

Australia develops its own foreign policy

Since Federation one of Australia's most important preoccupations was the way in which it needed to be concerned about its national security. It was, according to political scientist P. Henderson, a foreign policy based on "feelings of insecurity and fear" (Henderson 1985:304). This concern defined its strategic relations and foreign policy. The working assumption from 1901 was that Britain would come to the defence of Australia – for example as the British Navy patrolled Australian waters in the first years of Australian nationhood. Australia was a loyal member of the British Empire, sharing strong cultural, social and political links with Britain. The relationship went two ways. Australia supported Britain in the Boer War, and provided significant manpower in the First World War and again in 1939. Australian leaders were content to allow Britain to make decisions on Australia's behalf.

Australia's approach towards foreign affairs was itself very particular and though the External Affairs Department was established in 1901, it remained inside the Prime Minister's Department until 1934. It was considered a duty which Prime Ministers could and should handle directly themselves. Until 1940 Australia had no officials permanently stationed overseas other than London (Henderson 1985:305). It was therefore a strategic relationship with mother Britain that could guarantee its security and place in the globe. It was at the same time a *de facto* inability to entertain relations with many other nations such as Italy, except at the formal level. Booker explained the relationship eloquently. He states:

> Up to the Second World War we lived by the belief that the sole important connection was with the United Kingdom ... It was taken generally for granted that only enemies of Britain were likely to injure us, and that the only dangerous ones were in Europe. Our foreign policy therefore resided in the simple concept that we should give support to Britain when she needed it, and help in fighting her enemies in war (Booker 1976:11).

Italy in the post-war reconstruction period

When the Second World War ended, Italy, especially its industrial north, lay in ruins as one of the *de facto* defeated countries. Its priorities were political and economic reconstruction and they were urgent. The setting had changed and a new geo-political Cold War environment had set in. In 1946 a plebiscite ended the rule of the monarchy and a constituent assembly was elected to draw up plans for a new Republic. Communists had played a prominent part in the resistance movement in the latter years of the war and were triumphant in neighbouring Yugoslavia. What would now divide Italians would be the ideology of the capitalist market economy expressed through the Catholicism of the Christian Democracy supported by the United States versus the large Italian Communist Party supported by the Soviet Union. Eventually the elections of 1948 put a close to this political uncertainty and Italy loyally fell in place behind other Western nations electing a pro-Western Christian Democratic government. On 10 February 1947 Italy begrudgingly signed the Peace Treaty in Paris, ceding territory and colonial ambitions. Italian Prime Minister De Gasperi, remembering the chill as he entered the room in which his country's fate was to be decided, noted that at the end of his speech he received a sympathetic response from only one delegate: the Australian. The Cold War was well under way and, in 1949, amidst communist protests, Italy joined NATO. To help rebuild Italy's devastated state, the US implemented a European Recovery Program, or Marshall Plan, as it was known. With an intended objective of rebuilding the continent, it served as a key catalyst for the strengthening of Italy's economy and political system (Ginsborg 2003).

Australia emerged from the war as a more significant player on the world stage. Foreign Minister Evatt began playing a prominent role in the new global economic order – which included new structures such as the International Monetary Fund and the World Bank, culminating in the Bretton Woods Agreement – and the establishment of the United

Nations. Evatt was a member of the San Francisco Conference in 1945, which drew up the United Nations Charter, and was elected President of the General Assembly in 1948. Australia had now developed a taste for wholesale independence from London and during the war it had opened overseas missions in Singapore, Moscow, Wellington and New Delhi. Over the next five years Australia established a presence, including trade offices, in more than thirty countries.

As Australia settled down to the task of post-war recovery it very soon faced new challenges. Immediately after the war, important security questions emerged, including the rise of Asian nationalism and the independence of nations such as Indonesia, and the threat of Japan (Meaney 1985). In 1947 External Affairs Minister Evatt outlined the view towards Japan, which stated categorically:

> The first principle of our policy has always been the safety and security of the Pacific, including our own country. That calls for the disarmament and demilitarisation of Japan, destruction of its capacity to wage war, and a sufficient degree of supervision under the peace treaty to prevent re-growth of war making capacity ... (Progress towards democratisation, Dr. Evatt reports on his mission to Japan in August 1947 and the need for a Peace Treaty, cited in Meaney 1985:528).

Australia was beginning to also address the question of East-West Cold War tensions. Until 1949 the tensions were reflected through the prism of the outcome of the Second World War with the US and the USSR dividing the world into areas of influence. The Labor government of the time expressed a measured concern about communism, while the most pressing concern was the destruction of war-ravaged countries and the rise of nationalism, which was affecting large parts of Asia and beyond. Labor Prime Minister Chifley in 1948 spoke about the causal effect of poverty encouraging the growth of communism as it had occurred in Italy. He stated:

> Let us consider Europe. Could communism flourish there if the people were contented, and well fed, and enjoying decent living conditions? Given those conditions, communism could not have found a footing anywhere in Europe. Let us consider the situation in Italy, which is a great Catholic country. No church has put up a greater fight against the inroads of communism than has the Catholic Church. Nevertheless, in the great Catholic country of Italy, communism has grown and grown, not because the country is Catholic, but because economic conditions there provide a fertile bed in which communism can take root and flourish. Those who have studied the position in Italy today know that unless the problem of the landless farmer and the unemployed can be solved the recent triumph of the anti-Communist forces at the polls will prove to be a pyrrhic victory (Prime Minister Chifley, cited in Meaney 1985:546).

Australia, when turning to its strategic needs, knew it was a nation short of manpower and population. This brought up the need to populate the country and find new sources of labour for its growth and modernisation. This was the trigger for a large-scale migration program, which could help build a modern Australia.

Migration becomes a key priority

The Japanese threat to Australia was a wake-up call to "populate or perish". This was articulated and put into effect by Labor leader Arthur Calwell, who was appointed the first Minister for Immigration in the new Chifley government in July 1945. Calwell told the Parliament:

> If Australians have learned one lesson from the Pacific War it is surely that we cannot continue to hold our island continent for ourselves and our descendants unless we greatly increase our numbers. We are about 7 million people and we hold 3 million square miles of this earth surface ... much development and settlement have yet to be undertaken. Our need to undertake it is urgent and imperative if we are to survive (O'Connor 2012).

Although Calwell shared some of the prejudices of the community, he recognised that Australia could not rely solely on Britain and Ireland for its migration. Calwell's Melbourne constituency included Carlton, with a visible and prominent Italian community, but initially he was reluctant to turn to Italy as a major migration source. Despite this attitude many thousands of Italians came permanently to Australia during his tenure as Minister. Italy in the late 1940s was temporarily impoverished with a surfeit of population while Australia urgently needed significant human resources to develop its national potential. It was Calwell's successors who recognised how Italy might prove to be a prime and steady source of immigrants.

Chifley's government was defeated in the elections of 1949 and the Menzies led coalition, the Liberal-Country Party, took control. In 1950 Menzies made a brief visit to Rome, where he met his counterpart, Alcide De Gasperi, who drew his attention to Italy's one-and-a-half million unemployed, and the desirability to promote emigration to Australia. In 1951, with the Displaced Persons program coming to an end, Australia negotiated a series of migration agreements with European countries, beginning with The Netherlands. Though Italy signed the migration agreement with Australia in 1951, it was not able to win concessions, not even the promise of assisted passage, as enjoyed by British immigrants. Between 1945 and 1983 some 400,000 Italians came to Australia as "permanent and long term arrivals" though the bulk of this number arrived between 1952 and 1970 (Pascoe 1987:229). This not only laid the basis for a substantial relationship between the two countries but also played a key part in transforming Australia economically, socially and culturally.

Migration became one of the engines for Australia's post-war reconstruction and a key objective of successive governments for the country to develop an industrial and manufacturing base. Migrants brought labour power and new skills, not to mention the fact that they were consumers and paid taxes. Italians became the most numerous of the non-English speaking immigrants to join the labour market, with workers who for the most part had limited education and accepted poorer-paid, poorly-unionised and often dangerous jobs. The trade union movement tolerated this influx though English speakers, along with skilled northern Europeans, filled the better paid and more secure jobs.

The development of Australia's infrastructure provided employment for the new arrivals, as well as opportunities for enterprising Italians. The Snowy Mountains Hydro-Electric Scheme, which began in 1949, absorbed a great number of the new wave of workers. Even though most Italians employed had formerly been rural workers, they were concentrated in particular occupations such as masonry, tunneling and building retaining walls. They proved willing to work in adverse conditions for their future economic security (Panucci, Kelly & Castles 1992:60).

The first decade of mass migration

While many Italians went to work as unskilled labour, others established small family-oriented businesses. While some continued to be attracted to the sugar cane industry in Queensland, to mining and manufacture, a great number set up operations in market gardening, food and catering that partially served the Italian community (Pascoe 1987). As these businesses stabilised and prospered, Italian families were able to purchase their own home and even engage in property investment as a means of insurance for their families' future.

Though Italian migration is a success story, it came with hardship, language difficulties and cultural divide. Ingrained conservative views often provided unwelcome messages to these newcomers. Nonetheless they persisted and over time found ways of overcoming these discriminatory barriers.

The official Australian policy at this time was one of "assimilation", whereby migrants were expected to learn and only use English and so blend into the community. This was the policy adopted at all "welcome camps" like Bonegilla. As mass migration progressed, a credit squeeze and a doubling in unemployment hit Australia. In July 1952, 2,000 Italian men who had come to Australia on two-year contracts, with promise of work, rioted when they found they had no jobs and faced long delays in housing. Their complaints extended to the lack of heating and recreation facilities and the poor quality of food at Bonegilla. Italian authorities felt they needed to demand more for emigrants in Australia. In 1961 the Italian government under Prime Minister Fanfani refused to renew the migration agreement with Australia until Italian migrants were treated *on par* with British migrants. The Italian authorities were looking for assisted passage, settlement benefits and guarantees of employment (Pascoe 1987:229). All immigrants, including Italians, were the first victims of the cyclical downturn in 1952 and again in 1961.

The second decade of mass migration, from 1960 to 1970, saw a further 150,000 Italians arriving in Australia. As their numbers grew – with Italian emerging as the second most spoken and taught language in Australia after English – the impact of the Italian presence began to be felt. Most notably in food and related industries, with Italians prominent in city markets and the smallholdings that supplied them, including in restaurants run by Italians. The "chain-migration" element in the overall program reinforced this new diversity, as people joined other family or community members who had migrated before them.

Diplomatic developments between Australia and Italy

Australian representation was initially established in 1949 in Italy at the level of an Australian Legation (see Table 1.1) but was soon, upon recommendation from Paul McGuire, upgraded to Embassy status in Rome. In 1957 McGuire became the first Ambassador to Rome. His recommendation acknowledged that Italy was Australia's fourth largest wool customer and that already 10,000 migrants had gone to Australia. McGuire also observed that Rome was an extraordinary location for information and most nations had an established presence in Italy (Steele 2008). The Embassy in Rome has since been a location for career diplomats until the 2000s until the arrival of Amanda Vanstone. According to the Lowy report on Australian diplomatic representation, "Australia is over represented with missions in Europe compared with higher priority regions" (Oliver & Shearer 2011:37). This may not be good news for Australian representation in Italy.

According to Stirling (Ambassador from 1962 until 1967), Messina became the headquarters for Australia and Australian migration processing for Southern Italy and was known as the "Milan of the South" (Stirling 1973:124). In the same period Australia also had a small migration office in Genova, staffed by one person. In addition to Messina and Genova, there was also a small presence in Trieste, mostly for immigration processing purposes (Steele 2008). Italian President Saragat's visit to Australia in 1967 made significant steps forward in the relations between the two countries and the Italian community in Australia. During his visit, Saragat announced Italy's intention to offer a grant to assist the establishment of a welfare agency for Italians in Victoria (Mayne 1997) that became known as the COASIT (Committee of Assistance for Italian Immigrants), which would provide support for the new phase of Italian settlement in Australia (Gobbo 2010).

Table 1.1 Australian – Italian ambassadors serving in Rome or Canberra (1949 onwards)

Australian Ambassador	Period of duty	Italian Ambassador	Period of duty
C. W. Kellway (Minister)	1949-1954	Giulio Del Balzo di Presenzano	February 1949
Paul McGuire (First Ambassador 1957)	1954-1959	Silvio Daneo	June 1952
Hugh Smith	1959-1962	Silvio Daneo	March 1958
Alfred Stirling	1962-1967	Eugenio Prato	December 1958
Sir. Walter Crocker	1967-1970	Mario Tonarelli	December 1961
Malcolm Booker	1970-1974	Renato Della Chiesa d'Insasca	August 1962
John Ryan	1974-1977	Mario Majioli	January 1967
Robert Robertson	1977-1980	Paolo Canali	June 1971
Keith Douglas-Scott	1983-1985	Paolo Malajoni	June 1977
Gerald Nutter	1985-1989	Sergio Angeletti	March 1980
Duncan Campbell	1989-1994	Eric Da Rin	January 1986
Lance Joseph	1994-1997	Francesco Cardi	November 1989
Rory Steele	1996-2001	Marcello Spatafora	October 1993
Murray Cobban	2001-2004	Giovanni Castellaneta	January 1998
Peter Woolcott	2004-2007	Dino Volpicelli	June 2001
Amanda Vanstone	2007-2010	Stefano Starace Janfolla	June 2005
David Ritchie	2010-2013	Gianludovico de Martino	June 2009

Source: The author

It was also during this visit by Saragat to Australia that an agreement was reached on the establishment of a Consulate General for Milan, which was put into effect in March 1968. The first Consul General was Dudley Fagg, who led the post for the remainder of that year. From 1969 onwards it assumed the normal functions of a Consulate General with a significant proportion of its mandate being that of trade.

The Italian community in Australia, twenty-five years after the end of World War II, was, by now, well installed. Italian-language newspapers, social clubs and a range of official and semi-official facilities were established. The Italian language newspaper *Il Globo* was began publishing in November 1959 and, along with the older *La Fiamma* based in Sydney, was instrumental in providing relevant news and information to these newly arrived immigrants. The settling-in process was being aided not only by the establishment of COASIT but by other support services as well. In 1961 the Italian Cultural Institute in Melbourne was opened. In the mid-1960s the Abruzzo and Veneto clubs were both inaugurated, the Italian Trade Commission opened an office and country-to-country engagement took on a deeper meaning. The second generation born in Australia was making its mark, attending university and securing well-paid jobs. In the legal, medical and teaching professions, immigrants of Italian descent were increasingly to be found. Older Italians who had arrived long before were now in secure retirement, many returning to visit Italy and some electing to stay in their homeland while their children and grandchildren remained in Australia.

New and changing relations. Australia and Italy after immigration

Australia in the 1960s saw its foreign policy focused around Cold War and pro-US policies such as its participation in the Vietnam War. The Italian position on Vietnam was divided and depended on which party one supported. The official government position was tepid support of the American activities, as expressed by the then Prime Minister Aldo

Moro (Mammarella & Cacace 2006). However, when the question of conscripting "un-naturalised immigrants" for the Vietnam War was announced by Australia, Italy made known its objection. It involved recently arrived Italian youth being enlisted in Australia's armed forces, potentially bound for Vietnam. Italy, alongside a significant number of other emigrant countries, voiced its concerns to Australia, though no retaliatory actions took place (Edwards 1997:102). There was deep opposition to the bombing of Vietnam from the then strong Italian Communist Party, but these Italian views did not affect Australia and its participation in the US-led war. Equally important in the early 1970s was the question of Britain joining the European Economic Community (EEC), which provided a jolt to Australia and especially to its primary industry, which lost access to markets. The move was seen in Australia with distress and even with a sense of betrayal (Hudson 1988). It reinforced the view that Britain "had become for Australians a foreign country" as once expressed by Prime Minister Gorton in the late 1960s (Curran & Ward 2010:127). These events shifted Australian eyes further away from the European centre and acknowledged that European strategic interests had repercussions for the way Australia related to all of Europe and not just Britain.

Between 1970 and 1980 total yearly immigration from Italy fell below 30,000. By the early 1970s Australia had officially and definitively abandoned the White Australia policy and begun looking for migrants from other countries, notably in the Middle East and Asia. In 1973 the new Australian Labor Prime Minister Gough Whitlam visited Italy, reporting to Parliament afterwards that in Rome, in the absence of a meeting with Prime Minister Giulio Andreotti, he had outlined to a senior Italian minister his government's thinking on foreign policy matters:

> I found a close identity of views between our two Governments on all matters which we discussed, for example, the recognition of China and North Vietnam. I also explained to Signor Colombo

our attitude to continued French nuclear testing in the Pacific (Whitlam 2002, cited in Steele 2008).

Such high level visits in each direction gave sharper focus to the bilateral relationship. In 1975 Gough Whitlam made further visits to Italy where he met President Giovanni Leone and Prime Minister Aldo Moro. During this meeting Whitlam signed a cultural agreement – one of the first important agreements (after the 1951 immigration agreement) between the two countries (Whitlam 2002:12). On another front, relations with Italy during the 1980s progressed without too much grief or controversy. Richard Woolcott's gratitude to Italy in 1984 for its indirect support to Australia standing for membership of the Security Council was a sign of mutual recognition and respect (Woolcott 2003:191).

The emergence of internal ideological terrorism experienced in Italy throughout the late 1960s and 1970s culminating in the kidnapping and assassination of its former Prime Minister Aldo Moro in 1978, presented a very different side of Italy to Australian eyes. Australia had rarely seen this side of Italy as it habitually measured the country primarily for its emigration. The day of the Moro kidnapping, as well as the eventual recovery of the assassinated Moro's body two months later, produced strong media commentary in Australia. Its impact on the Italian community in Australia was well documented as demonstrated by *The Australian* under the title "Grief for migrants". It stated:

> Australia's 350,000 strong Italian community went into deep mourning yesterday after details of the Moro assassination were released. Special editions of Italian language newspapers were on the streets soon after dawn and early masses throughout the country were packed (*The Australian*, May 1978).

The article went on to record the views of other members of the Italian community, notably the then editor of the Italian newspaper *Il Globo*, Nino Randazzo:

Everyone understood a big game was being played in Italy at the moment – a game in which Italian democracy, even western democracy, was at stake, said Mr. Randazzo. But he hoped that some good might come from Mr. Moro's death in that the democratic system might be moved to defend itself more strongly (*The Australian*, May 1978).

In another editorial in *The Australian* on the eventual recovery of Moro's body in May 1978, the paper said "In Australia, we are at last becoming aware that we cannot forever take the risk of being spared from attack" (*The Australian*, 1978:8). The events of the Moro assassination shook Australia's perception of Italy.

The 1990s and the reaffirmation of going separate ways

Evans and Grant (1991) in their 1990s treatment of Australia's relations with Italy defined the relationship in the following terms:

> Australia's relationship with Italy has a solid human and historical basis – not least in the well over 600,000 Australians of Italian birth or ancestry – but it has taken on special importance over the recent years because of Italy's role as a major member of the EC, its membership of the G7, its direct economic importance to us and its booming economy (Evans & Grant 1991:290).

A sign that Italy was not at the top end of Australian Foreign Affairs priorities was exampled in the DFAT Annual Report for 1995-96. In the segment relating to "Western Europe" and the "European Union" while mention was made of the UK, Germany and France not a word was mentioned of Italy and its importance to Australia (DFAT 1996).

What also determined Australia's loosening its ties with Italy was the latter's leaning towards the European Union, especially its commitment to the Maastricht Agreement and eventually Italy's entry into the Eurozone, decided in May 1998. This diminished Italy's attention from Australia but at the same time the European Union was becoming a new entity that Australia needed to grapple with – for good or for bad.

During the late 1990s and into the 2000s, much of Australia's foreign and internal policy towards nations such as Italy and migration came clearer under the Howard government. The Howard government position on migration and multiculturalism was spelt out in very brutal terms, and ultimately reflected on most immigrant communities:

> John Howard ... in his first term in office ... cut the numbers [of migrants] sharply, skewed the intake to favour skilled migrants, removed the right of tens of thousands of foreigners to go on welfare and almost single-handedly wiped the word multiculturalism from the mainstream political lexicon (McGregor 1999:163).

Australian politicians often referred to Italy as a holiday attraction rather than a location for inter-government experience sharing. In one humorous incident in 1997, the then treasurer Peter Costello ridiculed the leader of the opposition (Simon Crean) for visiting Italy (Venice, Tuscany and Rome) to learn about how to reduce unemployment. The treasurer pointed out that Australia's unemployment was 8.6 [per cent] at the time while Italy's was 12.4 [per cent] (*The Age*, 1997, 'Roamer to Roma' Crean under attack: 8).

Australian Prime Minister Paul Keating, in his perceptive and provocative statement of Australia's global standing, made clear one thing: of the three countries whose interaction was shaping Europe [France, Germany and the UK], Britain was the one that loomed largest for Australia (Keating 2000:245). Not surprisingly, Italy, amongst the European nations, received no mention. Keating was very clear that Australia needed to pursue its own destiny. He said quite pointedly: "... Australia was not Asian or European or American or anything. This is what history and geography have delivered us. It is the only option we have and one we have every reason to celebrate" (Keating 2000:245).

Historical meeting and departure points

It is ironical that Italophile Gough Whitlam, Australia's most admired and simultaneously disliked Prime Minister in post-war Australia, would also occupy the seat of Werriwa in NSW, which had been previously occupied by an Australian politician with Italian ancestry, Hubert Peter Lazzarini. His origins date back to two protagonists of Italy's unification, Garibaldi and Mazzini (Whitlam 2002). Whitlam's expertise on Italy cuts across a range of cultural categories and especially his abounding knowledge of Italian art. On the question of Italian political affairs, it was surprising if not disappointing that Whitlam in his *Italian notebooks* (2002) made the surprising confession that Bob Santamaria was the most famous Italian name in Australian history. Santamaria was the National Civic Council leader and advocate for the Democratic Labor Party, which split from the Labor Party in the 1950s (Whitlam 2002:35). More surprising was his admission that Santamaria represented a reference point for things that were Italian (Whitlam 2002). What is curious about Whitlam's statement is that, while Santamaria was baited as being a "Catholic wog" (Grassby 1993:293), he was mostly known for his "Catholic anti-communism" rather than for his knowledge of Italy or Italians in Australia. More appropriately Jupp referred to Santamaria as "one of the most influential Catholic laymen of the 20th century [in Australia]" (Jupp 2009:261). While Santamaria defended the Italian migration program and took up the plight of Italian migrants, he was first and foremost a conservative Catholic. In his letter in 1952 to Marco Milano-Comparetti of the fiercely anti-Communist Catholic Action movement in Italy, Santamaria, while concerned about the plight of Italians arriving in Victoria, was equally concerned about their anti-clericalism, as when he wrote: "We are finding a frightening amount of anti-clericalism among Italians. This is manifested strangely enough, more against priests of their own nationality than against Australian priests" (Santamaria 2007:60). This raises the question of the influence of Italy and Italians through the presence of the Catholic religion in Australia. In the early part of the 20th century O'Farrell (1977) argues that Australian Catholicism supported Italy's intervention in the Spanish civil war and Mussolini's invasion of Abyssinia. O'Farrell posits:

> Mussolini's activities also drew on another Australian Catholic disposition, the tendency to be sympathetic towards Italy, particularly after Mussolini had made his peace with the Papacy in the concordat of 1926. The invasion revealed Catholic opinion to be confused and divided (O'Farrell 1977:388).

However, after the Second World War Italy and Italian priests seemed overwhelmed by the Irish control of the Catholic Church in Australia (Jupp, 2009) and, as Grech and Cahill (2005) point out, the Catholic Church in Australia was made up of diverse communities including Maltese, Italians, Lebanese, Dutch and Belgians. What is apparent is that while Rome (meaning the Vatican) imposed its authority on the Australian Catholic Church, especially after the Second World War, rarely was Italian foreign policy and Italy as a nation a consideration in this scenario.

Australia's understanding and knowledge of Italy has matured and grown from the days when Italy was viewed through the glasses of "migration". This is coupled with the unenviable fact that not only has Italian mass migration ended but it is being superseded by the presence of larger and newer migration, in particular that of Chinese and Indian immigration. The new demographic profile of Australia is a very different one from the 1970s. Not only are Italian communities in Australia declining, there is a decline in the use of the Italian language and in the readership of Italian language newspapers (*Il Globo* and *La Fiamma*). Italian-Australians are becoming a smaller cohort of the overall Australian demography.

Previously existing arrangements such as Alitalia flights to Australia ceased in 2000 (Steele 2008) and direct Qantas flights to Rome, which had been a feature for the Italian community for decades, ceased in 2003. In the Italian community there was a certain anger and protest against this decision but little came of the complaints. Qantas was redirecting its aircraft to other more lucrative markets such as the US. Italy was not a priority.

Bilateral arrangements and agreements

When asked, the official channels and representation from both Australia and Italy when speaking about each other will but only speak highly of the "warm and long-standing relationship underpinned by strong community ties" (DFAT website 2013). That is good diplomatic protocol but both sides will privately admit that today there is little to this bilateral relationship. The 2011 census claims that 916,116 Australians claimed Italian ancestry, including 185,402 Australian residents actually born in Italy. Those born in Italy are declining while Italian ancestry residents in Australia increase. While Australian government figures indicate that only 30,000 Australians live in Italy, the figure is understood to be much higher, even double the estimate, given the "softer" migration procedures and recording processes. Australia and Italy have concluded bilateral agreements covering culture, double taxation, air services, economic and commercial cooperation, reciprocal social security and health care benefits, and film co-production. The two countries have also signed a number of Memoranda of Understanding (MOUs) agreements covering science and technology cooperation, defence material, defence industry, motor vehicle safety certification, sports cooperation, game meat exports and trade cooperation. As has been noted by Steele (2008), the area of defence cooperation was more significant than would otherwise be known. For example:

> Defence in recent times has become a key area of complementarity, with both countries requiring state-of-the-art military capabilities. While Italy's industrial base is the more

significant, Australia has been able to provide offsets and to develop projects at home. Prominent among many areas of successful cooperation have been the Royal Australian Air Force's acquisition of Macchi trainers from Italy between 1967 and 1972, and the Royal Australian Navy's purchase of the Italian Gaeta minehunter, which was modified as the Huon Class to suit Australian conditions. In 1996 a Defence Office was set up in the Australian Embassy. Australian and Italian forces have served in United Nations (UN) peacekeeping operations, notably with Interfet in East Timor in 1999: Italy's generous contribution of a 640-strong contingent followed representations to that country by Australia (Steele 2008).

In July 2009 an MOU was signed regarding cooperation on the Square Kilometre Array, a proposed international advanced radio-telescope project. Many state governments have signed MOUs with Italian regional governments to promote cooperative activities and exchanges between the two parties.

Government-to-government relations also took place along city lines. Sister city agreements were developed between Sydney and Florence and ten years later Milan and Melbourne followed suit. In a less official capacity, as no formal arrangement was in place, there was a twinning arrangement between Victoria and the Veneto region and between Western Australia and Tuscany. The effectiveness of these arrangements is always questionable and neither country has gone to great lengths to promote them more than they needed. In the late 1990s negotiations began on working holiday arrangements for young people wishing to travel and work in either Italy or Australia. A bilateral Working Holiday Maker Arrangement finally became operative in January 2004, though as was noted by the then Ambassador Rory Steele, it required tremendous negotiation and considerable backdown by the Australian side to unblock the stalemate between Italy and Australia:

> ... the working holiday visa issue, we were dragging our heels. We were asking the Italians to consider our system of a one

stop shop in terms of visas and things like that. With us, you
get this one type of visa for work and everything. We wanted
reciprocity, but it was difficult. We wrangled about it for years.
The Italians wanted to have a working holiday arrangement with
Australia but they couldn't match our bureaucratic approach.
They said: "on our side, because of our constitution, we have to
have different types of security, at the national level and at the
regional level, the Ministry of the Interior and the *Carabinieri*
have to consent. Our history dictates that we must have a three
stage process of approvals for someone who wants to come
and work in Italy on this basis, whereas Australia required one
hurdle only to overcome before you got your visa. We argued
over that for a long time and I think we just caved in or we found
a way around it ... (cited in Mascitelli, Steele & Battiston 2010:
104-105).

A different form of incomprehension between Italy and Australia
occurred on the question of dual citizenship. Again, as Ambassador
Steele at that time noted, the Italian community was up in arms over
the contradictory approach in allowing dual citizenship once having
obtained Australian citizenship for Italians living in Australia. Steele
described the debate in the following manner:

> There was a similar policy issue then with dual citizenship. This
> wasn't something where there was pressure from the Italians in
> Italy, rather it was all the community in Australia. Again we went
> through 180 degrees saying no, no if you want dual citizenship,
> if you're Australian and you take out Italian citizenship for
> example, then you'll lose your Australian citizenship. And we
> shifted 180 degrees on that – so suddenly from no, no, no we
> went yes, yes, yes. I think that was a common sense decision in
> Australia as we woke up to the fact that we could actually lose
> citizens. We wanted to get citizens, we are a migrant receiving
> country, we wanted to gain migrants so there was a sudden
> switch. There was pressure from Italian community groups

in Australia saying current policy is mad, those who had one citizenship namely Australian and wanted to take out Italian citizenship ... (Steele interview in Mascitelli, Steele & Battiston 2010:105-106).

Expatriate voting and the Australian view

Intense relations between the Italian and Australian government were renewed when Italy implemented the Italian expatriate vote and representation in 2001. Greater levels of consultation and interaction became the norm in the preparation of the expatriate vote in Australia, which was one of the nations with a significantly large Italian population located in the cities of Melbourne and Sydney. At first Australia was opposed to permitting the Italian expatriate vote due largely to the (unfounded) fears that the large Italian community might engage in unsocial activities and possible political violence. However in late 1999 Australia abandoned its opposition to the Italian expatriate vote (Mascitelli, Steele & Battiston 2010:12). In an internal memo entitled "Italy: Voting rights for citizens abroad", sent in March 1999 from the then Ambassador Rory Steele, the concern, very eloquently expressed, stated:

> There are of course other Australian concerns which we have routinely presented to our interlocutors here [Rome]. Namely the extraterritoriality of Italy's new legislation; the potential for divisive Italian issues to be imported into Australia; the undesirability of having election campaigns for another country carried out on Australian soil; possible damage to bilateral relations; and the precedent it might set for other countries/ communities in Australia. These are all matters which have in the past in a similar way also exercised Canada, alone among the major destinations of Italian migrants (Internal DFAT memo, "Italy: Voting rights for citizens abroad", 4 March 1999, cited in Mascitelli, Steele & Battiston, 2010:307).

Italian expatriate voting throughout the globe has provided

an extra window for Australia to see Italy in a different light. Australia monitored Italian expatriate voting insofar as it related to its sovereignty and eventually saw it as harmless and non-invasive regarding Australia sovereignty (Mascitelli, Steele & Battiston 2010). While there are different views on the issue of expatriate voting and especially the Italian model, there is little doubt that two Italian Australian parliamentarians sitting in the Italian parliament have raised the Australian profile in Italian political quarters.

Conclusion

The aim of this chapter has been to explore and separate the rhetoric from the reality in terms of the relationship between two countries that have, for their specific motives, pursued quite distinct directions in foreign policy, especially since the 1970s. In many respects this was a partial conclusion reached by Steele in his 2008 paper when he concluded by saying:

> There are many ... reasons why the relationship has failed to realise its undoubted potential, and most of them have nothing to do with government, although it is true that over the past couple of decades both Canberra and Rome have increasingly concentrated on priorities within their own region (Steele 2008).

This was, by Steele, a "positive and hopeful" summary of the relationship. It is difficult to see how this relationship can be sustained. Things have changed between the two countries. Since 2006 the Lowy Institute has promoted an information census on "What Australians think of other countries". Its aim was to examine what Australians thought of almost 40 countries that included France, Germany, the UK, India, China and the United States (Hanson & Oliver 2013). Italy was not considered for this census (2013) despite the presence of large numbers of Italians in Australia. This non-consideration of Italy is but an example of the dismal nature of this relationship and a theme of this book.

Italy and Italians in Australia are an important part of Australia's immediate past and much less so of its immediate future. The human, cultural and socio-political vestiges of the Italian presence in Australia are today nostalgically cherished but in the overall picture of Australian history will be but one phase of its development. There is nothing wrong with this outcome nor should be there be concern. It is stating the obvious. In changing and uncertain geo-political fortunes, the two countries pursue their strategic national interests that, as it turns out, are one of separateness, as they were prior to the onset of the migration program in the late 1940s.

References

Andrews E.M., 1978, *Patterns in Australian Foreign Policy, from Selected Readings in Australian Foreign Policy*, Ed. David Pettit & Anne Hall, Sorrett Publishing Victoria.

Blainey G., 2005, *A Short History of the 20th century*, Penguin Books, Victoria.

Booker M., 1976, *The Last Domino: Aspects of Australia's Foreign Relations*, Collins Publishers, Melbourne.

Bosworth R.J.B., 2007, *Mussolini's Italy: Life Under the Fascist Dictatorship, 1915-1945*, Penguin Putnam, USA.

Cresciani G., 2003, *The Italians in Australia*, Cambridge University Press, Cambridge, UK.

Cresciani G., 1980, *Fascism, Anti-Fascism, and Italians in Australia, 1922-1945*, ANU Press, Canberra.

Curran J. & Ward S., 2010, *The Unknown Nation: Australia After the Empire*, Melbourne University Press, Melbourne.

Curtin J., 1941, The tasks ahead, 27 December 1941, http://john.curtin.edu.au-/pmportal/text/00468.html accessed 23 May 2013.

Department of Foreign Affairs and Trade (DFAT), 2013, website Italy: Country profile, Bilateral relations, http://www.dfat.gov.au/geo/italy/italy_brief.html, accessed 2 October 2013.

Department of Foreign Affairs and Trade (DFAT), 1996, *Annual Report*, Commonwealth Government, Canberra.

Department of Foreign Affairs and Trade (DFAT), 1999, Internal DFAT memo from the Australian Embassy, Rome, "Italy: Voting rights for citizens abroad", 4 March 1999, cited from B. Mascitelli, R. Steele & S. Battiston, *Diaspora parliaments: How Australia faced the Italian challenge,* 2010, Connor Court Publishing, Ballan, Victoria: p. 307.

Edwards P., 1997, *A Nation at War*, Allen & Unwin, Sydney.

Evans G. & Grant B., 1991, *Australia's Foreign Relations: In the World of the 1990s*, Melbourne University Press, Victoria.

Fitzgerald R., 2003, *The Pope's Battalions: Santamaria, Catholicism*, University of Queensland Press, Brisbane.

Ginsborg P., 2003, *A History of Contemporary Italy, 1943-1988*, Palgrave Macmillan, London.

Gobbo J., 2010, *Something to Declare: a Memoir*, The Miegunyah Press, Melbourne.

Grassby A., 1993, *The Australian Republic*, Pluto Press, NSW.

Grech J. & Cahill D., 2005, The Catholic Church and the Australian Nation – Monolithic or Multicultural, A paper delivered at the Australian Catholic Bishops conference, Sydney NSW.

Hanson F. & Oliver A., 2013, The Lowy Institute Poll on Australia and the world: Public opinion and foreign policy, in: edited by M. Fullilove and A. Bubalo, *Reports from a Turbulent Decade* – Lowy Institute, Penguin Viking, Melbourne, Australia.

Henderson P., 1985, *Parliament and Politics in Australia*, Heinemann Educational Australia, Victoria.

Henig R., 2005, *The Origins of the Second World War*, 1933-41.

Hudson W. 1988, *The Australian People and Foreign Policy, in In pursuit of National Interests: Australian Foreign Policy in the 1990s*, Edited F. Mediansky & A. Palfreeman, Pergamon Press, NSW.

Jupp J., 2009, *The Encyclopaedia of Religion in Australia*, Cambridge University Press, UK.

Keating P., 2000, *Engagement: Australia Faces the Asia-Pacific*, Pan MacMillan Australia, Sydney.

Lenzi G., 2011, Diplomats, politicians and foreign policy in post-war Italy, *UNISCI Discussion Papers*, No. 25, January 2011, p. 25, http://pendientedemigracion.ucm.es-/info/unisci/revistas/UNISCI%20DP%20 25%20-%20LENZI.pdf, accessed 7 June 2013.

Mammarella G. & Cacace P., 2006, *La politica estera dell'Italia*, Editori Laterza, Bari-Roma.

Mascitelli B., Steele R., & Battiston S., 2010, *Diaspora Parliaments: How Australia Faced the Italian Challenge*, Connor Court Publishing, Ballan, Vic.

Mayne A., 1997, *Reluctant Italians? One Hundred Years of the Dante Alighieri Society of Melbourne*, Dante Alighieri Society, Melbourne.

McGregor R., 1999, Silencing the immigrant song: Closed doors or open minds? in: Ed. P. Kelly, *Future Tense: Australia Beyond Election 1998*, Allen Unwin, NSW.

Meaney N. 1985, *Australia and the World: A Documentary History from the 1870s to the 1970s*, Longman Cheshire, Melbourne.

Metcalf B., 2011, *Utopian Fraud: The Marquis de Rays and La Nouvelle-France*, Utopian Studies, Vol. 22, No. 1, 2011, The Pennsylvania State University, University Park, PA, http://www98.griffith.edu.au/dspace/bitstream/handle/10072/45489/76210_1.pdf;jsessionid=AA8BB9E1BB4 53D72D1BD6A996C8D6F6D?sequence=1, accessed 27 June 2013.

Mortara G., 1925, *La Salute pubblica in Italia durante e dopo la Guerra*. New Haven: Yale University Press.

O'Brien I., 1988, *Australia's Italians, 1788-1988*, The Italian Historical Society and The State Library of Victoria, COASIT, Victoria.

O'Brien I., 2007, Citizenship, Rights and Emergency Powers in Second World War Australia, *Australian Journal of Politics and History*, 48, 3 June 2007, pp.207-222.

O'Connor B., 2012, Arthur Calwell Memorial Lecture, 3 April 2012, Speech delivered in Melbourne, http://www.minister.immi.gov.au/media/cb/2012/cb185365.htm, accessed 3 May 2013.

O'Farrell P., 1977, *The Catholic Church and Community in Australia: A History*, Nelson Limited, Melbourne.

Oliver A. & Shearer A., 2011, Diplomatic disrepair: Rebuilding Australia's diplomatic infrastructure, in: Ed. M. Fullilove & A. Bubalo, 10th anniversary collection, *Reports from a Turbulent Decade,* Lowy Institute, Sydney.

Panucci F., B. Kelly & S. Castles, 1992, Italians help rebuild Australia, in: *Australia's Italians: Culture and Community in a Changing Society*, Ed. S. Castles, C. Alcorso, G. Rando & E. Vasta, Allen & Unwin, Sydney.

Pascoe R., 1987, *Buongiorno Australia: Our Italian Heritage*, Greenhouse Publications, Richmond, Vic.

Pesman R., 2000, Italian studies in Australia: Past, present and future, Ed. P. Genovesi & W. Musolino, *In Search of the Italian Australian into the New Millennium*, Conference Proceedings, Melbourne, 24-26 may 2000, Italian Australian Institute, Melbourne.

Rando G., 2005, Italo-Australians during the Second World War: Some perceptions of internment, University of Wollongong, Research Online, http://ro.uow.edu.au/cgi/viewcontent.cgi?article=1123 accessed 25 May 2013.

Santamaria B., 2007, *B.A, Santamaria: Your Most Obedient Servant – Selected letters: 1938-1996*, Ed. Patrick Morgan, The Miegunyah Press, Melbourne, Australia.

Steele R., 2008, 20th-century diplomatic and trade relations, in: *Australians in Italy: Contemporary Lives and Impressions*, Edited by Bill Kent, Ros Pesman & Cynthia Troup, http://books.publishing.monash.edu/apps/bookworm/view/Australians+in+Italy/52/xhtml/part01chapter02.html, accessed 1 October 2013.

Stirling A., 1973, *On the Fringe of Diplomacy*, The Hawthorn Press, Melbourne.

Stone N., 2009, *World War One: A Short History*, Basic Books, New York.

The Age, 1997, 'Roamer to Roma' Crean under attack, 1 October 1997, p. 8.

The Age, 1940, Contemptible! Italy's action: Scathing attack by Mr. Menzies, *The Age*, 12 June 1940 http://news.google.com/newspapers?nid=130

0&dat=19400612&id=Ip-ZVAAAAIBAJ&sjid=KpcDAAAAIBAJ& pg=7144,3969277, accessed 20 September 2013.

The Australian, 1978, Editorial: Democracy must go to war – or die, 19 May 1978, p. 8.

The Australian, 1978, Grief for migrants: Families pack masses as 350,000 mourn, 11 May 1978.

Whitlam G., 2002, *My Italian Notebook*, Allen & Unwin, NSW.

Woolcott R., 2003, *The Hot Seat: Reflections on Diplomacy from Stalin's Death to the Bali Bombings*, Harper Collins Publishers, Sydney.

2
Italo-Australian cultural relations after the Second World War: The case of the Frederick May Foundation for Italian Studies

Gianfranco Cresciani

Since the formation of nation-states, cultural exchanges, like sporting events, have served the purpose of encouraging, facilitating and promoting economic, diplomatic, military and political interaction and penetration in countries deemed, rightly or wrongly, to belong to one's sphere of interest, or having an ideological affinity, or being potential rivals. A case in point was the "ping-pong diplomacy" in 1971 that paved the way to a visit to Beijing by President Richard Nixon. At best, cultural contacts aimed at convincing "the other" of your good intentions, of your wanting to establish a climate of "peaceful coexistence". At their worst, it was an expression of cultural imperialism, seen with deep suspicion by "the others", who perceived in "foreign" efforts of cultural rapprochement a threat to their cultural independence and uniqueness. A menace aptly described by Virgil in his *Aeneid* when he wrote, referring to Greek city-states, *timeo Danaos et dona ferentes* (I fear the Greeks, even those bearing gifts).

Naturally, the strength or the weakness of any cultural relationship is dependent upon the proximity or the distance of the countries in question, not only in geographic terms, but also in social, economic, historical and geopolitical ones. This is the case for the cultural relations between Italy and Australia, two countries at the opposite side of the world, the former with an ancient, rich and complex cultural heritage, yet constantly – one would say to the present day – in the process of 'inventing' Italians. Massimo d'Azeglio's apocryphal phrase "we have made Italy, now we must make Italians" is perhaps paradigmatic of the country's failed attempts to instil in its fractious inhabitants what the Germans call *Staatsrecht,* the sense of the State. Italy's popular Northern League is a case in point. Its leaders, Bossi and Maroni, are today as divisive and racist as d'Azeglio, who in 1860 wrote in his *Epistolario*: "the union with Neapolitans is scary, it is like going to bed with a person taken ill with smallpox".[1]

Australia, also an ancient land, with its 40,000 years of indigenous history, followed by 200 years of "white invasion", is still in the throes of creating its national mythology. For many years, despite the fact that both were liberal democracies, several factors contributed to discourage meaningful cultural contacts with Italy: a different language, religion, political system, economic development, the one being a European nation, the other a British Commonwealth nation. In short, both countries had a different *Weltanschauung,* a fundamentally diverse place in the world. During the Depression, the chasm between the two nations was also favoured by rampart xenophobia in Australia, exemplified by the anti-immigrant riots in Kalgoorlie in 1934 and by the establishment in Queensland of the British Preference League; and in Fascist Italy, by Mussolini's henchman, Mario Appelius' insane catchcry *Dio stramaledica gli inglesi* (God curse the English many times over). When it came to rampant xenophobia, there was not much to choose between the two. The Italians were rather good, like the Australians, at murdering blacks as well. The fact that Italy and Australia fought against each other during the Second World War inhibited contacts, cultural or otherwise, between the warring countries, despite the fact that some Australians maintained a cultural connection with Italy by virtue of their Catholic tradition, faith, anti-British Irishness, classical education or class. Also, travel, the wool trade, being gay in a British imperial way tempered their perception of

Fascist Italy. Similarly, Italians in Italy strove through the International Red Cross, sometimes successfully, to keep in touch with their next-of-kin who had emigrated to Australia before the war and were now either interned as enemy aliens or living precariously in an understandably hostile environment, one that was often nonetheless much more cosy than in an Italy at least partially affected by real war.

Some tentative cultural contacts can be traced back to the 19th century, well before the unification of Italy and the Australian federation. For instance, the palace of Portici in Naples, royal residence of the monarchs of the Kingdom of the Two Sicilies, in the 1830s had a private zoo that included kangaroos. In 1820 Ferdinand II negotiated the acquisition of eighteen kangaroos in exchange for an equal number of papyruses from Herculaneum. The king acquired his kangaroos but Australia did not gain his scrolls, which remained in the hands of the British consul in Naples.[2] Interest in Australia increased during the second half the 19th century, during Italy's Liberal governments' quest to acquire a colonial foothold in the South Pacific. As well as sending its warships to Australian waters in a futile effort of gun diplomacy and beginning to export emigrants to the Antipodes, Italy took part in the two International Exhibitions held in Sydney in 1879 and in Melbourne in 1888. Italian "cultural" artefacts on show were marble statues, jewellery, Venetian glassware, furniture and alabaster. Australian universities were of course teaching the classics and priests were moving to and from papal Rome.

Both Liberal and Fascist Italies paid scant interest in pursuing an ongoing, formal cultural liaison with the new Australian nation, which reciprocated with indifference. *Bella Italia* and *Terra Australis Incognita* were the private domain of cultured Italians and British settlers in Australian colonies (before there was an Australia), the latter captivated, during their Grand Tour, by the treasures of classical Rome, Renaissance Florence or romantic Venice and, in contrast, feeling revulsion for the "lesser breed" natives with whom they were perforce coming into contact, especially at Naples, often the first port of call. Theirs was merely part of a general British or Anglo-Saxon response, shared by travellers from other European countries. For instance, French historian, travel writer and observer of social mores Pierre Jean Grosley (1718-1785) was disgusted by some Neapolitan habits: "the courtyards of palaces and hotels, the porches, staircases and landings of private houses are places used by passers-by for the discharge of their urgent needs".[3] Adelaide Ironside was interested in fresco painting, Sir Samuel Griffith in translating Dante's *Divine Comedy*, Randolph Bedford in 'discovering' Florence and the Renaissance through Anglo-Saxon eyes. Many middle-class Australian women who took their "duty free" voyage of discovery of Italy and "the continent" are representative of people who left Australia in search of excitement, engagement and entertaining in a different and, to them, exotic country.[4] Likewise, Australia attracted the interest of Italian travellers, such as ethnographer Enrico Giglioli, botanist Giuseppe Canali, astronomer Pietro Baracchi and surgeon Tommaso Fiaschi.[5] During the first half of the 20th century, Italian culture of a kind was spread in Australia by the chapters of the Dante Alighieri Society, by the lonely activities of anti-fascist Omero Schiassi, Reader in Italian at Melbourne University and by lectures given at the Fascist Branches by the few local intellectuals supporting the Regime, such as Antonio Baccarini, Ferdinando and Maria Bentivoglio and Lamberto Yonna. The universities taught some Italian and so did the Catholic Church. Not even Fascism, with its policy of spreading internationally its credo, despite claims that it was not an item for export, was planning to make a concerted cultural foray in Australia. Its only credible attempt to establish in 1938 a venue in Melbourne, a *Casa d'Italia,* which would spread Italian culture in this country, failed miserably when the person in charge of collecting money donated by Italian migrants, a pound sterling for a *mattone* (brick), embezzled its proceedings. Italy attracted Australians' attention only intermittently, for instance when airman Francesco De Pinedo flew from Rome to Sydney in 1925, or on the occasion of famed soprano Toti Dal Monte's wedding in Sydney in 1928, or when press reports on Mafia and *Mano Nera* (Black Hand) murders were blown up out of proportion. Likewise, Australia was seldom mentioned in Italy, except in rare circumstances, for example when pioneer Australian aviator and Fascist sympathiser Bert Hinkler crashed in Tuscany in 1933 during a solo flight from England to Australia and was buried, on Mussolini's orders, with full military honours in the Protestant cemetery at Florence.

It was only after the Second World War, with the beginning of mass migration from Italy to Australia, mainly from the impoverished South, improvement in communications, Italy's 'economic miracle' of the 1950s and 1960s and its cultural revival, spanning from cinema with its neo-realist films by Rossellini, De Sica, Bertolucci, Fellini and Visconti to literature with Moravia, Calvino, Levi and Pasolini and the establishment of diplomatic relations between the two countries in 1948 that formal cultural contacts were made. On 4 February 1949 Giulio Del Balzo, the first Italian representative, arrived in Sydney, where the Italian Legation was situated, and C. V. Kellway, his Australian counterpart, reached Rome on 9 November 1949.[6] However, it is interesting to note that, while an Australia-Italy Migration Agreement was signed in Melbourne by Harold Holt and Giulio Del Balzo on 29 March 1951, it took another twenty-four years for the two governments to enter into an Agreement of Cultural Co-operation, signed in Rome on 8 January 1975 by prime ministers Gough Whitlam and Aldo Moro. As always, trade, even its human variation, took precedence over culture.

From the 1950s, cultural contacts between Italy and Australia developed in quantity and sophistication, also in view of the fact that in 1958 the Australian Legation in Rome had been upgraded to the status of Embassy, its first Ambassador being the Catholic D. P. McGuire.[7] These exchanges involved all tiers of government, the universities, the business world, private institutions, individuals and the media. Australian journalist, author and playwright Desmond O'Grady resided and worked in Rome after 1962, writing about the Vatican Council II and on Italian affairs ranging from politics to culture and travel, mainly for the *Sydney Morning Herald* and the *Melbourne Age*. It would be impossible to mention all exchanges that took place in the last sixty years. They included aspects of artistic and cultural endeavour, and established a framework upon which to build future initiatives. At federal government level, Australia was quick to mark its presence. The prestigious Venice Biennale was a forum where Australian artists represented their country after 1954. In that year, Sidney Nolan, Russell Drysdale and William Dobell exhibited their works, as in 1958 did Arthur Streeton and Arthur Boyd. In future years, Australia's presence would be a recurrent affair, especially after 24 June 1988, when Industrial Relations Minister Ralph Willis officially opened an Australian Pavillion at the Giardini. The Pavillion, designed by Architect Phillip Cox, was constructed by Franco Belgiorno Nettis' company Transfield. In 1973 he had established the Biennale of Sydney, and would remain one of its most important financial supporters.

The federal government, through its arts funding bodies, the Australian Council for the Arts, created by prime minister Harold Holt in 1967, the Australia Council, established in 1974 by Gough Whitlam, and its Department of the Arts, was instrumental in organising and supporting several major initiatives throughout the years, namely the funding of major blockbuster exhibitions, among them *Pompeii* in 1980-81. The Australia Council also managed several artists' studios in Italy, where writers, musicians and visual and performing practitioners could go to perfect their skills. The studios were located in Venice, Rome, at Besozzo, near Milan and at Il Paretaio in Tuscany. Of lasting influence was the cultural activity by Bernard Hickey as a teacher of Commonwealth literature at the University of Venice from

1968 and as a professor of English literature at the University of Lecce from 1988 until his death in 2007. Academic Brian Matthews, who met Hickey for the first time in 1974, described him as "a rotund, slightly gnome-like figure with a shock of just-greying hair, and a huge smile that managed to appear both joyous and mischievous".[8] With the financial support of the Australia Council and the network of contacts in Italian academia and among prominent exponents of Venice's *dolce vita* – Hickey was a socialite, friend of American millionaire Peggy Guggenheim –, he organised seminars on Australian literature that were attended by academics and writers from Australia and Italy. In 1979, he funded *Società Italiana di Studi Australiani* (SISA), that held seminars at Bologna (1979), Turin (1980), Sicily, Florence and Pisa (1981-2), Udine, Venice and Rome (1982). Bernard Hickey became a kind of roving cultural ambassador in Southern Europe and behind the Iron Curtain. In Lecce, he established a Centre for Australian Studies in the Mediterranean, to which he bequeathed his library of 7,000 volumes on Australian literature, albeit seldom consulted by Italian readers.

The Italian government reciprocated in kind. Under the aegis of the Ministry for Foreign Affairs, it opened at Punt Road, Melbourne an Italian Institute of Culture, which in 1974 moved to larger premises in South Yarra. The Institute comprised meeting rooms and a library of 9,000 books, periodicals, CDs and video cassettes. Another Institute of Culture opened in Sydney in 1977. It published three issues of an informative bulletin entitled *Italian Cultural Activities* before being closed in 1982. Its last Director, having been posted from francophone Beirut, did not speak English. It reopened on 12 February 1986. During 1991-1995, under the direction of Gerlando Butti and the guidance of Consul-General Fabio De Nardis (1949-2008), Sydney's Institute contributed significantly to bring Italian culture to Australia. Exhibitions on the *Barocco Emiliano,* on *Rediscovering Pompeii,* on *The Scale of Space. Contemporary Italian Architects* and on

Renaissance Drawings from the Uffizi, just to mention a few, were possibly due to the Consul-General's personal intervention. De Nardis was also instrumental in facilitating a series of lectures in Sydney by distinguished Italian architects, among them Renzo Piano, who designed in Sydney the Aurora Place office and accommodation towers, Gae Aulenti, who refurbished Paris' Gare d'Orsay, Mario Bellini, who was commissioned to plan the extension to Melbourne's National Gallery of Victoria and Paolo Portoghesi, the architect of Rome's Islamic mosque. With foresight, De Nardis saw the potential of spreading Italian culture in this country as a means of redefining its dominant Anglo-centric mythology. In 1994, the year before being posted to Paris as First Counsellor at that Embassy, he wrote a seminal paper, *La cultura italiana in Australia come elemento di forza del paese,* in which he advocated a greater presence of Italian design, architecture, cuisine, youth initiatives, literature and technology.[9]

During the second half of the 20th century Italian art blockbusters proved a most popular and successful medium in Australia. In 1982, Sydney University hosted *Spelt from Sybil's Leaves. Explorations in Italian Art,* an exhibition from the Padiglione d'Arte Contemporanea in Milan. The Art Gallery of New South Wales staged several exhibitions with Italian themes, among them *The Renaissance in Venice* in 1988 and one on Italian painter Giorgio Morandi in 1997. In 1997 the National Gallery of Victoria displayed *San Marco in Venice,* and in 2000 Sydney's Powerhouse Museum exhibited *Leonardo Da Vinci. The Code Leicester.* In 2002 Sydney's Museum of Contemporary Art hosted an exhibition on *Arte Povera. Art from Italy 1967-2002,* from the Castello di Rivoli Museo d'Arte Contemporanea in Turin. In 2002 Canberra's National Gallery of Australia staged *The Italians,* a major review of three centuries of Italian art, and in 2011-12 an exhibition of 70 Renaissance paintings from Bergamo's Accademia Carrara, including masters such as Bellini, Botticelli, Mantegna and Raphael.

Perhaps the most significant presence by Italy in Australia took place in 1988, during the celebrations for this country's Bicentenary of white settlement. Entitled *Italy on Stage* and attended by President Francesco Cossiga and Prime Minister Giulio Andreotti, the event included a concert by the orchestra of the National Academy of Santa Cecilia directed by *Maestro* Giuseppe Sinopoli, a recital by soprano Katia Ricciarelli, costumes from the Teatro La Scala, an exhibition of Roman jewellery from Pompeii and a film festival. The kermess, funded with unusual largesse, was marred by disorganisation. The orchestra played to a half empty Opera House, as few people had been admitted to the invitation-only event. On his part, from 1997 until 2001, the Australian ambassador to Italy, Rory Steele, organised an Australian Film Festival on Rome's Isola Tiberina. In recent years, the British School in Rome greatly expanded its Australian contacts, mainly for economic reasons.

Of public interest were also the visits to Australia by Italian academics and intellectuals, such as Sergio Romano, then Italian Ambassador to the USSR and former Director of Cultural Relations at the Ministry for External Affairs. During his stay in Sydney, Romano gave a lecture on Italian foreign policy at the Australian Institute of International Affairs and sought a meeting with the Coalition's Shadow Minister for Foreign Affairs, John Spender, husband of Italo-Australian fashion designer Carla Zampatti. At that time Romano was assessing the global impact of the Soviet Union's mammoth energy development in Siberia, and wanted to know what was the Opposition's policy on this issue. Spender, showing remarkable political narrow-mindedness, could not understand the relevance of this question, because in his opinion the USSR's booming construction of gas and oil pipelines and massive energy exports to Europe and China were not affecting Australia's economic and strategic interests. Romano and his American wife spent their last days in Sydney buying vacuum-packed beef, as it was unsafe to purchase meat in post-Chernobyl Moscow. In 1998 Claudio Magris, writer and foremost Italian expert on German literature, took part in Sydney's Writers' Festival and so did novelist Niccolò Ammaniti in 2003. Distinguished historian Paul Ginsborg, teaching at Florence University, spoke several times at Melbourne and in 2012 at the University of Sydney on "Italy and the European Crisis: Problems and Prospects". Italy's musical prestige was enhanced in 2004, when Maestro Gian Luigi Gelmetti was appointed Chief Conductor and Artistic Director of the Sydney Symphony Orchestra. In 2003, Patrizia Piccinini, born in Reggio Emilia but Australian citizen, was selected to represent Australia at the Venice Biennale.

Italian emigration to Australia, particularly after the Second World War, has been significant, peaking in 1971 when, according to the Australian census, some 289,476 people born in Italy resided in this country. The Italian organisation that over the years paid particular attention to the cultural history of migrants was Rome's Centro Studi Emigrazione of the Scalabrinian Order. Under the leadership of Gianfausto Rosoli, it dedicated several issues of its journal *Studi Emigrazione* to the Italian presence in Australia. Documents and memorabilia of Italian migrants from New South Wales were included in a major exhibition organised by Rosoli at Ellis Island, New York, entitled *The World in My Hand. Italian Emigration in the World. 1860-1960*. The exhibition was opened on 23 June 1997 by the Italian Minister for Foreign Affairs Lamberto Dini.

At State government level, NSW established with Venice's International Centre Cities on Water an annual six-month exchange residency and a scholarship of $9,000 for research on architectural and environmental issues relating to the quality of life, design and urban development of cities on water such as Sydney and Venice. It was named, upon Gianfranco Cresciani's suggestion to Premier Carr, after academic and urban architect Max Kelly. At that time Cresciani was managing the exchange on behalf of the NSW Ministry for the Arts. Between May 1995 and 2002 several young Italian architects came annually to Sydney to study and research, and an equal number of

Australians resided in Venice to appraise themselves on the problems and solutions adopted by that city. The first Australian winner was historian and planner Greg Young, who used his time in Venice to develop a planning and promotional concept for the islands, foreshores and waterways of Sydney Harbour National Park, drawing on Venetian and other models for cities on water. In March 1998 scholars Jennifer Hill (Australia) and Davide Longhi (Venice) took up residency. In 1999 Marco Migotto completed his research on *Conservation and reuse of industrial architecture in Venice,* while in 2000 Alessandro Costa researched on the remediation and redevelopment of Homebush Bay Olympic Site, and in 2001 Caron Mountsey-Smith examined *Master Planning in Venice.* The International Centre Cities on Water, under the leadership of architect Rinio Bruttomesso, was particularly interested in Sydney's infrastructure development. In 1994, Cresciani, Kelly and former NSW government Architect Colin Still spoke at the Faculty of Architecture of Venice University on "La baia di Sydney. Progetti culturali in cantiere e recupero del patrimonio edilizio". In 1997 the Centre hosted a lecture by Cresciani on the "Sydney Cove Waterfront Strategy" and in 1998 an address by the same speaker on "Culture and Port Redevelopment of the Walsh Bay Port Area".

During the 1990s the NSW government and Frederick May Foundation Scholarship, valued at $5,000, was set up to assist people to travel to Italy to gain experience of that country's cultural forms. In 1997 the scholarship was awarded to singer Nadia Piave, to undertake a course in the Baroque vocal style and performance in Urbino and Siena. The State government was also represented on the Council-run Sydney-Florence Twin City Committee. In 1994 the NSW Ministry for the Arts organised the staging in Rome of an exhibition of 37 prints and five oils by the distinguished Italo-Australian painter Salvatore Zofrea, and a photographic exhibition of 57 panels on the history of Italian migration to Australia. The shows were staged at the prestigious Acquario Romano, under the aegis of the tenth program of cultural co-operation implementing the cultural agreement between Italy and Australia for the years 1994-97. It was officially opened on 7 July by Rome's Mayor Francesco Rutelli and by the NSW Minister for the Arts Peter Collins.

Beside the above-mentioned contacts, several other organisations pursued exchanges with Italy, among them the Italian Committee of Assistance (COASIT) in Sydney and Melbourne, through its Italian Historical Society; Victoria University, with its Italian Australian Records Project, established with funding from the Australian Research Council; the Italian Australian Institute in Melbourne, whose founding chairman was entrepreneur Rino Grollo; the Italians in NSW Project of the State Library of NSW; Melbourne's Vaccari Foundation, which was formed in 1990 from donations to Victoria University Library and later the Australian Institute of Multicultural Affairs Library. Its collection contains over 4,000 titles. From the Italian side, to ensure the continuation of the study of Italian language and culture at tertiary level, in 1999 Treviso's Cassamarca Foundation donated $6 million over six years to fund 11 lectureships, scholarships and a chair in Latin Humanism at Perth's University of Western Australia. At the expiry of the term, the Foundation extended its commitment with a gift of 900,000 Euros per year over 13 years, its total value being approximately $22.5 million dollars. Perth-based Australasian Centre for Italian Studies (ACIS) is the Foundation's main instrument in Australia.

Important aspects of Italy's attraction to Australians include its centuries-old cultural accretion, evidenced by its Greek, Roman, Norman, Arab, Spanish, French and German pasts, its cuisine and the myth of *Bella Italia*. Many Australian artists, especially after the Second World War, elected to reside in that country in order to draw inspiration and work there. In 1991, among the many painters and sculptors living in Tuscany and Umbria were Jeffrey Smart, Justin O'Brien, Ken Whisson, Keith Looby, Lorri Whiting and Barbara

Campbell. Poet Bernard Whiting and wife Lorraine Fraser, sculptor, painter and sister of former Prime Minister Malcolm Fraser, lived in Rome since 1955 and bequeathed their apartment in Trastevere to the Australia Council, to be administered as a term residence for Australian writers. Many Australian artists, novelists and even some academics escaped in some way to some version of Italy, mainly because they were Catholic or gay or both.[10]

Despite Australia's obvious attraction to Italians, there is no institutional presence in Italy promoting Australian culture, as a counterpart to Italy's Institutes of Culture in Sydney and Melbourne. With the exception of the Centre for Australian Studies in the Mediterranean, established at the University of Salento in Lecce and Monash University's European Studies Centre in Italy (MESCI) in Prato, which opened on 17 September 2001 with the financial assistance of the Grollo family, the establishment of an Australian cultural institute in Italy did not take place. Although in late 2005 the Monash Centre held in Prato an important symposium on "Australians in Italy", it could not have the same impact as a federal institution would have, properly funded and pursuing a coherent, long-term cultural policy. However, a case to the contrary could be made that such institutions in a globalised and technologised world are hopelessly dated and irrelevant, and much better might be to try to place culture where quality already exists, that is, in the best universities. In reality, an attempt to reach an understanding with the Italian government to open in Rome a cultural institute was made at the meeting of the Mixed Commission to re-negotiate the Italo-Australian Cultural Agreement, held in Rome on 26-28 September 1989. The Italian delegation was prepared to identify a building in Rome to be assigned to Australia for this purpose, provided the Australian government would guarantee funds for its refurbishment, maintenance and running. This pledge was not given, and Article 17 of the IX Program of Cultural Co-operation inconclusively resolved that "the Italian side, in welcoming the prospective opening of an Australian Cultural Centre in Rome, gives its assurances that it will assist as far as possible in the realisation of this initiative". The issue of a permanent, physical Australian presence in Rome was not raised again at future meetings.

The framework informing Italo-Australian cultural relations is the 1975 Agreement of Cultural Co-operation, renegotiated every four years ever since by a Mixed Commission comprising bureaucrats from the respective Foreign Ministries. The agreement provides the essential, official context for Australian activities in Italy and Italian ones in this country. Obviously, not all initiatives programmed become a reality, but the Mixed Commission meetings are a useful forum where proposals and projects can be canvassed, discussed, supported or rejected. The agenda is wide-ranging, including items such as the teaching of languages and the dissemination of culture, universities and scientific co-operation, scholarships, publishing, libraries, archives and museums, the protection of cultural assets, cinema, radio and television, sport and tourism, youth exchanges and the arts. By the end of the 1990s both parties felt that their bilateral relationship should be enhanced, not only politically and economically, but also culturally. On 6 February 1997 foreign ministers Lamberto Dini and Alexander Downer issued a joint declaration entitled "Australia and Italy in the 21st Century", where the establishment of an Australia-Italy Economic and Cultural Council was announced, in order to "intensify our cultural exchange and to ensure that our bilateral relationship remains dynamic and meets its full potential". However, economic reality and the "tyranny of distance" precluded a significant enhancement of cultural contacts, even if these were traditionally receiving a temporary burst during the visits to Australia by Italian Presidents Giuseppe Saragat in 1967, Francesco Cossiga in 1988 and Oscar Luigi Scalfaro in 1998, and by Popes Paul VI in 1970 and John Paul II in 1986.

The most significant and intense period of cultural interaction between Italy and Australia was between 1976 and 1999, when the Frederick May Foundation for Italian Studies at the University of Sydney, established on 7 June 1976, undertook a series of high profile initiatives. It was named after May, a Londoner who at the end of 1963 took up the first Chair of Italian at an Australian university and until his death on 11 January 1976 remained a controversial and idiosyncratic figure, with his sandals, shabby dress, unkempt hair, plastic bag full of books that he was loath returning to the library and unconventional exams papers, with the questions sometimes arranged like "concrete poetry". His charisma was still intact in 1985, twenty years from his death, when a journalist from Sydney's gutter newspaper *L'Opinione* described him as a "toothless libertine ... a pornographic clown ... [enjoying] a hackneyed reputation of being an immoderate genius".[11] Initially, the Foundation, set up by Silvio Trambaiolo, then Acting Head of the Italian Department, had three objectives: to promote Italian studies at academic level, to encourage the study of the Italian language and culture at pre-tertiary level, and to enlarge the collection of Italian books and periodicals in the University's Fisher Library. This predominantly literary thrust was confirmed by the series of memorial lectures held in June-July 1976 on themes concerning Italian writers Verga, Pasolini, Leopardi, Montale, Pirandello and Manzoni. One of the speakers was Gino Rizzo, Professor of Italian and Comparative Literature at City University, New York, who compared Pirandello's writings with those by Brecht and Artaud. The Foundation's major activity for 1977 was a symposium, held in May, on the Italian Baroque, with public lectures, seminars, plays and exhibitions on Italian history, art, literature and music of the Baroque period. These activities reflected the – at that time – cultural interests of serving Council members. At its meeting of 29 November 1967, Council approved that only the Departments of Fine Arts, Italian and Music be represented.[12]

In mid-1977 May's successor was appointed in the person of

Rizzo, who during the Resistance fought with the partisans of the Osoppo brigade in his birthplace, the Veneto region, and in the United States had been instructor in Italian to the American Army, but with decidedly modest levels of academic output. From the outset of his tenure, it became evident that a wider objective ought to be pursued, aimed at establishing direct contacts and exchanges with Italian business, academia and the economic and political world, bypassing the filter of Anglo-Saxon intellectuals who, until then, had been the privileged "exporters" of Italian culture to Australia. At its meeting on 6 December 1976, the University Senate appointed Paul Sonnino to the position of Chairman of the Foundation. Sonnino was a wealthy textile merchant who, during the early 1940s, together with his friend Claudio Alcorso, a Jewish refugee like him, had been one of the founders of Melbourne's anti-Fascist movement Italia Libera, which published from 1944 until 1956 the newspaper *Il Risveglio*. Other generous sponsors were Renata Salteri, wife of Carlo, one of the founders of the Italian construction company Transfield; arts philanthropist Vivian Chaldwin, who was also appointed as one of the Foundation's Governors; the Italian companies Alfa Romeo, Olivetti Australia and the Italian Consulate-General and its Institute of Culture.

In 1977, the idea of publishing a book of Italian studies with a predominantly literary content in memory of Frederick May was canvassed. The volume, edited by Trambaiolo and Nerida Newbigin, entitled *Altro Polo. A volume of Italian Studies,* was launched in 1978. It contained a contribution by Umberto Eco, 'Pirandello *Ridens*'. In order to widen the Foundation's sphere of interest, on 16 June 1977 Richard Bosworth, Cresciani and Roslyn Pesman put forward a proposal to hold in August 1978 the First Australian Conference on Italian Culture and Italy Today. Bosworth and Pesman were then charismatic teachers – in critical vein – of a year-long undergraduate course in Italian history at Sydney University, that began with the present, went back to the Renaissance and then delved on the

Risorgimento and Fascism, while Cresciani was employed by the Italo-Australian construction company Electric Power Transmission. The proposed event, encompassing history, politics, sociology, literature, music and fine arts, would require, the proponents stressed, "financial support from private industry, airline companies, the Australia Council and other Federal and State bodies interested in the advancement of Italian culture in Australia".[13] The net had been cast wide. On another important development, the Senate of the University of Sydney, at its meeting on 1 August 1977, noted the appointment of Rizzo as director of the Foundation, a move that has been preannounced by the Foundation's Chairman, Sonnino, at the Foundation's Council meeting on 16 June 1977.[14]

One year of intense planning and programming followed. The purpose of the Conference – and it would remain the same for other events that will follow – was "to provide an international and interdisciplinary forum for the study and interchange of ideas on the political, cultural and social conditions of present-day Italy ... Cultural relations between Italy and Australia have been few and uncoordinated. Media coverage tends to be alarmist and superficial ... Italy has presented a tripartite image to Australia: the 'poetic country' of art, music and Mediterranean sun; the poor country which offers itself to cheap tourism and which sends its sons to be labourers in Australia; the complicated country of perennial political crisis, of Fascism and Communism, of scandals and corruption, and yet the world's seventh industrial power ... The Conference aims at an analysis of the character of modern Italy, its cultural and political traditions, and its points of contact with modern Australia."[15]

Several Italian academics were contacted and invited to attend, among them Lucio Coletti, Alberto Asor Rosa, Pietro Scoppola, and Renato Zangheri, but were unable to accept. Of the overseas attendees who intervened at the conference on 27-31 August 1978 were Renzo De Felice of Rome University, who spoke on "Italian historiography since the Second World War": Giuliano Procacci of the University of Florence, who delivered a lecture on "The workers' movement from its beginning to Fascism"; Paolo Valesio of Yale University, on "Decoding ideological messages"; Giorgio Spini of Florence University, on "Death and rebirth of Italian socialism, 1925-1946" and on "The political life of Michelangelo"; Francesco Alberoni of the University of Catania, on "The Italian crisis, 1968-1978"; Eugenio Battisti of Cosenza University, on "The visual arts in contemporary Italy"; Pietro Spinucci of Padua University on "Patrick White in Italy" and Giuseppe Bartolucci of Rome's Theatre on "Images of the Italian *avant-garde* theatre".

The participation of such eminent Italian scholars was a coup for the Foundation, as it raised its profile and attracted interest among Australians interested in Italian affairs, academia and the Italian Ministry for Foreign Affairs. De Felice was the acknowledged biographer of Mussolini and had a keen interest in the history of Italian emigration to South America, Canada and Australia. His wife, Livia De Ruggiero, daughter of Neapolitan historian of European Liberalism Guido De Ruggiero, in 1979 translated Cresciani's book on *Fascism, Anti-Fascism and Italians in Australia. 1922-1945,* which De Felice had it published by Bonacci Editore, Rome. Procacci, author of a book on the *Storia degli Italiani,* was a prolific writer on the labour movement, international affairs and Marxist ideology. Later he would be appointed Senator to the Italian Parliament, representing the Italian Communist Party. Spini was a charismatic figure in the Socialist movement and author of many works on the history of Protestantism, among them *Italian Protestantism in the 20th Century.* Alberoni was the leading sociologist of the time. His main work was *Movement and Institution*, one of the first books on the sociological analysis of movements, their start, development and end. Alberoni had been influenced by the teachings of Franciscan friar and sociologist Agostino Gemelli.

As well as the plenary sessions held at the Stephen Roberts

Theatre of Sydney University, meetings and discussions were held, upon suggestion by Bosworth, at Wollongong University, at FILEF (Federation of Italian Workers and their Families), Friends of the Labor Party, the Australian Communist Party, with the State Minister for Education, Eric Bedford, and at Melbourne's Italian Institute of Culture. Also, a photographic exhibition of 58 panels on "The History of Italian Anti-Fascism In Australia", curated by Cresciani, was held at the Stephen Roberts Theatre. The conference was a big success, with over 500 people attending. Its budget of $31,088 was not exceeded, the total cost having been $26,787. Major contributors were Chalwin ($5,000), the Australia Council ($8,000), the Italian government ($4,200), the Italian Cultural Institute ($1,220) and Wollongong University ($2,250). De Felice sent to the conservative newspaper *Il Giornale* a reportage entitled *Come ci vedono agli Antipodi* (How they see us from the antipodes), and Battisti to the Communist *Paese Sera* his own account on *Italia e Australia: due culture con parecchi punti di contatto* (Italy and Australia: two cultures with many meeting points).

Buoyed by the results achieved with the First Conference, the Foundation began planning future initiatives that would establish it as the engine house of Italian culture in Australia. In July 1979 a second *Altro Polo* was launched. Its editors, Bosworth and Cresciani, published in it the Conference papers by Procacci, De Felice and Spini as well as contributions from Trieste's historian Elio Apih and Belgrade's scholar Dragan Zivojinovic. At the Foundation's Council meeting, held on 21 June 1979, Sonnino retired from the Chairmanship, to be replaced by Chalwin, and Adrienne Lussu was elected Vice-Chairman, in place of the previous office bearer, C. Cobianchi, Managing Director of Pirelli Cables. Adrienne's husband, Lucio Lussu, was Chief Executive Officer of Agip Australia. Over the years, Chalwin and the Lussus contributed substantially to the Foundation's initiatives, for instance underwriting the publishing costs of the second issue of *Altro Polo*, beside contributions from Olivetti Australia and Electric Power Transmission.

During 1979, other activities emphasised the Foundation's long-term planning to influence Australian culture by means of direct contacts with Italian institutions and academics. In July Bosworth delivered a lecture on the 1908 Messina earthquake and arranged a photographic and book exhibition at Fisher Library on this subject. His paper drew attention to the long-standing problems of poverty and alienation in the Italian south. Concurrently, an exhibition of some 350 Italian books was opened in the Rare Book Library at Fisher Library and in October Italian experimental films were shown at Paddington. The final activity for 1979 was a Book Fair held on 15-16 December at the *Casa d'Italia* in Surry Hills. Made possible by the generous conditions offered by several major Italian publishers and with the sponsorship of Alitalia Airlines, the Foundation offered for sale at discounted price some 4,000 books dealing with history, politics, sociology, literature, music, cinema, theatre and fine arts. By the end of 1979, the Foundation had increased its paid membership to 120, as against 85 members at the end of 1978. Paradoxically, despite the crucial contribution given for more than one year by Bosworth and Pesman to the planning of the First Australian Conference on Italian Culture and Italy Today, by the end of 1979 the Department of History was still not officially represented on the Foundation's Council. A proposal to change to this effect the Foundation's Constitution was put forward at the Council's meeting of 10 November 1977, and on 30 March 1978 Council approved that "one member of the Department of History, who shall be a member of the Foundation and shall be elected by all the teaching members of the Department of History" be elected to the Council.[16] One of the reasons why this obvious and necessary amendment took so long to be approved was the persistent, subterranean opposition to it by staff of the Italian Department, who venerated the memory of May and held in contempt Rizzo and his progressive ideas.

They never forgave him for introducing "politics" in the Foundation, for allegedly favouring "history" over "literature". On his part, Rizzo was not shy of making scathing remarks on allegedly untrustworthy members of his Department. This endemic tension was also reflected in the relationship between the so-called Italian community, if a body of such nature ever existed, towards the Foundation. Its self-appointed "leaders", some suspected of Mafia and 'Ndrangheta connections, paternalistic and still sporting a fascist mindset, shunned or openly criticised the Foundation for its engagement in a critical assessment of modern Italy, while they were anxious to avoid such "communism".

March 1980 saw the Foundation holding its third annual general meeting. Guest speaker on that occasion was former Prime Minister Whitlam. In an address entitled "The Italian Inspiration in English Literature", he proposed that a companion to Italian literature be compiled, "from Frederick II to Frederick May Australia", he went on, "is well situated and equipped to produce a work which will be useful and attractive to scholars and students of both English and Italian and to the pilgrims who will always take the many roads which lead to Rome". On this occasion, Whitlam indicated his willingness to be associated with future activities of the Frederick May Foundation by accepting to become its Honorary Governor. In 1980 the Foundation published the former Prime Minister's address as well as the third issue of *Altro Polo,* a critical anthology of contemporary Italian poetry edited by Raffaele Perrotta. On 12-13 July 1980 a symposium was held on Andrea Palladio. It consisted in a series of lectures on various aspects of Palladian art, a photographic exhibition of Palladian buildings and an exhibition of models.

The Foundation's major commitment for 1980 was a three-day conference, held on 25-27 July, on "The Roots of Fascism, Italy 1900-1922". On that occasion, visiting speakers were Franco Ferraresi, Professor of the Sociology of Labour at the University of Turin, who spoke on "The Image of Fascism in contemporary Italy", and Giovanni

Sabbatucci of the University of Macerata, one of De Felice's pupils who in later years would become one of Italy's leading historical commentators, who delivered a paper on "Soldiers and society in war and *dopoguerra*". The conference was opened by Sergio Angeletti, Italian Ambassador to Australia, and Whitlam took part in the round-table discussion on the theme "Fascism – before and after". In August Ferraresi and Sabbatucci also spoke at Melbourne's Italian Institute of Culture, and Ferraresi published in September, in Milan's *Il Sole – 24 Ore*, two long articles on Australia under the prime ministerships of Whitlam and Fraser. The conference, well attended by many Italian migrants, struck a cord with them, in particular the plea made by the conference's convenor, Bosworth, who in his address exhorted them to "read Italian history ... Italians in Australia will only be real citizens of this country when they master their own history both in Australia and in Italy".

Other initiatives taken were the sponsoring on 18 June of a public lecture by Professor Cecil Grayson of Oxford University on "Italian literature and the concept of the Renaissance", and a lecture on "Problems of the Italian economy today", given on 15 October by distinguished economist Paolo Sylos-Labini of "La Sapienza" University, Rome. The year 1980 closed with a sad note, as Chalwyn died on 5 October. He had been a sincere friend of Italy, a personal friend of Frederick May and a generous benefactor. Adrienne Lussu succeeded him to the position of Chairperson of the Foundation.

Already at its meeting on 12 June 1980, the Foundation's Executive Committee began planning for the Second Australian Conference on Italian Culture and Italy Today, to be held in 1982. An approach made by Cresciani to Sergio Romano, Director-General for Cultural, Scientific and Technical Co-operation of the Italian Ministry for Foreign Affairs, gave positive results. On 24 September 1980 Romano wrote: "we could examine the possibility of supporting the initiative with a Ministry's contribution towards the realisation of a Conference promoted by the Frederick May Foundation, concerning Italo-Australian relations in the historical, cultural and migration fields'.[17] In October and November, Rizzo and Cresciani held discussions in Rome with Romano concerning the 1982 Conference. By the end of 1980, the prestige and influence of the Foundation was strengthened by co-opting to its Council Lorenzo Borla, General Manager of Ferrero Australia. Lucio Lussu for Agip Australia and Franco Belgiorno-Nettis for Transfield were its Governors. Borla was appointed to the position of Foundation's Deputy Chairman.

Meanwhile, during 1981 contacts with distinguished Italian academics continued. On 30 July Franco Venturi gave a lecture on "The Role of Intellectuals in Modern History" at the University of Sydney. Venturi, author of the multi-volume *Settecento Riformatore,* was an Italian historian, essayist and journalist, a scholar of the Enlightenment in Italy, of the history of Russia and an anti-fascist, active in the Resistance. On 17-21 May distinguished linguist Raffaele Simone gave a seminar on "Italian language and civilisation". During the year, work proceeded towards the preparation of the fourth issue of *Altro Polo,* a volume of Italian Renaissance studies, edited by Conal Condren and Pesman, which was published in 1982. Also, most of the year was spent in the preparation of the 1982 Conference, contacting possible speakers, raising funds, booking venues, planning activities and securing the official participation by the Italian Ambassador and by the Premier of New South Wales. By March 1982, the Foundation had 146 paying members.

The Second Australian Conference on Italian Culture and Italy Today, held on 3-8 August 1982, arguably was the largest, most expensive and most successful enterprise until then undertaken by the Foundation. Twenty speakers and guests from Italy were invited, and another ten flew to Australia at their expense to attend its proceedings. Funds totaling approximately $70,000 were raised through contributions from Agip, Alitalia, the Australia Council, Banca

Commerciale Italiana, the Italian Cultural Institutes of Sydney and Melbourne, the Italian Ministries of Education and Foreign Affairs, the NSW government, the Universities of Sydney and Wollongong, Transfield and Westfield. On 20 April 1982 Cresciani was successful in negotiating in Rome with Saverio Avveduto, Director-General of Education, the sending *in missione* to Australia of Professors Bertelli, Zambelli and Fabbri at that Ministry's cost. On 14 January 1982, Neville Wran, Premier of New South Wales, accepted the invitation to open the Conference.[18]

The Italian speakers who attended represented the best of Italian culture and academia at that time. Vittore Branca of the University of Padua and Vice-President of the Cini Foundation in Venice, an international authority on Italian humanism of the 14th and 15th centuries, spoke on "Boccaccio and other early illustrations of the Decameron". Sergio Bertelli, Professor of modern history at the University of Florence, gave a lecture on "Politology in the Florentine Republic"; Paola Zambelli, Professor of Philosophy at the same University, read a paper on "Magic and astrology in Renaissance Italy"; in his second lecture Sergio Bertelli dealt with "*Il Gruppo*, an unorthodox comment on Italian Communism"; Emilio Gentile, of the University of Camerino, spoke on "Italian right-wing radicalism: myth and organisation"; Paolo Fabbri, from the University of Bologna, delivered a paper on "Television in Italy: decoding the media"; Claudio Gorlier, of the University of Turin, addressed the issue of "Italian characters and stereotypes in Australian literature"; Alberto Asor Rosa, of the University of Rome, dealt with "Trends in contemporary Italian literary criticism"; Vittorio Gregotti of the University of Venice spoke on "Architecture and the urban environment, 1970-82"; Pier Maria Lugli, an architect from Rome, illustrated the topic "The Utopian tradition in Italian urban planning and design"; Luigi Ballerini of New York University spoke on "Exploration in Italian art" and Giuseppe Bartolucci of Teatro di Roma on "Theatre as communal celebration".

Upon his return to Italy, Branca published in Milan's *Corriere della Sera* two articles on Australia and the Foundation.

Umberto Eco, the charismatic Professor of Semiology at the University of Bologna, wrote his intervention while the previous speaker was giving his lecture, and delivered a captivating speech on "New developments in the mass media of contemporary Italy". Marcello Colitti, Deputy Chairman of Agip, spoke on "The role of Italian state industry". The Conference included also two round table discussions, moderated by Whitlam and by Eco. On 6 August the Conference moved to the University of Wollongong, where the causes and effects of emigration and immigration were discussed. Two speakers from Italy took part: Ercole Sori, from the University of Ancona, who addressed the issue of "Economic factors behind Italian emigration", and Gianfausto Rosoli, Director of Rome's Centro Studi Emigrazione, who dealt with "Catholicism and the issue of migration, 1880-1980". Among related activities were an exhibition of contemporary Italian art, *Spelt from Sybil's Leaves: exploration in Italian art,* and performances by Rome's *avant-garde* theatre group La Gaia Scienza, *Gli insetti preferiscono le ortiche.*

The second Conference confirmed that the May Foundation was Australia's main vehicle for cultural contacts with Italy. By 1982, its members had established working relationships with a spate of European and international institutions, among them Milan's Brodolini Foundation and the Centro di Politica Estera e Opinione Pubblica, Belgium's Groupe Europeen de Recherche et d'Information sur l'Italie, Rome's Centro Studi Emigrazione, the History of Immigration Research Centre of the University of Minnesota, Bologna's John Hopkins School of Advanced International Studies, the United States Association for Italian History, the Friedrich Ebert Stiftung, the Istituto Socialista di Studi Storici and the Institut zur Geschichte der Arbeiterbewegung at the Rurh Universität in Bochum.[19]

By then, its importance was recognised by Italian and Australian authorities. Already in April 1981 Giovanni Migliuolo, Italy's Director-General of Emigration and Social Affairs had written to Romano, recommending that the "May Foundation's initiative be encouraged and supported financially, for no other reason than the considerable number of our nationals living in Australia and the positive attitude taken by Australian authorities towards the culture and traditions of the Italian community".[20] In November of the same year, Angeletti issued a communiqué, stating that "I wish to express my own personal support for the Frederick May Foundation for Italian Studies. In the few years of its activities, the Foundation has already established itself as a committed cultural organisation for the purpose of promoting the different facets of the Italian society. I think that the Foundation is a worthwhile and unique organisation not only for the scope of its activities, but also because it enjoys the full operational structure of the University of Sydney".[21] Earlier, R. H. Robertson, Australian Ambassador to Italy, had made the remark that "one can only hope that ... the sort of commonality of records that exists between the United Kingdom and Australia ... be developed to the same degree with Italy".[22] Following the 1982 Conference, Eco wrote to Rizzo, commenting that "I have seldom seen a conference so 'total', successful in dealing with a large number of issues and making a cross-examination (*spettrografia incrociata*) of Italian culture in Italy and in Australia. I wish that also in other countries our culture be spread with such vivacity and passion ... Sydney's and Australia's Italian community have a strong sense of identity, few complexes, a lot of energy and many ideas ... I seldom had this impression in other countries".[23]

Starting from these solid foundations and encouraged by public and international response, the Foundation began planning its 1983 activities. During that year it published two issues of *Altro Polo*, one co-edited by Bosworth and Rizzo on "Intellectuals and their ideas in contemporary Italy", the other, also co-edited, by Peter Groenewegen and Joseph Halevi, on "Italian economics. Past and Present". The latter volume further widened the Foundation's academic sphere of interest. On 24 November 1983, Ambassador Angeletti launched at Sydney University the volume *Australia, the Australians and the Italian Migration,* edited by Cresciani. It had been published in Milan, both in English and Italian, as one of the *Quaderni di Affari Sociali Internazionali* by Franco Angeli and contained the papers on issues relating to migration that were given at the Second Conference.

The most significant initiative of that year was the preparation by Bosworth and Cresciani of a "Promemoria on the cultural relations between the Italian Republic and the Commonwealth of Australia – Position of the Frederick May Foundation for Italian Studies". The document, drafted on 25 April, stressed that "the Foundation is in the enviable position of acting, for many Australian circles, as a basic reference point for the many projects here which aim to make better known Italy as it is today, rather than merely engaging in superficial celebrations of the past Italy of the Roman Empire and the Renaissance ... The continuous and fundamental ambition of the Foundation", the document went on, "has been to create the political basis necessary for a direct diffusion and development of Italian culture in Australia by eliminating the traditional mediation of British and American networks". The authors recognised that "institutionally speaking, the Foundation exists inside the structure of the University of Sydney, and thus has certain institutional and constitutional limitations. For example, it cannot expand and open branches in other Australian cities. In addition, it must concentrate on the spread of Italian culture in Australia, rather than acting directly to spread Australian culture in Italy". In order to overcome these obstacles, the Foundation was asking from the Italian government four things: joint planning for an Italian cultural policy in Australia; co-ordination with the activities of the Italian Institute of Culture in Melbourne (Sydney's one had just been closed); official recognition and support by the Italian State; ongoing financial support.[24]

Bosworth and Cresciani also endeavoured to secure a similar arrangement with the Australian government. They sought a meeting with Barry Cohen, Minister for Home Affairs, on 16 May held discussions in Canberra with officers of the Department of Foreign Affairs and were authorised by Ambassador Angeletti to convey his official encouragement and support for their bid. On 15 June, Bill Hayden, Minister for Foreign Affairs, diplomatically signalled his appreciation for this initiative. However, the May Foundation request was rejected. On 23 August 1983, the Department of Foreign Affairs wrote that "at least for the present, it would not be appropriate to give the Frederick May Foundation a formal, continuing role in the management of official-level cultural relations between Australia and Italy. To give the Foundation what would amount to semi-official status would bring it into competition with several Commonwealth Organisations ... the Department cannot give any undertakings to provide diplomatic or financial support for the Foundation's activities or to liaise with it in respect of Departmental programs". In order to make his refusal less painful, the Department's Assistant Secretary gave the generic assurance that "there will be occasions when it will be mutually beneficial for the Department and the Foundation to act in concert ... [then] the Department will extend to the Foundation recognition and assistance appropriate to the circumstances".[25] The Commonwealth's refusal to grant the Foundation official status dashed its hope to become the official, main 'conveyor belt' of cultural exchanges between the two countries. From now on, it could rely almost exclusively on its strength and contacts.

Three major activities took place in 1984. On 30 April, the University of Milan organised a seminar on "Australia, la cultura australiana e i rapporti tra Italia ed Australia". Australian contributors were Pesman, who spoke on "Australian Images of Italy", Veronica Brady ("David Campbell's Poetry"), Newbegin ("Studi italiani in Australia") and Christopher Koch ("The Year of Living Dangerously"). In July,

Emilio Gentile, of the University of Camerino, gave a lecture on "Gli italiani e il mito di Mussolini". Gentile, a pupil of De Felice, was one of the leading historians of Fascism. Upon invitation by Bosworth, he also taught for a term undergraduates at the History Department of the University of Sydney.[26] However, the main commitment was the staging, on 11-13 August, of the mini-conference on "Art, Science and Perception in the Italian Renaissance". On that occasion, guest speakers from Italy were Amedeo Quondam of the University of Rome, who gave a lecture on "The Description and Representation of Space: The Renaissance Geographical Discourse between Ptolemy and Atlas". Franco Ferrucci, from Rutgers University, spoke on "Christian and Classical Mythologies in Italian Renaissance Literature". During the year another *Altro Polo,* edited by Anne Reynolds, was launched. Its theme was "The Classical Continuum in Italian Thought and Letters". The volume included contributions by Quondam and by American and Canadian scholars.

By 1985, the Foundation's international cultural relations were recognised for their wide-ranging impact, even in the United States. On 29 April, Richard Gardner, US Ambassador to Italy from 1977 to 1981 and Professor of Law and International Relations at Columbia University gave a lecture on 'An American Ambassador in Rome, 1977 to 1981".[27] Not all Italian academics saw with favour the intrusive interest by American scholars in Italian culture. Sergio Bertelli, one of the participants to the 1982 Conference, in a letter to Rizzo lamented "the overbearing imperialism of our Anglo-American colleagues ... we are a victim of, and accomplices in a situation that is also political-diplomatic. The absolute dependency by our government led to an equal dependency by our intellectuals".[28]

By this time, it had been the May Foundation's policy to plan for a major international conference every four years and for a smaller event in the intervening years. 1986 was the year chosen to host the Third Australian Conference on Italian Culture and Italy Today.

Throughout 1985, the Foundation's several committees embarked on the task of raising funds, contacting prospective speakers, advertising the event and securing venues. In view of past achievements, the Italian government was quick in pledging financial support. On 27 December 1985, Rizzo asked the Ministry of Education to send *in missione* four Italian academics, Luciano Cafagna, Paolo Ceccarelli, Maria Corti and Gianfranco Folena. Saverio Avveduto, the Ministry's Director-General, a few days later, approved the request.[29] So did the Italian Ministry for Foreign Affairs, which on 6 March 1986 pledged 15 million *lire* towards the Conference.[30] In 1985, the Foundation also established an annual, joint NSW government-May Foundation Scholarship, valued at $5,000. The Scholarship aimed at providing opportunities for people to travel to Italy to gain experience "from Italian cultural forms and organisations". A main event sponsored by the Foundation was the First Australian Congress of Classical Archaeology, held at the University of Sydney on 9-14 July 1985. Fourteen scholars from Italy took part in the event, as well as specialists from France, Bulgaria, Germany, the USA and UK, Austria, Greece, Spain and the U.S.S.R. The year ended with the sad note of the departure of the Italian Ambassador, Angeletti, posted to Ethiopia. Angeletti had been an indefatigable supporter and a strong advocate of the Foundation with his superiors in Rome.[31] Lucio Lussu also left, having been appointed Director of Foreign Affairs for the ENI Group in Rome, and the Foundation's Deputy Chairman, Lorenzo Borla, after ten years in Australia, was transferred back to Italy by Ferrero. These were momentous changes, precluding even more dramatic upheavals at the end of 1986 and in 1987. Still, the Foundation's prestige was running high, a fact reflected by the statement made by John Ward, the University's Vice-Chancellor, who described the Foundation as "was a warm testimony to the force of a good idea".[32]

Considerable effort was made early in 1986 to organise the Third Australian Conference on Italian Culture and Italy Today, which took place from 29 August to 2 September 1986 at the University of Sydney. Patron of the event was Sir Ninian Stephen, Governor-General of Australia. It was officially opened by Bob Carr, State Minister for Heritage and the Environment, in the presence of Eric Da Rin, the new Italian Ambassador to Australia who had replaced Angeletti. It turned out to be the largest initiative ever organised by the Foundation, thus becoming, as Romano, then Italian Ambassador to the Soviet Union and one of its participants quipped, "a staging post of Italian culture in the Antipodes ... [that] could also count on a vast Italian hinterland and on that 'nationalism in reverse', at the same time nostalgic and a little querulous, which always characterises Italian communities abroad".[33] Italian historians, sociologists, linguists, scholars of feminism, emigration, architecture, art and literature were invited. Among them were Romano, who spoke on "Culture and Italian foreign policy"; Enrico Serra from Bologna University and head of the Archivio Storico-Diplomatico of the Italian Ministry for Foreign Affairs ("The bureaucracy of Italian foreign policy"); Luigi Goglia of the University of Rome ("Outline of fascist colonial imperialism"); Pietro Spinucci of Verona University ("Australian literature in Italy: a personal encounter"); Gianfranco Folena of the University of Padova ("Travellers' images of Australia"); Rudolph Vecoli of the University of Minnesota ("Italians in the USA: a comparative perspective"); Robert Harney of the Multicultural History Society of Ontario ("Italians in Canada: a comparative perspective"); Raffaele Simone and Serena Ambroso from the University of Rome, who respectively spoke on "Maintaining the Italian language outside Italy" and "Linguistic minorities in Italy"; Laura Balbo, Member of the Italian Chamber of Deputies ("Recent developments in Italian sociology"); Gianfranco Poggi from Edinburgh University ("The crisis of ideologies"); Alberto Asor Rosa of Rome University ("The Italian Left today: between politics and ideology"); Franco Ferraresi from the University of Torino ("The New Right in postwar Italy"); Marcello

Colitti of ENI, Rome ("Italian state industry: the ENI perspective"); Marina Zancan of L'Aquila University ("The contribution of women to Italian literature"); Remo Bodei from the Scuola Normale Superiore di Pisa ("Philosophy and psychology in the development of Luigi Pirandello's work"); Paolo Ceccarelli of Venice University ("Venice: art, science and urban development"); Eugenio and Giuseppina Saccaro Battisti of Rome University, who respectively presented a paper on "Mannerism and baroque in recent art criticism" and "The historiography of Renaissance thought in the 17th century". Vecoli and Harney also spoke at Melbourne's Vaccari Italian Historical Trust. The Conference budget, totalling $59,200, was funded through grants and the financial support from Alitalia, ENI, the Australia Council, the Italian and NSW governments and the Universities of Sydney and Wollongong. At the conclusion of the proceedings, Conference delegates unanimously approved a motion requesting, among other things, that "the Italian government be urged to establish and support, through the Frederick May Foundation, an institute for the study and maintenance of Italian language and culture in Australia and the preservation of the history and heritage of Italian migrants in this country". Their plea was not successful, as the government in February of that year had re-opened its Institute of Culture in Sydney, a move that some academics considered to be a "bad idea", since they opposed the establishment of national cultural institutes in foreign countries, favouring instead inter-university exchanges. Similar lack of success was met by the Foundation seeking representation on the Federal government's recently established Italy-Australia Promotion Committee, under the Chairmanship of Franco Belgiorno-Nettis, who had been one of the Foundation's Governors. Canberra belatedly replied that "your Foundation might be represented on a Cultural Sub-Committee".[34] Another rebuff was received from Barrie Unsworth, Premier of NSW, who ignored the Foundation's suggestion to be allocated the $1 million that he had announced it to be used by the

Italian community for a Bicentennial project. Money would be spent, Rizzo said, "to expand its initiatives in areas not yet fully developed, such as a Centre for Migration Studies and Oral History, a Migrant Language Institute, and the creation of an Italian Migrant Archive in Sydney, the need for which is being increasingly felt given the size and the ageing of the Italian community".[35]

Upon their return, some of the participants published in the Italian press their account on the Conference and on Australia in general. Serra wrote an article in Turin's newspaper *La Stampa* entitled "Italian flags raised in Sydney. The increasing role of immigrants on the cultural scene"[36] and Romano had two reports published in Milan's *Corriere della Sera*, "The Australian mosaic: a continent in search of its identity" and "The day on which Sydney discovered Pirandello: Italian culture in Australia".[37]

Other Foundation's activities during the year included the launch of another *Altro Polo,* edited by Camilla Bettoni. The volume, with a preface by eminent Italian linguist Tullio De Mauro, was sub-titled "Italian Abroad" and dwelled on studies on language contact in English-speaking countries. Also, the Foundation's inaugural scholarships were presented to successful applicants. On 10 April, Ambassador Da Rin awarded the ENI-Enrico Mattei Scholarship, valued at $8,000, to Hugh Harley, to pursue his studies in economics at Cambridge. The Frederick May-NSW Government Scholarship was presented by Evan Williams, Director of the Office of the NSW Minister for the Arts, to Alison Leitch, to do field work in social anthropology at Carrara, Italy.

Given the considerable financial and organisational effort made in 1986, activities in the following year were necessarily modest. On 12 May, Italian novelist Dacia Maraini, then visiting Australia, was hosted by the Foundation to deliver her lecture on "Immaginario femminile e seduzione maschile in letteratura", and the following day Gian Giacomo Migone, a historian on Italian emigration to the US and editor of Turin's literary journal *L'Indice,* spoke on "The role of literary journals and small publishing houses in Italy". On 28-30 August, a symposium on 15th century architect Filippo Brunelleschi was held at the Art Gallery of NSW. Salvatore Di Pasquale, Dean of the Faculty of Architecture at the University of Florence was a guest speaker on that occasion.

The end of 1986 and the year 1987 represented a watershed in the history of the Frederick May Foundation. In June 1986, Edoardo Daneo, who represented ENI-Agip, was elected Chairman and Governor of the Foundation, replacing Adrienne Lussu, returning to Italy.[38] On 20 October 1986, Bosworth, who for years had been the Foundation's Deputy Director, announced that he would take up the Chair of History at the University of Western Australia, and would leave Sydney and the Foundation in January 1987. The Council resolved to appoint Cresciani as Deputy Director to replace Bosworth. Some eight months later, at the Foundation's Council meeting on 8 July 1987, Rizzo, on the eve of his retirement and relocation to Venice, announced his resignation as Head of the Italian Department and as Director of the Foundation. At the same Council meeting, confronted by Rizzo's claim that the Deputy Directorship was "an honorific position rather than executive", Cresciani immediately submitted his resignation as Deputy Director, considering the Director's remarks offensive as he, like Bosworth, had played for many years an executive role.[39] Trambaiolo was appointed Director of the Foundation, despite the fact that during the previous ten years his relations with Rizzo had been less than cordial. On 9 November 1987, Cresciani tendered his resignation as Deputy Chairman and Honorary Governor of the Foundation, as well as a member of its Council. He considered Rizzo's appointment of Trambaiolo, to be, at best, an inexplicable surrender to those who had consistently undermined him since his appointment, at worst, a betrayal of the Foundation's policy of "opening to the world" and a marked lack of interest on his part, *après moi le déluge,* in the future of the body to which he had given so much.[40] The loss of four of its most active members suddenly deprived the Foundation of a wealth of contacts, funding sources, and inspiration that had made it the most authoritative vehicle of cultural exchange with Italy. Most importantly, Italian Ministries, Australian Departments, the bureaucracies of both countries and the Italian business community in Australia, who for the previous ten years had identified these office-bearers with the Foundation, lost in them a point of reference, a trusted interlocutor, a committed exponent of Italian culture. Other people took over, among them Giovanni Carsaniga, who followed Rizzo at the headship of the Department and the Foundation, until his retirement in July 2000, Pesman, Mario Benanzio, Newbigin, and Lou Klepac, who was the Foundation's President from 1991 to 1995.

Activities progressively dwindled, although an important landmark was the publication in 1988 of *Altro Polo*, edited by Ian Grosart and Trambaiolo, containing mainly papers delivered at the 1986 Conference. Another important initiative was the Fourth International Conference on Italian Culture and Italy Today, subtitled "Italy and Europe" and held on 11-14 July 1991. Key Italian guests were the politologist Massimo Salvadori, Giuseppe Schiavone (Professor of International Relations, Institute of European Studies "Alcide De Gasperi"), Pino Arlacchi (University of Florence), Guido Neppi Modona (University of Turin), Remo Bodei (University of Pisa), Anna Dolfi (University of Trento), Alfredo Luzi (University of Macerata) and Paolo Ramat (University of Pavia).

The Frederick May Foundation for Italian Studies was officially closed in 1999. The April 2012 web site of the Department of Italian Studies of the University of Sydney claimed unconvincingly and perhaps put what might be read as a desperate attempt at self-justification that "the Foundation did not succeed in transforming its reserves of goodwill and energy into financial capital ... the Foundation was no longer able to receive direct financial assistance from the Italian government, and other organisations, which are able to receive funding, have taken over the Foundation's role in supporting Italian language and culture in the Australian community. It has therefore been appropriate to refocus the Foundation's energies on activities that are directly related to the University's principal activities of research and teaching".[41]

Some conclusions can be drawn from the Frederick May Foundation's successes and its demise. Its promising beginnings can be ascribed to the convergence, at that particular time, of several concomitant circumstances. The enthusiasm for Italian studies among students and the community aroused by Frederick May before his death facilitated the University approving the creation of a Foundation after his name. Sydney University's financial and logistic support over the years, as well as the reputation attached to being an official institution of Australia's oldest and most prestigious University made of the Frederick May Foundation the most important pole, one would argue the only *polo,* of Italian studies in this country. Another factor was the international network of contacts with academia, governmental institutions, business and the media that Rizzo, Lussu, Bosworth and Cresciani brought to the Foundation. Their capacity to attract the interest and participation in Foundation's activities by Italy's most respected academics and to maintain, indeed to increase over the years, the presence in Australia of experts in so many aspects of Italy's political, economic, social, artistic and historical life made of the Foundation the pivot upon which cultural contacts with Italy developed during the 1970s and 1980s. This time also was coincidental with the peak of Italian migrant presence in Australia, as well as with the beginning of its decline. The 1971 Census registered 289,476 people, the one of 1981, 275,883.

The Foundation's pre-eminence was also due to the fact that it was the only voice promoting Italian culture in the absence of other centres of Italian studies in Australia. At the very time when the Italian government was closing Sydney's Italian Institute of Culture, it afforded generous, preferential financial treatment to the Foundation. This situation lasted until the late 1980s. Also, the presence in Australia of enlightened managers of Italian multinationals, who saw in the Foundation a vehicle that could be used in the pursuit of their economic interests, was to the Foundation's advantage. At its functions, Italian captains of industry, business and finance mingled with their Australian counterparts, with Australian premiers, politicians, diplomats, bureaucrats, lobbyists, socialites and people who 'count'. Italians were firm believers that culture was the proverbial Trojan Horse necessary to penetrate business and financial circles, and they masterly rode that horse. Of great importance to the Foundation's success was the policy of multiculturalism enacted in 1972 by the Whitlam government and carried further by Fraser, that literally opened Australia to the world and secured respect and legitimacy to those which were euphemistically called "minority" cultures. Whitlam, a man of culture, in 1983 appointed Australian ambassador to UNESCO, strongly believed in the importance of cultural contacts among nations. In his speech on 23 November 1973 at the opening of the first Biennale of Sydney at Sydney's Opera House, he stated that "there remains an invincible element of philistinism in all societies, including our own, that exhibitions like this will help to break down".[42] The May Foundation, of which Whitlam was Honorary Governor and an active participant to its events, strove to break down the barriers of nationalism and chauvinism that, even in the cultural field, were a traditional obstacle to the understanding of the point of view of the "other". For pursuing this policy, the Foundation was at times accused of being "left-wing" and "anti-Italian". Italy's conservative historian Rosario Romeo, in an article published in *Il Giornale,* called Bosworth an "Italy hater". A typical example of this siege mentality was an article in Melbourne's *Il Globo* Italian newspaper that in 1983 lambasted the Foundation for "presenting to Australians, Italy and its culture in a warped Marxist key".[43]

It must be said that even some members of the Foundation viewed with uneasiness its foray in areas of study that lay outside the traditional, "safe" ones of teaching language and literature. "Left-wingism" was deeply resented, even if in the silence of their consciences. Indeed, it was to "traditional" university teaching, as previously mentioned, that the Foundation resorted when the *troika* of Rizzo, Bosworth and Cresciani left its leadership, when public and private funding dwindled and eventually dried up, also as a result of the economic crisis of the late 1980s, when international cultural contacts entertained in previous years ended, when no more cutting edge *Altro Polo* were published. The audacity, enthusiasm, determination and perseverance to become the indispensable conveyor belt of cultural exchanges between the two countries gave way to the proven, even if staid, practice of withdrawing behind the walls of a cultural ivory tower and shunning the challenges and dreams of forging in Australia an Italian cultural alternative, an *Altro Polo.*

The new millennium that began one year after the demise of the Frederick May Foundation does not augur well for Italian cultural exchanges. The Italian community is ageing and rapidly dwindling, there are no meaningful cultural structures comparable to the defunct May Foundation, cultural funding by both governments is reduced to a trickle, there is no long-term cultural policy, there are no new *troikas* galvanising the community, business and governments into cultural action, Italian multinationals moved to other, more profitable countries and the policy of multiculturalism is called in question. On the eve of the Italian political elections of 24-25 February 2013, in a letter to Italians abroad, Giulio Terzi, Minister for Foreign Affairs, seemed to delegate the pursuit of cultural relations, among other impossible tasks, to the two candidates elected in the ridiculously vast *circoscrizione elettorale* (electoral college) *Africa, Asia, Oceania e Antartide*: "Members of Parliament elected abroad contribute to strengthen Italy's global influence by fostering friendly relations and economic and cultural exchanges in countries where Italians reside".[44] Italy has become even more culturally distant while Australia has enthusiastically embraced the "Asian Century". The future of cultural exchanges with Italy is thus in the hands of future generations of Italo-Australians who hopefully will still see in Italian culture a mandatory reference point to define who they really are, although, for good or ill, they are more likely to be citizens of a globalised world.

Endnotes

1. http://cogitoetvolo.it/fatta-litalia-ora-bisogna-fare-gli-italiani/accessed 18 January 2013.
2. Harold Acton, *The Bourbons of Naples,* London, 1956, p. 660.
3. On this, see the impressions by travellers to Italy in: Ercole Sori, *La città e i rifiuti. Ecologia urbana dal Medioevo al primo Novecento,* Il Mulino, Bologna 2001, p. 19.
4. On Australians travelling to Italy, see: Roslyn Pesman Cooper, 'Randolph Bedford in Italy', in: *Overland,* No. 120, Spring 1990, pp.12-15; 'Australian visitors to Italy in the 19th century', in: Gianfranco Cresciani (Ed.), *Australia, the Australians and the Italian Migration,* Franco Angeli, Milano 1983, pp.124-141; 'Sir Samuel Griffith, Dante and the Italian Presence in Nineteenth-Century Australian Literary Culture', in: *Australian Literary Studies,* Vol. 14, October 1989, pp. 199-215; 'Majestic Nature – Squalid Humanity: Naples and the Australian Tourist 1870-1930', in: *Australian Cultural History,* No. 10, 1991, pp. 46-56; 'Some Images of Italy in Nineteenth Century Australia', paper given at the History '84 conference, Melbourne University, August 1984; 'Australian Tourists in Fascist Italy', in: *Journal of Australian Studies,* No. 27, November 1990, pp. 19-31; 'An Australian in Mussolini's Italy: Herbert Michael Moran', in: *Overland,* No. 115, August 1989, pp. 44-53; *Duty Free. Australian Women Abroad,* Oxford University Press, 1996. For a contemporary account on the Australian presence in Italy, see: Bill Kent, Ros Pesman and Cynthia Troup (Eds), *Australians in Italy. Contemporary Lives and Impressions,* Monash University ePress,

Clayton, Victoria 2008. Also: Gough Whitlam, *My Italian Notebook*, Allen & Unwin, Sydney 2002.

5. On Italians' impressions of Australia, see: Flavio Lucchesi, *L'esperienza del viaggiare. Geografi e viaggiatori del XIX e XX secolo*, Giappichelli Editore, Torino 1995; Alan Mayne, 'An Italian Traveller in the Antipodes: An Historical Rite of Passage', in: *Australian Cultural History*, No. 10, 1991, pp.58-68; Roslyn Pesman Cooper, 'Some Italian Views of Australia in the Nineteenth Century', in: *Journal of the Royal Australian Historical Society*, Vol. 70, December 1984, pp. 171-193. For a biography of Tommaso Fiaschi, see: Ivo Vellar, *Thomas Fiaschi. Italo-Australian patriot, surgeon, soldier and pioneer vigneron*, Publishing Solutions, Melbourne 2012.

6. James Jupp (Ed), *The Australian People. An Encyclopedia of the Nation, Its People and Their Origins*, Angus & Robertson, Sydney 1988, p.614.

7. McGuire's previous posting had been Ambassador to the Irish Republic. Born in Adelaide, he published on Australian and international affairs, as well as travel books, novels and poems. He lectured on modern history at the University of Adelaide. http://trove.nla.gov.au/ndp/del/article/18375232 accessed 30 December 2012.

8. http://books.publishing.monash.edu/apps/bookworm/view/Australians+in+Italy/52/xhtml/part06chapter24.html accessed 30 December 2012.

9. Cresciani Archive, Frederick May Foundation Papers (hereafter CRAMP) Fabio Claudio De Nardis, 'La cultura italiana in Australia come elemento di forza del paese', un-published essay, 1994.

10. Peter and Susan Ward, *In a Different Light. Australian Artists Working in Italy*, University of Queensland Press, 1991. On Italy's attraction to Australian gays, see: Robert Aldrich, *The Seduction of the Mediterranean: Writing, Art and Homosexual Fantasy*, Routledge, London 1993.

11. Guido Cicinelli, 'No, Luigi no, così non va', in: *L'Opinione*, Sydney, 6 May 1985.

12. CRAMP, Minutes of the Frederick May Foundation Council meeting of 29 November 1976.

13. CRAMP, Bosworth, Cresciani, Pesman, Memorandum, 16 June 1977.
14. CRAMP, Minutes of the Frederick May Foundation Council meetings of 16 June and 10 November 1977.
15. CRAMP, 'First Australian Conference on Italian Culture and Italy Today', Draft Programme by R. J. B. Bosworth, Acting Secretary, undated, in the 1978 file.
16. CRAMP, Minutes of the Frederick May Foundation Council meetings of 10 November 1977 and 30 March 1978; revised Constitution, dated 2 May 1978.
17. CRAMP, Sergio Romano to Sergio Angeletti, Ambassador of Italy to Australia, 24 September 1980.
18. CRAMP, Wran to Rizzo, 14 January 1982.
19. CRAMP, Rizzo and Bosworth to John Ward, Vice-Chancellor and Principal, The University of Sydney, 28 September 1982.
20. CRAMP, Giovanni Migliuolo to Sergio Romano, 8 April 1981.
21. CRAMP, Sergio Angeletti, communiqué, 27 November 1981.
22. CRAMP, R. H. Robertson to Cresciani, 24 July 1980.
23. CRAMP, Eco to Rizzo, 21 August 1982.
24. CRAMP, Bosworth and Cresciani, 'Promemoria on the cultural relations between the Italian Republic and the Commonwealth of Australia – Position of the Frederick May Foundation for Italian Studies', 25 April 1983.
25. CRAMP, Bosworth to Barry Cohen, 2 May 1983; Bosworth and Cresciani to Bill Hayden, 19 May 1983; Bill Hayden to Cresciani, 15 June 1983; Max Loveday, Assistant Secretary, Information and Cultural Relations Branch to Cresciani, 22 August 1983.
26. See *La Fiamma* newspaper, Sydney, 26 July 1984.
27. See *La Fiamma* newspaper, Sydney, 2 May 1985.
28. CRAMP, Bertelli to Rizzo, 15 October 1985.
29. CRAMP, Rizzo to Avveduto, 27 December 1985; Avveduto to Rizzo, 29 January 1986.

30. CRAMP, Rizzo to Bartolomeo Attolico, Director-General, Cultural Relations, 23 December 1985; Schmidt to Rizzo, 6 March 1986.
31. See *Il Globo* newspaper, Melbourne, 9 December 1985.
32. CRAMP, May Foundation Sixth Annual General Meeting, 7 April 1983, minutes.
33. Sergio Romano, 'E Sydney un giorno scoprì Pirandello. La cultura italiana in Australia', in: *Corriere della Sera*, Milano, 24 September 1986.
34. CRAMP, Rizzo and Bosworth to Prime Minister Robert J. L. Hawke, 6 June 1986; Jon Nicholson, Senior Private Secretary, Office of the Prime Minister to Rizzo, 26 November 1986.
35. CRAMP, Rizzo to Unsworth, 18 August 1986.
36. Enrico Serra, 'Cresce nella cultura il ruolo degli immigrati. Bandiere italiane a Sydney', in: *La Stampa*, Torino, 1 October 1986.
37. Sergio Romano, 'E Sydney un giorno scoprì Pirandello', op. cit.; 'Un continente alla ricerca della propria identità: il mosaico australiano', in: *Corriere della Sera*, Milano, 13 October 1986.
38. Edoardo was the son of Silvio Daneo, the first Italian Ambassador to Australia, who arrived in August 1952, during the crisis of the Bonegilla riots. In his report back to Rome, Daneo underlined "the racism that he deemed endemic in Australian society and the general crudity and boorishness of what he defined as the "rustic democracy" of the locals" [James Jupp (Ed), *The Australian People. An Encyclopedia of the Nation, Its People and Their Origins*, Angus & Robertson, Sydney 1988, p.614].
39. CRAMP, Frederick May Foundation for Italian Studies, Minutes of the meeting of the Council, 8 July 1987.
40. CRAMP, Cresciani to Trambaiolo, 9 November 1987.
41. http://sydney.edu.au/arts/italian/research/societies.shtml Accessed 20 December 2012.
42. National Archives of Australia, Sydney, Series M533, item 193, Speech by Mr Whitlam.
43. See *Il Globo* newspaper, Melbourne, 5 September 1983. Giulio Terzi, Circular letter to Italians Abroad, Roma, 12 January 2013.

3
The Anglo-Italian Treaty: Australia's imperial obligations to Italian migrants, 1883-1940

Catherine Dewhirst

Between 1883 and 1940 Italian migrants' rights were legally classified as equal to those of British subjects in Australia, whether naturalised or not. They were protected by international law under the 1883 Treaty of Commerce and Navigation between the United Kingdom and Italy (the Anglo-Italian Treaty). That the Anglo-Italian Treaty stipulated access by the "respective subjects" of both powers to equal "civil rights" within their sovereign territories, including "dominions and possessions" (Great Britain. Foreign Office 1931: 369, 372-373), proved contentious for the Australian government after 1901. In practice, the terms of the Treaty for reciprocal rights to travel, residency and property-ownership were frequently violated in Australia as a result of the fractured nature of the political and legal framework, influenced by Queensland's colonial legacy. A series of negotiations over legal interpretations and power struggles punctuate the history of Australia's imperial obligations to Italian migrants that lasted almost 60 years.

While nation-building from 1901 engineered the White Australia policy to target non-'white' peoples, the cultural landscape from the 1920s began to shift for European migrants. Certain groups of Europeans, including Italians, were cast as racially inferior to the more preferable British due to fears about an unemployment crisis, which dovetailed with rising ultra-nationalistic attitudes. This led to immigration restrictions on Europeans, straining the federal government's obligations under the Treaty. But the disputes about the rights of Italians to purchase land and take up cane cutting jobs in Queensland made matters worse. In the context of the global economic climate and Australia's preferences for British migrants, a prolonged debate ensued over Italian migrants' legal entitlements. There was not only a conflict with the spirit and the letter of the Treaty but also with Queensland's legislation. Examining diplomatic correspondence from Australia's federal and state politicians, Italy's consular representatives, and British authorities reveals the extent of how Queensland contravened the Treaty. There were two influences here. First, wider community anxieties about foreign nationals in the sugar industry created difficult circumstances for negotiations. Second, the machinations of imperial politics intervened to resolve the conflict in a devious way.

The Treaty's erosion can be dated back to a "Gentlemen's Agreement" from the Queensland sugar industry in 1930, which had a powerful influence on the state government's legislative processes to resist bending to the Treaty's terms. This led to a decision within the British government in 1935 to resolve the dilemma, which effectively silenced the Italian Consul General's complaints while also duping the power of the Australian Prime Minister. Yet, while a profound deterioration of perceptions about Italians developed, Italian migrants had supporters, many of whom were influenced by the action that a small group of migrants took in defending their rights. This chapter focuses on Australia's imperial responsibilities to the British Empire and Italy that accidentally protected Italian migrants, charting the legal ramifications from international negotiations and the natural justice expected by Italian migrants. Tracing the history of the Treaty goes to the heart of the consistent injustices that Italian migrants experienced in Australia that culminated in the internments from

1940. To appreciate why negotiations failed to uphold the Treaty is, to a large extent, to comprehend the nature and degree of anti-Italian sentiment in Queensland.

The foundations of Australia's and Italy's imperial obligations

The Anglo-Italian Treaty was one of many agreements that European nations were sanctioning during the last quarter of the 19th century. It symbolised the traditional friendship between Great Britain and Italy but also spoke to the geopolitical context of imperialism. The contemporary British historian Leonard Woolf (1919:24) describes the general ambiance of European relations from the 1880s as being "dominated by rival imperialism, colonial policies, spheres of influence, commercial treaties, markets, and tariffs". From the mid-1870s, the British Empire was threatened by what Gaston (1982:318-319, 323) refers to as a "transitional period" in global trade terms, stemming from the rising industrial strength of Germany and the United States. Up to the 1880s, imperialism produced heightened diplomatic tensions between Britain, France and Italy over Tunis, and, by 1884, over strategic and commercial control of East Africa (see Woolf 1919:88-119, 156-157; Lowe and Marzari 1975:21-24). Britain was concerned about its colonial territories in Africa and the strains on its commercial markets. As such, the British Foreign Office directed its energies to clawing back the Empire's export power through a number of agreements on free trade with European nations.

Italy was dependent on international agreements at this time. There was much to gain, including recognition as a great power. Industrial underdevelopment as well as the global agrarian crisis contributed to the need for international treaties (Lowe and Marzari 1975:10; Tosi 1989:787-788). From the 1880s, Italy developed imperial policies through a formal colonial program of aggressive expansion into the Mediterranean region and East Africa, and irredentism, and through informal economic ties across the diaspora (see Choate 2008:1-20).

Export power was central to Italy's economic sustainability, which first expanded through Italy's Chambers of Commerce abroad (Choate 2008: 82-83). In this light, the Anglo-Italian Treaty manifested an alliance to counter French imperial intentions to expand into East Africa while also aiming to protect British and Italian interests there and elsewhere. At a time when migration hardly factored into international agreements, it could not have been foreseen that Italian migrants' rights would disturb colonial laws that Australia inherited when the Commonwealth was created in 1901.

The historiography on the Treaty began with diplomatic historical interest from the late 1920s, which emphasised Australia's desire for autonomy from Britain in governing its own foreign affairs. According to Bailey (1929: 190), Australia had more flexibility in negotiating commercial rather than political agreements prior to Federation despite legal obligations to 24 British treaties up to this time. There was a general understanding over the second half of the 19th century that Britain's international negotiations required consultation with the colonies. Indeed, a precedent had been set in Newfoundland in 1855 when this colony declined to be party to an Anglo-French treaty (Stirling 1934: 28). Both Bailey (1929: 191) and Stirling (1934: 30) remark, however, on the exceptional case of the 1883 Treaty because of Australia's inability to withdraw from it. The Australian government attempted to do so on two occasions before the First World War and on another in the early 1920s on the basis of the country's commercial and immigration needs.

What made withdrawal so impossible? "Italy refused", states Stirling (1934:30). Nicholson (1955:133) points out that this became "a source of embarrassment" for Australia not only due to the government's lack of power in negotiating another agreement but also because of Australia's reliance on trade with Italy. Indeed, Italy was one of the greatest importers of Australian products up to 1934 (Nicholson 1955:134). But the Treaty was also exceptional in that it was the only commercial treaty that Australia had with a foreign power to survive the First World War (Nicholson 1955:24). The history and implications of the Treaty have since received surprisingly little attention with the exception of some references in Italian-Australian studies and Southern European immigration history (see: MacDonald 1958:126; Cresciani 1985:37; Langfield 1991a:5-6, 11; Douglass 1995:194-195; Dewhirst 2008:39-40). Although the political discrimination and racialisation of Italians posed a paradox for the Treaty's effectiveness, the failure of the federal government to resolve the political agitation in Queensland marks Australia's powerlessness in enforcing domestic cohesion and handling foreign relations.

Italy may have refused to release Australia from its Treaty obligations, but the peculiarities of Australia's colonial politics and 'race' relations emerged as more pressing problems. On the one hand, this had to do with the federal government's desire for autonomy from the British Empire, which was "ubiquitous" through economic, legal and patriotic ties (Macintyre 2001:125-126). On the other, the government had to manage what Macintyre (2001:113) terms the "obdurate independence" of the states and various sectors of society, inherited from the colonial days, for the benefit of national cohesion. Although the federal government oversaw trade and immigration, the states maintained the infrastructure, governing on matters of property, education, health, public services and moral behaviour (Macintyre 2001:95). It is notable, however, that these peculiarities proved to be legally impotent against the strength of the Treaty until the period between 1935 and 1940.

Little thought would have been given to Italian migrants in colonial Australia when British Ambassador to Italy Augustus Berkeley Paget met with the Italian Minister of Foreign Affairs Pasquale Stanislao Mancini in Rome on 15 June 1883 to sign the Treaty.[1] Prominent in their minds was no doubt the reciprocal commercial ties and the means for securing trade between Great Britain and the Kingdom of

Italy. In less than a year, on 10 March 1884, the Treaty was ratified by the colonies of Natal, Newfoundland, New South Wales, Queensland, Tasmania, Victoria, Western Australia, and New Zealand. Later the Orange Free State and the Transvaal, the Irish Free State, India, Southern Rhodesia and Malta also acceded (see Great Britain. Foreign Office 1931:375). With Federation, the Australian government "fell heir to the treaty obligations of the States"[2] and took responsibility for any communications on behalf of the five colonial signatories (Bailey 1928:176). When issues arose in 1908, 1912 and 1923 the government attempted to withdraw from the Treaty.[3]

The Treaty officially lasted until 1947, despite some confusion about whether it was in operation during the Second World War.[4] Italy's invasion of Ethiopia in 1935, which contravened the League of Nations Covenant, resulted in Australia passing the 1935 Sanctions Act although these trade sanctions were quite soft and lasted less than a year (see Nicholson 1955:136). When Italy entered the Second World War on 10 June 1940, the Treaty was suspended with all Italian consular staff setting sail for Japan by the end of the month (Nicholson 1955: 24; Cresciani 1980:86-87). This state of suspension lasted for the duration of the war until "Italy" was "deleted" from the list of Australia's trading partners by proclamation in 1945 (Nicholson 1955:24). The Treaty was officially repealed six months after the 1947 Peace Treaty with Italy by the federal government's decision not to reactivate it (Nicholson 1955:24-25).

Australia's "unconditional withdrawal"

The significance of the 1884 colonial accords slipped from importance for Australia in 1901 as the duties of self-government took priority. It is not clear why Australia desired to withdraw from the Treaty in 1908. However, considerable anxiety had been expressed during the first decade of Federation about the arrival of Southern Europeans and Italians specifically. The Closer Settlement Acts from the 1880s opened up the opportunity for the development of farms (Dewhirst 2008:33), which gained momentum after 1901. Between 1905 and 1908 the editors of the Italian weekly newspaper, *L'Italo-Australiano*, led a public campaign to explore opportunities for large groups of Italian migrant families to access agricultural settlement schemes in New South Wales and Queensland through the Closer Settlement Acts until after 1901 (Dewhirst 2008:33-40, 43). The Italian government was supporting a similar venture in Western Australia at the same time (see Zunini [1906] 1997:45). More is known about Australia's attempt to withdraw from the Treaty in 1911-1912. What transpired here was that Italian migrants wanted to purchase land in Queensland. At this time there were officially only 6,719 Italians in Australia, 929 of them residing in Queensland (Census of Commonwealth of Australia 1911:129, 207).

Following a request by Australia's Governor-General Lord Denman in 1911, Rennell Rodd of the British Foreign Office wrote to Italian Minister of Foreign Affairs Antonino di San Giuliano to enquire whether Italy would be prepared to discuss the withdrawal of "the self-governing dominions of the Empire" but "without impairing the Treaty as respects the rest of the Empire".[5] Britain offered to facilitate negotiations for one "such Dominion" to withdraw after the required 12-month period. This would allow discussions towards a provisional agreement for "reciprocal concessions of the most favoured nation treatment" to take precedence before Australia and Italy signed a new treaty. But the Italian government considered the idea of a provisional agreement to be "inopportune and complicated temporarily", preferring the "logical and simple proposal" to move directly to negotiating the new treaty. As the Italian Minister emphasised, any withdrawal from the Treaty was solely to redraw a new treaty in order to support "the needs of produce, commerce and industries" between the two nations. While the Australian government's circumstances were to change in 1912 – with a Navigation Bill for "conventional tariffs with foreign countries" being tabled for parliamentary debate – Italy's response was not what the Australians wanted at all. Prime Minister Arthur Fisher put it succinctly when he replied to Minister di San Giuliano that Australia wanted "the unconditional withdrawal" from the Treaty.[6] It is worth considering the wording of Articles I, XIII, XV and XX, which became the most contentious.

Article I specifies the means for "reciprocal freedom of commerce and navigation" by permitting full access by the "ships and cargoes" of Great Britain and Italy "to all places, ports, and rivers in the dominions and possessions of the other" (Great Britain. Foreign Office 1931:369-370). It explains that, "subject to the laws and regulations in force", both powers would expect "the same rights, privileges, liberties, favours, immunities, and exemptions in matters of commerce and navigation" as local subjects have, without any more taxes or duties than these subjects pay. Article XIII outlines the particular privileges of those foreigners who enter the other's sovereign territory and whose rights are conditional on "the laws of the country" through four stipulations: first, their access to "full liberty, with their families, to enter, travel, or reside in any part of the dominions and possessions"; second, the authorisation for them "to hire or possess the houses, manufactories, warehouses, shops and premises" to carry out their work and livelihood; third, the approval for them to "carry on their commerce either in person or by any agents"; and fourth, that "their persons or property, or in respect of passports" or "commerce or industry" will not be subject to greater "imposts or obligations" than those "imposed upon native subjects" (Great Britain. Foreign Office 1931:372-373). Article XV states that each power's subjects are to have "full liberty to exercise civil rights, and therefore to acquire, possess, and dispose of every description of property, movable and immovable" (Great Britain, Foreign Office 1931:373). This extended, "under the same conditions as national subjects", to the "purchase, sale, donation, exchange, marriage, testament, succession ab intestate, and in any other manner", and to their descendants accordingly. Article XX ends with the conditions for a 12-month notice for withdrawal (Great Britain. Foreign Office 1931:375). The latter clause did not appear to be misunderstood under the Fisher government but later governments queried it as a possible loophole.[7]

Since Italy was not partial to the idea of a provisional agreement, Prime Minister Fisher resolved the problem by having a clause inserted into the Commonwealth Leases to Aliens Restriction Act to clarify migrant rights generally but also suggesting the origins of the dissent:

> Nothing herein contained shall prejudice the rights of any of the subjects of a foreign power between which and the United Kingdom of Great Britain and Ireland there is now subsisting, or shall hereafter subsist, any treaty of commerce whereby reciprocal civil rights of the subjects of such treaty Powers are reserved, granted, or declared, and to which treaty the State of Queensland has acceded or shall hereafter accede.[8]

The negotiation highlights that Queensland's state laws were out of sync with both the Treaty and the rest of the Commonwealth. As would become clear, Queensland harboured a discriminatory culture against foreign nationals that clashed with the government's legal framework as far as Italians and Maltese were concerned. The amendment would not save either migrant group from further discrimination in the 1930s. Queensland's Premier and Governor would prefer to adhere to the state's earlier colonial Aliens Act of 1867 and Real Property Acts, 1861-1929, and the more recent Lands Acts, 1910-1932.

It is worth pointing out that not all states had problems conforming to the Treaty's articles as one case in New South Wales reveals. Two Italians, Domenico Piccoli and P. V. Trelfo, were successful in their application to buy agricultural land in 1914, in spite of being non-naturalised.[9] The purchasing of property was no doubt less complicated in individual cases and in rural areas where there was little job competition. Greater numbers of Italians, however, were problematical. It took decades to address the legal inconsistencies between Queensland and the rest of Australia, which stemmed from intensified fears about job security, especially in the very profitable sugar industry in Queensland.

Freehold rights "in all States but Queensland"
The 1920s and 1930s marked a shift in Australia's approach to immigration policy towards Europeans for a number of reasons. A sense of "widespread unease" that emerged has to be placed within the context of the flood of post-war migrants, the United States immigration restrictions of 1921 and 1924, and the generous land settlement schemes being offered (Langfield 1991a:1-3). Cole (1971:511) describes the period as characterised by a growing "ethnocentrism" based on British-Australian bonds and justified by the strength of racial, national and imperial ties dating back to the late 19th century. The "ethnic consciousness of being British" equated to "being white" but also "morally white" (Cole 1971:516). This meant that, although Europeans were officially exempt from the 1901 Immigration Restriction Act, cultural characteristics and practices disqualified many. Some people doubted the capacity of Jews, Southern Europeans, Eastern Europeans and even the Irish to be loyal and patriotic (Cole 1971:517). The question was how could they be relied upon to uphold the moral standards needed to defend the nation from a potential Asian invasion?

Following the end of the First World War, the Treaty entitlements of Italians were initially respected in spite of some continued confusion. But the 1920s witnessed an "intense desire in many quarters to maintain a 'white Australia'" by encouraging British immigration but applying "restrictions and regulations" on Europeans (Langfield 1991a:13). This approach first manifested in a reliance on the mechanism of the dictation test. MacDonald (1958:132) states that 12 Italians were refused entry between 1902 and 1914, one on the basis of failing the dictation test, although Langfield (1991a:4) claims that two Italians who failed the test in 1913 and 1922 were accepted all the same. Their cases were similar to a number of Maltese who failed yet were permitted entry because of their British subject status (Douglass 1995:330, n.115). The administration of the dictation test was used increasingly to deny entry to Europeans from the 1920s, exacerbating 'race' relations (Langfield 1991b:3-4). The government also took more stringent measures with specific countries to control "Australia's racial purity" through passports, visas and landing permits (Langfield 1991a:5-6, 13).

Despite the extant Treaty, Italy and Australia cooperated with Australia's need to curb immigration over the 1920s (see Douglass 1995:153-154). First, Italy agreed to reduce the approval of passports by a criterion based on proof of sufficient funds (Price 1963:88, 90, n.12). Then in 1923 the federal government attempted to withdraw from the Treaty again, only to abandon the idea "owing to the likelihood of reprisals on the part of the Italian government which would adversely affect the Commonwealth's trade with Italy".[10] Italy's fascist government was enforcing tighter administrative controls and cohesion over emigration (Cresciani 1980:10-11) by this time. However, in 1924, Australia began prohibiting all Europeans, including Italians, without a sponsor's written guarantee or, alternatively, a landing fee of £40 to process arrival (Price 1963:88). A quota system increased the cost of landing permits for those without a personal guarantee and was universally applied to migrants of non-British birth (Langfield 1991a:4-5). This coincided with the unpleasant Royal Commission of 1924 into the impact of increasing foreign workers in North Queensland, which exposed Southern Europeans and Southern Italians in particular, to inferior racial stereotypes, endorsing racism. By 1928, the Australian government communicated with the Royal Consul General of Italy about enforcing a cap on Italian arrivals, basically to reduce their annual numbers from 7,000 to 3,000, to which the Consul General agreed (Langfield 1991a:8, 12-13; Cresciani 1980:27). However, the protection of Italian rights to purchase land would be raised within a year, prompted by a gentlemen's agreement in Queensland.

Between 1929 and 1935 Italy's consular representatives approached the Queensland state government, the Australian federal government, the Italian government and the Italian Embassy in London about breaches against the Treaty rights of Italians to own land in Queensland. As the Royal Italian Consul in Townsville (Francesco Pascale) first pointed out to Queensland's Premier Arthur Moore in 1929: "the Queensland legislation dealing with the rights of [Italian] aliens to own freehold property [...] conflicts with the provision of the Treaty ..." whereby the legislation only permitted Italians "to acquire a lease of realty for a term not exceeding twenty-one years".[11] This dated back to Queensland's Aliens Act of 1867, but the Real Property Acts, 1861-1929, and the Lands Acts, 1910-1931, were also implicated. Queensland's Aliens Act of 1867 conflicted with the Treaty on the basis that it:

> ... provides that every alien being the subject of a friendly State may hold personal property except chattels real as fully and effectually to all intents and purposes as if he were a natural born subject of the United Kingdom. The Act further provides that alien residents may hold lands for a term not exceeding twenty-one years.[12]

Queensland's Lands Acts, 1910-1931, and Real Property Acts, 1861-1929, were similar in that:

> ... certain laws of the State of Queensland put disabilities on aliens, apparently including also Italians; thus the "Land Acts 1910-31", Sections 59, 62 and 94 and Regulation 12, impose certain conditions on aliens who desire to acquire or sublease

selections and goes so far as to say that "all his rights, title and interest in such selection shall be forfeited if he does not become naturalized within 5 years[."] And again, the interpretation given by the "Real Property Acts" of Queensland [...] is that "the applicant or his nominee must not be an alien".[13]

Premier Moore was only prepared to consider changing the legislation if there was evidence of "mutual reciprocity" of freehold ownership in Italy, Great Britain and elsewhere in Australia. As the Department of External Affairs expressly put it in a press release several years later: "Out of the total British population of 6,800 in Italy very few are Australians, whereas at the last census there were over 14,000 Italians in Australia".[14] But the Queensland Premier had not understood the seriousness of the Treaty's terms, which could not be measured by comparisons. In any case, as Sydney's Acting Consul General Mario Carosi discovered and informed the Prime Minister, "foreign subjects have a right to freehold in all States but Queensland".[15] The Acting Consul General enclosed a copy of the 1884 proof that Queensland had acceded to the Treaty.

Premier Moore no doubt felt relieved to resolve the problems by stating that Italians were entitled to "full liberty to become the full beneficial owners of freehold [as well as] ... leasehold land".[16] In fact, he instructed the relevant authorities to interpret the Real Property Acts quite liberally. And, he declared that the 25-year restriction of the Leases to Aliens Act in Queensland "was not to be made to apply in respect of Italian Nationals". Nevertheless, property-ownership was conditional on a trustee system – "a Nomination of Trustees" – with a further condition being "that the Trustee was British born or naturalized". Unfortunately, the Premier had not remedied the issue at all. But pursuing the continued violation of the Treaty proved untimely because of the global economic crisis. It took political changes in both the Queensland government and the Italian Consulate over 1932 and 1933 for the issues to reemerge. The debate from this time turned to a "Gentlemen's Agreement" proclaimed in 1930 by the dominant players within Queensland's sugar industry.

The "Gentlemen's Agreement" and the Petition

The three most powerful bodies within Queensland's sugar industry were alarmed by the impact of the economic depression and the number of foreign nationals employed on farms. The Australian Sugar Producers' Association, the Queensland Cane Growers' Association, and the Australian Workers' Union organised a conference on 12-13 June 1930, which resulted "a Gentlemen's Agreement".[17] This Agreement not only caused a number of Italian migrant workers' particular grievances but also triggered debate in the federal government over the outstanding legal matters infringing on Australia's imperial obligations. Based on parts of the Sugar Industry Award, the objective of the Gentlemen's Agreement was to reserve jobs in the industry for "British cutters". They were defined as "all those who are born in Australia" by whom it was meant Australian-born workers of British ancestry, thus protecting their jobs from "naturalized British subjects" and, in particular, "Maltese or naturalised Italians".[18] Ultimately, the three organisations put their weight behind ensuring that no less than 75 per cent of British-Australians held the most lucrative jobs – cane cutting – in most of the North Queensland mills.

The first of the Agreement's 11 clauses reiterated the first part of clause 22(1) of the Sugar Industry Award; that:

> ... no person other than a financial member of the Australian Workers' Union shall be employed, or continue in employment as a cane cutter or farm hand after the date of this agreement.

It neglected the second part of the Award, which stated: "... provided there are members of this Union willing, ready, and competent to perform the work to the satisfaction of the employer."[19] Although the Agreement allowed a small percentage of jobs to go to the non-

British-born – largely as farm hands – wind of the move to deny them jobs angered a number of Maltese and naturalised British subjects who were paying members of the Union. Their voices mattered little at a time when the federal government was enforcing immigration restrictions due to the effects of the global recession.

By the end of 1930, the Department of Home Affairs requested a "very urgent" draft "Proclamation" from the Attorney-General's Department in accordance with the Immigration Act of 1901-1930. This "Proclamation" declared a ban on the immigration of "any alien of an European nationality" because of "the unemployment conditions now existing in the Commonwealth" with the exception of temporary tourists, visitors or authorised permit-holders.[20] But within four days of the initial request, it became apparent that the "Proclamation" might be in "breach of Article 13 of the Anglo-Italian Treaty" if it prohibited "entry into Australia of immigrants of any European nationality, including Italians".[21] Another question arose within the Department of Home Affairs which sought legal advice from the Attorney-General's Department:

> I shall be glad if you will also confirm the verbal opinion recently given that the restriction placed on the entry into Australia of a number of Italian migrants who failed to pass a dictation test applied to them under Section 3(a) of the Immigration Act, did not constitute a breach of the Article referred to.

The Acting Solicitor-General replied that a further definition of the kind of "prohibition" would be required: "In my opinion the unqualified prohibition of the entry into Australia of any class of person which included Italian would amount to a breach of Article XIII." On the other hand, the Treaty would not be breached as far as applying the dictation test to Italians as – in the words of the Treaty – they had "to conform themselves to the laws of the country" they sought to enter.[22]

Prime Minister Joseph Lyons hesitated. What would the British government do? Did it consider there to be any violation against the Treaty in its own issuing of labour permits to Italian migrants? He cabled the High Commissioner's Office in London to seek legal advice with the reply telegram reading:

> Home Office advise permits required in respect of any aliens who desire to land in order to enter the service of an employer in the United Kingdom. Aliens not allowed to land for the purpose of seeking employment. There is general international understanding that appeal shall not be made to the terms of the commercial treaty against immigration control provided that it is applied to aliens of all nationalities alike.[23]

The key here was not to be seen to be discriminating against Italians in particular so the Australian government could follow suit. However, 1933 marked a turning point with the influence of the sugar industry Gentlemen's Agreement re-emerging.

It is significant that the percentage required in the Agreement for British cutters had crept up from 75 percent in 1930 to 86 percent by 1933.[24] A dispute erupted in 1933 at the Kalamia Sugar Mill, described by the *Townsville Daily Bulletin* as "racial feuds".[25] In May 1933 the naturalised British subjects of the Ayr district reacted to the move to reduce their employment quota by formalising a Petition to the Governor-General and the King about their exclusion from the sugar industry.[26] Their Petition was forwarded to the Prime Minister, with whom they were able to speak when he visited North Queensland. The Petition drew attention up front to the fact that, "on renouncing the nation of our origin [we] have taken upon ourselves under oath all the obligations and duties which our new status of citizenship imposes upon us", with "all the rights and protection" of the King.[27] The petitioners argued that the Agreement had contravened its own terms firstly by increasing the percentage of British-Australians and secondly because they too were British cutters. They emphasised that they were "excluded from the benefits granted to Britishers" and were "being systematically so excluded". They contested three new clauses being introduced to amend the Sugar Prices Acts, 1915-1931, which were "directed against the naturalised British subjects", quoting Mr Justice W. F. Webb, who was meant to ensure "no discrimination" and their protection from "victimisation": "I suppose if we do not insert the clauses in the award, we will be charged with going out of our way to protect foreign labour." And, they claimed "full loyalty to the Throne, to the Empire and to our new country of adoption", signing the Petition: "B. Tapiolas-Vila (farmer), P. Coppi (farmer), G. Granzotti (cane cutter), G. Capra (cane cutter), on behalf of the naturalised British subjects of the Ayr district." The Petition brought Italy's newly appointed Consul General into the debate about Treaty violations.

It "would be inconsistent with the spirit, if not the letter of the Treaty"
Royal Consul General of Italy Marquis A. Ferrante took up the Italian migrants' cause when he wrote to both Queensland's Premier and the Minister for External Affairs, suggesting that Queensland was still violating the terms of the Treaty. Ultimately, Consul General Ferrante wanted a similar clause inserted into Queensland's Acts to the one that Prime Minister Fisher had authorised in 1912 in the Leases and Aliens Act. He pointed to the "evident contradiction" that required "remedial measures ... to restore the rights of the Italian citizen in Queensland".[28] He was reacting to advice from Premier William Forgan Smith who had taken up office in 1932. In his own enquiries, the Premier discovered that his predecessor's 1929 instructions, allowing Italians property-ownership via a trustee system under the Real Property and Leases to Aliens Acts, were still in place.[29] However, as he explained to Consul General Ferrante, his predecessor had taken "no action" to amend the Queensland's Aliens Act and Land Acts, hence "no finality appears to have been reached".[30] Yet, as the Premier soon confided in the Governor of Queensland Sir Leslie Wilson, pandemonium would be unleashed if

he were to adhere to the Consul General's solution:

> The introduction of such an amendment would be viewed with considerable hostility by all parties in the State, and would without doubt provoke anti-Italian feeling in the North, which is undesirable especially as such cordial relations exist at present.[31]

More to the point, he was also reported to have warned that "North Queensland will be in danger of becoming in fact an Italian Colony secured by means of peaceful penetration" if Italians were "permitted to take up land on equal terms with British subjects" (cited in Douglass 1995: 195-196). He explained the paradox to the Governor, which presented a quandary not only for Queensland but for Australia as a whole:

> ... in many instances, Italians proposing to become naturalized give as their reason for taking such action the desire to comply with the law in order that they may acquire freehold titles to their lands. Obviously, if Italian Nationals could get all the advantages of British Citizenship without undertaking its obligations, the incentive to become naturalized British Subjects would be reduced.

The Consul General's solution would instigate "considerable hostility" and lead to unnecessary complications over the naturalisation law. While the Premier waited for a response from the Governor, he announced to the Consul General that: "it has been decided in all the circumstances not to introduce any amendment of the existing law in the direction indicated".[32] Referring to problematic Acts and the measures taken by his predecessot, he stated that, after all:

> ... these laws were passed in their present form many years ago by a Parliament of which I was not a member and it is only within recent years that any claim has been advanced that they conflict with the provision ...

He claimed that there was "no impediment to non-naturalised Italians holding land in Queensland".

In the meantime, the Consul General had paid Prime Minister Lyons a visit to discuss "the Italian question in Queensland",[33] a question that was becoming progressively public since the sugar industry's Gentlemen's Agreement. The Prime Minister then wrote to Premier Forgan Smith "to learn whether any action was eventually taken with a view to the amendment of Queensland legislation in the direction desired by the Consul".[34] At the same time, and acting no doubt in response to the naturalised British subjects' Petition, the Attorney-General's Department began examining the legalities of the Agreement. The Department's Secretary, George Knowles, raised concern about the "racial limitation [...] imposed" on cane cutter jobs.[35] This was not a matter of interfering with the selection of workers by an employer. As Southern European migrants themselves had understood, the Agreement "infringes the rights acquired by them under section 11 of the Nationality Act" by which they had "all political and other rights, powers and privileges to which a natural-born British subject is entitled", and thus equality in status with the "British cutters". Even though the Attorney-General's Department incorrectly noted that Queensland could legislate by excluding naturalised Italians from working as cane cutters, the fact was that Italian and other Southern European workers had joined the Union. As Secretary Mr Knowles put it:

> One of the objects of the Australian Workers' Union is to promote the general and material welfare of the members. In the preface to the Constitution of the Union reference is made to "the high and noble aim of the Union" and each member is urged to become an active unit in the Great Army of Reform – "active as an agitator and true to his comrades as a unionist always is – etc." The treatment meted out by the union to certain of its members (who happen to be Maltese or naturalized Italians) *does not appear to be in accord with the aims of the union as set out in its Constitution.* [Emphasis in original.]

The Department of the Interior agreed that the treatment of Maltese and Italian migrants as "inequitable".[36] While Mr Knowles concluded that the federal government had no power to intervene, within a few days the Solicitor-General asked: "Can a State by legislation affect the rights conferred by prior naturalization under the [Commonwealth] Act?".[37] The answer was no. Yet, the Department of Trade and Customs drew attention to the fact that:

> ... various sugar agreements have been based on the principle enunciated by the Prime Minister in 1923 whereby matters of domestic interest [...] were to be the sole responsibility of the Queensland government or agencies under its jurisdiction *unless expressly included in a sugar agreement*.[38] [Emphasis in original.]

In matters of national and international law, however, the industry could not rely on a principle enunciated by a Prime Minister ten years earlier.

The existence of the Treaty then began to catch wider attention. Francis Michael Forde, then MP for Capricornia, Queensland, requested a copy of the Treaty from the Prime Minister's Department because of a "complaint".[39] He was referring to a letter from Archbishop James Duhig who wanted Mr Forde's "opinion on the position of the Italians in the North."[40] As the Archbishop had asserted: "You know the Treaty of 1883 between Great Britain and her Dominions and Italy has never been adhered to". But the Queensland government was about to introduce a Bill to amend the Regulation of Sugar Cane Price Act which, in the words of Consul General Ferrante, would "be an attempt to prevent a naturalized Australian obtaining sugar land".[41] He wrote to the Minister for External Affairs about "the great discontent which has been created amongst the Italian community of Queensland" as a result of the Bill.

In late 1933 the Prime Minister requested a copy of the Bill from the Queensland Premier.[42] But the Bill had already been passed. Not surprisingly, the relevant insertion in the state's recent Act, as the petitioners had warned in May 1933, specified the approval of the Central Sugar Cane Prices Board as necessary for "the sale or lease of assigned land" and contingent on "a fit and proper person to hold the assignment".[43] Premier Forgan Smith "emphatically and definitely denied" any discrimination against any nationality, noting specifically that the section inserted had been "for the express purpose of protecting purchasers and lessors of assigned lands from exploitation, irrespective of nationality". External Affairs set to work to examine the situation, finally articulating the crux of the problem: the Queensland government had made a mistake in acceding to the Treaty; the then colony had not been "in a position to give full effect to the Treaty" which it "apparently overlooked" in 1884.[44]

With Queensland feigning Italian property-ownership through the trustee system and Premier Forgan Smith refusing to introduce any amendments to the Aliens Act of 1867 – instead introducing controversial Bills – the Prime Minister reminded the Premier in March 1934 of the Consul General's view that all three of the state's Acts "continue to apply to Italians in respect of the leasing of land.[45] But there was nothing more that the Premier would say.[46] In fact, it would later be revealed by the British Representative in Australia, E. T. Crutchley, that the Colonial Office in London had not objected to Queensland's Lands Act of 1910 and, in any case, "to remove the incompatibilities" would have been "a practicable impossibility."[47] Clearly, Britain had 'overlooked' the implications of its Treaty obligations with Italy as well. The only thing left for the Consul General to do was to alert the Italian government and the Italian Embassy in London.

Throughout the rest of 1934 correspondence travelled between Australia, the United Kingdom, and Italy. Queensland's Governor Sir Leslie Wilson had already briefed the Permanent Under Secretary of the Dominions Office, Sir Edward Harding, about the legal mess. As the Governor put it: "a somewhat difficult situation may arise in connection with the correspondence which the Premier has received from the Royal Consul General of Italy".[48] The Governor explained that there were two situations. The first was that it was impossible, "from a political view", to amend Queensland's Acts with a clause inserted in the manner of the 1912 clause in the Leases to Aliens Restriction Act. The second was that this was now a racial problem:

> As you are doubtless aware, there has been considerable feeling on the subject of Italians in the sugar cane fields amongst Australian cane growers, and to attempt to put them on the same standing, as regards the acquisition of land, as is possessed by naturalised British subjects, would arouse keen resentment.

It took nine months before Under Secretary Harding could reply. His advice was to try to convince the Italian authorities that Queensland's trustee system met the Treaty's provisions with the only difference being a theoretical one. As he put it:

> The question whether Italian nationals get what they are entitled to is one of fact, and provided that no breach of the Treaty occurred in practice, the fact that the terms of the law were not in conformity with the practice would not, we think, entitle them to protest, although of course the legislation itself does not constitute a fulfillment of the Treaty obligation. It seems, therefore, that, as things stand, the most satisfactory solution would be for the Italians to be persuaded that the trustee system described in your letter under reference does, in fact, for all practical purposes satisfy their treaty rights.[49]

Two alternatives remained, according to Mr Harding: either "the Italians [...] could presumably take the point to arbitration under the Protocol to the Treaty of 1883"; or the British Empire as a whole could denounce the Treaty since Queensland could not withdraw alone. While the latter would not happen, the former needed to be avoided at all costs. Predictably, this kind of interpretation would not do for the Italian government. In London, Counsellor Leonardo Vitetti, who was the Chargé d'Affaires of the Italian Embassy, had received word from Consul General Ferrante. Just as the Consul General had argued, Counsellor Vitetti pressed for the insertion of a clause to amend Queensland's legislation when he wrote to E. H. Carr of the British Foreign Office in late 1934. According to the Counsellor, such an insertion "would certainly be sufficient to remedy that which today would appear to be an infringement of art.15 of the Italo-British Treaty of Commerce caused by the [...] Queensland Land Acts."[50]

Premier Forgan Smith and Prime Minister Lyons were still at loggerheads by the end of 1934. The Premier stipulated in a letter to Governor Wilson that the Queensland government was already substituting practice for theory.[51] The Prime Minister, for his part, was still expressing concerns to the Premier in early 1935 about "the serious dissatisfaction which appears to exist in connection with discrimination against the classes" of Maltese British subjects.[52] But a deal was about to be struck in London, involving British Representative Crutchley. After Counsellor Vitetti contacted Mr Carr about the only acceptable solution from the Italian government's position, Mr Carr handed the matter over to the Head of the Southern Department, Owen O'Malley. Siding with the Queensland Premier, Mr O'Malley advised Counsellor Vitetti that, "for practical reasons which I explained to you verbally, the Queensland Government would very much depreciate anything being done to put them on a different basis to that on which they now stand".[53] However, this was a "semi-official letter", based on an informal meeting between Mr O'Malley and Counsellor Vitetti, and to be finalised after Mr Crutchley confided in the Secretary of the Prime Minister's Department, J. H. Starling. We gain further insight into these deliberations from the correspondence between these two men.

"My dear Starling", wrote Mr Crutchley, Mr O'Malley had relied on Counsellor Vitetti's own advice.[54] According to Mr Crutchley, the Foreign Office had shared the draft reply with Counsellor Vitetti, who it was claimed, had advised that "it would be better to omit from the draft anything which would give the legal department in the Italian Foreign Office an excuse for writing argumentative minutes and drafts as the legal points involved were, in his opinion, susceptible of being argued almost indefinitely". Mr Starling was thrilled, but had one piece of advice to polish the draft and rid the country of further recourse from the Consul General of Italy in Sydney:

> I think the matter is skillfully handled, and hope that it will now be allowed to drop. In this respect, however, I do not think the last paragraph of the reply would appeal to the Queensland Government, as it may give further opening to the Italian Consul-General, and it has been our experience that local consuls are apt to raise issues needlessly and on their own volition.[55]

Thus, the British government sealed the matter once and for all.

Perhaps the stalemate between the Queensland Premier and both the Consul General and the Prime Minister could not have been resolved any other way. We can only ponder what might have followed had the British Foreign Office supported Italy and backed the Consul General's solution. But, in the deal between Mr O'Malley, Mr Crutchley and Mr Starling, there was no mention of the wider context of the Gentlemen's Agreement or the migrants' Petition. Counsellor Vitetti's disloyalty might also be questioned as being based on false representation. Ultimately, Queensland had managed to usurp the Prime Minister through his own department. Ironically, the federal government could inform a Brisbane legal firm, Tully & Wilson, in 1937 that the Treaty was "still in force".[56]

The "principle of equality of treatment"

The Treaty emerged one final time in 1938 over the cost of landing permits for the purpose of reducing Italian immigrant numbers in particular. The government wished to adopt a policy of ministerial discretion in order to allow exemptions for "a desirable type" of Northern European without appearing to discriminate against Italians because of their incapacity to assimilate. They would have to pay the increased cost.[57] As the Acting Secretary for the Department of the Interior pointed out, there had been more than 3,000 arrivals from Italy over the past year but the less than 100 per year from Denmark, Holland, Norway and Sweden. He wanted to know whether "special concessions" could be given "to alien immigrants from Northern European countries without the government laying itself open to challenge for showing discrimination unfavourable to Italians". While the Solicitor-General from the Attorney-General's Department confirmed that there would be no problem, he raised the point that the provision "departs from the principle of equality of treatment":

> As it is well know that Italian migrants are by far the more numerous class of alien migrants to Australia in recent years, I think the Italian authorities would have grounds for invoking the understanding.[58]

A scribbled piece of paper, headed "Mr Knowles" and noting "prepared by Mr Lyons", can be found in the National Archives of Australia. Its "Alternative Opinion" read: "In my opinion, the suggested rule would be inconsistent with the spirit, if not the letter of the Treaty, and it would also be inconsistent with the understanding referred to [by the Home Office in 1930]".

Australia's inability to withdraw from the Anglo-Italian Treaty before the 1920s speaks to the strength of global trade agreements made during the imperial age. Australia and Italy discovered mutual benefits in this respect. Increasing European immigration and economic pressures from the 1920s posed new problems. The federal government put in place measures that supported a rise in nationalist and xenophobic feelings, which resulted in breaching Italians' rights under the Treaty in Queensland. When the federal government attempted to mediate between Italy and Queensland, it became embroiled in a conflict that challenged its imperial obligations and political leadership. This was frustrated by two deceitful deals between Queensland's state politics and the sugar industry, on the one hand, and between individuals in the British government and the Prime Minister's Department, on the other. There is no doubt that emerging imperial tensions leading to the Second World War overshadowed the Treaty. However, the Treaty's history reveals a significant number of perhaps unexpected supporters for the migrant cause, not least the naturalised petitioners of 1933 themselves.

Bibliography

Bailey, H. K., 1929, 'Australia's Treaty Rights and Obligations', *Journal of Comparative Legislation and International Law*, Third Series, Vol. 11, No. 4, (1929): 190-193.

Bailey, K. H., 1928, 'Australian Treaty Rights and Obligations', in P. Campbell, R. C. Mills, G. V. Portus (eds), *Studies in Australian Affairs*, Macmillan and the Melbourne University Press, Melbourne: 156-178.

Census of the Commonwealth of Australia, 1911, Volume II, 1911, Part II– Birthplaces, Australian Bureau of Statistics, Canberra.

Charteris, Professor, 'Our Treaty with Italy. Effect on Migration', *The Sydney Morning Herald*, Wednesday, 16 July 1930, p. 17.

Choate, M., 2008, *Emigrant Nation: The Making of Italy Abroad*, Harvard University Press, Cambridge, MA, and London.

Cole, D., 1971, '"The Crimson Thread of Kinship": Ethnic Ideas in Australia, 1890-1914', *Historical Studies*, Vol. 14, No. 56, (April 1971): 511–525.

Cresciani, G., 1985, *The Italians*, Australian Broadcasting Corporation.

Cresciani, G., 1980, *Fascism, Anti-fascism, and Italians in Australia, 1922-1945*, Australian National University Press, Canberra.

Dewhirst, C., 2008, 'Collaborating on Whiteness: Representing Italians in Early White Australia', *Journal of Australian Studies*, Vol. 32, No. 1, (2008): 33-49.

Douglass, W., 1995, *From Italy to Ingham: Italians in North Queensland*, Queensland University Press, St Lucia, Qld, 1995.

Gaston, J. W. T., 1982, 'Trade and the Late Victorian Foreign Office', *The International History Review*, Vol. 4, No. 3, (August 1982): 317-338.

Great Britain. Foreign Office, 1931, *Handbook of Commercial Treaties, etc., with Foreign Powers*, 4th edn, His Majesty's Stationery Office, London.

Langfield, M., 1991a, '"White aliens": The control of European immigration to Australia 1920-30', *Journal of Intercultural Studies*, Vol. 12, No. 2, (1991): 1-14.

Langfield, M., 1991b, 'Attitudes to European immigration to Australia in the early 20th century', *Journal of Intercultural Studies*, Vol. 12, No. 1, (1991): 1-15.

Lowe, C. J. and Marzari, F., 1975, *Italian Foreign Policy 1870-1940*, Routledge & Kegan Paul, London and Boston.

MacDonald, J. S., 1958, 'Migration from Italy to Australia with Special Reference to Selected Groups', unpublished PhD thesis, Department of Demography, The Australian National University, Canberra.

Macintyre, S., 2001, *The Oxford History of Australia: The Succeeding Age, 1901-1942*, Volume 4, Oxford University Press, South Melbourne.

National Archives of Australia: A11804, 1912/155, Anglo-Italian Treaty of Commerce 1883.

National Archives of Australia: A432, 1930/2393, Proposed proclamation under Sec. 3K of Immigration Act 1930/31. Question as to whether Art. 13 of Anglo-Italian Commercial Treaty of 1883 would be affected.

National Archives of Australia: A432, 1938/1047, Anglo-Italian Treaty 1883: Question of effect restricting alien immigration into Australia.

National Archives of Australia: A981, TRE358, Anglo-Italian Commercial Treaty, 1883. Operation of the treaty in Queensland.

Nicholson, D. F., 1955, *Australia's Trade Relations: An Outline History of Australia's Overseas Trading Arrangements*, Cheshire, Melbourne.

Price, C., 1963, *Southern Europeans in Australia*, Oxford University Press, Melbourne.

State Records of New South Wales: 10/32037, 14/1161, Administration of Closer Settlement: 'Re rights of foreigner not naturalized taking up Settlement Purchase'.

Stirling, A., 1934, 'Australia and Treaty-Making', *The Australian Quarterly*, Vol. 6, No. 24, (December 1934): 28-41.

Tosi, L., 1989, 'L'Italia e le origini dell'Istituto Internazionale di Agricoltura', in L. Pilotta (ed.), *La formazione della diplomazia italiana 1861-1915*, Franco Angeli, Milano: 784-823.

'The Kalamia Dispute. Meeting of A.W.U. Position Outlined', *Townsville Daily Bulletin*, Tuesday, 6 June 1933, p. 5.

'The Kalamia Dispute. Naturalised Subjects. Petition Prime Minister', *Townsville Daily Bulletin*, Tuesday, 27 June 1933.

The Townsville Daily Bulletin, Wednesday, 21 June 1933, p. 4.

Woolf, L., 1919, *Empire & Commerce in Africa: A Study in Economic Imperialism*, The Labour Research department and Allen and Unwin, London.

Zunini, L., [1906] 1997, *Western Australia as it is Today*, M. Melia and R. Bosworth (eds and trans), The University of Western Australia Press, Perth.

Endnotes

1 MS, National Archives of Australia: A981, TRE358, letter to the Minister of Foreign Affairs, Rome, from Savile Lumley, 10 March 1884.

2 Professor Charteris, 'Our Treaty with Italy. Effect on Migration', *The Sydney Morning Herald*, Wednesday, 16 July 1930, p. 17.

3   MS, National Archives of Australia (NAA): A981, TRE358, memorandum from the Department of External Affairs, 27 June 1930, p. 3.

4   MS, NAA: A432, 1938/1047, letter to the Secretary of the Department of External Affairs from the Secretary of the Attorney-General's Department, 24 June 1943; letter to the Attorney-General's Department from Jos. Francis, 25 October 1944.

5   MS, NAA: A11804, 1912/155, letter to the Governor-General from Rennell Rodd, 28 December 1911, enclosing translation of a memoradum from the Ministry of Foreign Affairs, Rome, 24 December 1911.

6   MS, NAA: A11804, 1912/155, letter to the Governor-General from the Prime Minister, 22 July 1912.

7   MS, NAA: A981, TRE358, letter to the Premier of Queensland from the Royal Consul General of Italy, 13 July 1933; copy of 'Extract from Treaty of Commerce and Navigation between Great Britain and Italy. Signed at Rome, June 15, 1883'.

8   Cited in MS, NAA: A981, TRE358, letter to the Governor of Queensland from the Premier of Queensland, 18 September 1933.

9   MS, State Records of New South Wales: 10/32037, 14/1161, Administration of Closer Settlement: 'Re rights of foreigner not naturalized taking up Settlement Purchase'.

10 MS, NAA: A981, TRE358, memorandum from the Department of External Affairs, 27 June 1930, p. 3.

11 MS, NAA: A981, TRE358, letter to the Prime Minister from the Premier of Queensland, 23 September 1929.

12 MS, NAA: A981, TRE358, letter to the Secretary of the Department of External Affairs from the Solicitor-General of the Attorney-General's Department, 9 March 1934, p. 3.

13 MS, NAA: A981, TRE358, letter to the Premier of Queensland from the Royal Consul General of Italy, 13 July 1933.

14 MS, NAA: A981, TRE358, 'For the Press: Anglo-Italian Commercial Treaty of 1883', from the Department of External Affairs, 8 November 1933.

15 MS, NAA: A981, TRE358, letter to the Secretary of the Prime Minsiter from the Acting Consul General for Italy, 26 November 1929; copy of letter to the Minister of Foreign Affairs, Rome, from Savile Lumley, 10 March 1884.

16 MS, NAA: A981, TRE358, letter to the Governor of Queensland from the Premier of Queensland, 19 Septmber 1933.

17 MS, NAA: A981, TRE358, copy of "'Gentlemen's Agreement". The Sugar Industry', 12-30 June 1930. The agreement was signed by C. V. Hines (Australian Sugar Producers' Association), W. H. Doherty (Queensland Cane Growers' Association) and W. J. Riordan (Australian Workers' Union).

18 MS, NAA: A981, TRE358, copy of "'Gentlemen's Agreement". The Sugar Industry', 12-30 June 1930; minute paper, 'Cane Cutters – Gentlemen's Agreemeny – Employment of Cutter not born in Australia', from the Attorney-General's Department, 27 October 1933.

19 MS, NAA: A981, TRE358, copy of "'Gentlemen's Agreement". The Sugar Industry', 12-30 June 1930.

20 MS, NAA: A432, 1930/2393, letter to the Secretary of the Attorney-General's Department from the Assistant Secretary of the Department of Home Affairs, 12 December 1930; letter to the Secretary of the Department of Home Affairs from the Acting Secretary of the Attorney-General's Department, December 1930, enclosing draft 'Proclamation'.

21 MS, NAA: A432, 1930/2393, letter to the Acting Secretary of the Attorney-General's Department from the Assistant Secretary of the Department of Home Affairs, 16 December 1930.

22 MS, NAA: A432, 1930/2393, 'Opinion', from the Attorney-General's Department, December 1930. Section 3(a) of the Immigration Act of 1901 reads: "Any person who when asked to do so by an officer fails to write out at dictation and sign in the presence of the office a passage of fifty words in length in an European language directed by the officer". Dictation tests were used to control numbers of intending European immigrants (Langfield 1991: 4).

23 MS, NAA: A432, 1938/1047, telegram, 16 December 1930, cited in letter

to the Secretary of the Attorney-General's Department from the Acting Secretary of the Department of the Interior, 7 September 1938.
24 'The Kalamia Dispute. Meeting of A.W.U. Position Outlined', *Townsville Daily Bulletin, Tuesday, 6 June 1933*, p. 5.
25 *The Townsville Daily Bulletin*, Wednesday, 21 June 1933, p. 4.
26 MS, NAA: A981, TRE358, 'The Italian Question in Queensland – the "Gentlemen's Agreement"', from the Department of External Affairs, 31 October 1933, p. 1.
27 'The Kalamia Dispute. Naturalised Subjects. Petition Prime Minister', *Townsville Daily Bulletin, Tuesday, 27 June 1933*, p. 5.
28 MS, NAA: A981, TRE358, letter to the Minister for External Affairs from the Royal Consul General of Italy, 13 July 1933; letter to the Premier of Queensland from the Royal Consul General of Italy, 13 July 1933.
29 MS, NAA: A981, TRE358, letter to the Governor of Queensland from the Premier of Queensland, 18 September 1933.
30 MS, NAA: A981, TRE358, letter to the Royal Consul General of Italy from the Premier of Queensland, 15 August 1933.
31 MS, NAA: A981, TRE358, letter to the Governor of Queensland from the Premier of Queensland, 18 September 1933.
32 MS, NAA: A981, TRE358, letter to the Royal Consul General of Italy from the Premier of Queensland, 15 November 1933.
33 MS, NAA: A981, TRE358, memorandum to the Secretary of the Prime Minister's Office from the Prime Minister's Private Secretary, 20 October 1933.
34 MS, NAA: A981, TRE358, letter to the Premier of Queensland from the Prime Minister, 26 July 1933.
35 MS, NAA: A981, TRE358, minute paper, 'Cane Cutters – Gentlemen's Agreemeny – Employment of Cutter not born in Australia', from the Attorney-General's Department, 27 October 1933.
36 Cited in MS, NAA: A981, TRE358, 'The Italian Question in Queensland – the "Gentlemen's Agreement"', from the Department of External Affairs, 31 October 1933, p. 2.

37 MS, NAA: A981, TRE358, copy of comment by the Solicitor-General of the Attorney-General's Department, 31 October 1933.

38 MS, NAA: A981, TRE358, 'The Italian Question in Queensland – the "Gentlemen's Agreement"', from the Department of External Affairs, 31 October 1933, p. 2.

39 MS, NAA: A981, TRE358, letter to the Prime Minster's Department from F. M. Forde, 21 November 1933.

40 MS, NAA: A981, TRE358, letter to the to Prime Minster from F. M. Forde, 1 December 1933.

41 MS, NAA: A981, TRE358, letter to the Minister for External Affairs from the Royal Consul General of Italy, 8 December 1933.

42 MS, NAA: A981, TRE358, draft letter to the Premier of Queensland from the Prime Minister, 14 December 1933; note from the Department for External Affairs, 15 March 1934.

43 See MS, NAA: A981, TRE358, letter to the Prime Minister from the Premier of Queensland Smith, 8 January 1934.

44 MS, NAA: A981, TRE358, draft letter to the Premier of Queensland from the Prime Minister, 14 December 1933; note by the Department for External Affairs, 15 March 1934.

45 MS, NAA: A981, TRE358, letter to the Premier of Queensland from the Prime Minister, 29 March 1934.

46 MS, NAA: A981, TRE358, letter to the Prime Minister from the Deputy Premier of Queensland, 30 April 1934.

47 MS, NAA: A981, TRE358, letter to the Secretary of the Prime Minister's Department from the Representative in the Commonwealth of Australia of His Majesty's Government in the United Kingdom, 24 July 1935.

48 MS, NAA: A981, TRE358, extract from a letter to the Permanent Under Secretary of the Dominions Office from the Governor of Queensland, 21 September 1933.

49 MS, NAA: A981, TRE358, letter to the Governor of Queensland from the Dominions Office, 19 June 1934.

50 MS, NAA: A981, TRE358, letter to the British Foreign Office from the Italian Embassy, London, 14 August 1934.

51 MS, NAA: A981, TRE358, letter to the Queensland Governor from the Premier of Queensland, 22 November 1934.

52 MS, NAA: A981, TRE358, letter to the Premier of Queensland from the Prime Minister, 4 January 1935.

53 MS, NAA: A981, TRE358, draft letter to the Italian Embassy, London, from the British Foreign Office, 12 June 1935.

54 MS, NAA: A981, TRE358, letter to the Secretary of the Prime Minister's Department from the Representative in the Commonwealth of Australia of His Majesty's Government in the United Kingdom, 8 July 1935.

55 MS, NAA: A981, TRE358, letter to Representative in the Commonwealth of Australia of His Majesty's Government in the United Kingdom from the Secretary of the Prime Minister's Department, 1 August 1935. The concluding paragraph read: "I am sure that the Queensland Government would be happy to discuss the whole question at any time with the local Italian Consul-General if the latter so wished."

56 MS, NAA: A981, TRE358, letter to Messrs Tully and Wilson from W. R. Hodgson of the Department of External Affairs, 29 July 1937.

57 MS, NAA: A432, 1938/1047, letter to the Secretary of the Attorney-General's Department from the Acting Secretary of the Department of the Interior, 7 September 1938.

58 MS, NAA: A432, 1938/1047, 'Opinion', from the Solicitor-General of the Attorney-General's Department to the Acting Secretary of Department of the Interior, [n.d.] 1938.

4
Australian-Italian Relations in World War II: The Italian Consul General and the Australian Government

Karen Agutter

Introduction

In the years prior to the First World War direct relations between Italy and Australia were limited both by distance and as a consequence of imperial policy. At the highest level, Australia, as a dominion of the British Empire, generally deferred to Britain for negotiations with European nations and Australian relations with Italy were no exception. Interactions were in the main conducted through the Secretary of State for Colonies in London. At a commercial level, burgeoning trade links between Italy and Australia were similarly influenced by British and Italian trade agreements, but also by distance and the lack, at this time, of regular and direct steamships routes. At an individual or personal level, financially able Australians certainly travelled to Italy during these years, generally en route to other destinations or as part of the 'grand tour', while for the Italian emigrant population, Australia was a distant and lesser known destination, with the majority of sojourners and settlers travelling to the Americas and other European nations.

In comparison with immigrant Italian populations in countries such as Canada and the United States, the Italian born population in Australia in the years leading up to the First World War was small and according to the 1911 census numbered only 6,719, of which 5,543 were male. Even following the larger influxes that occurred as a consequence of the Italo-Turkish War in Libya, this figure only increased to approximately 12,000 by 1914.

In Australia probably the best known and most well documented of relations between these two nations in the late 18th and early 19th centuries was that of the unwanted immigrant. The Italian was most commonly portrayed as the swarthy, knife-welding mafia agent, a danger to Australia's economic and social wellbeing. With the outbreak of War in 1914 this attitude toward Italian immigrants in Australia was further compounded, initially by Italy's alliance to Germany, and then by a period of neutrality and uncertainty. From this emerges what can only be described as a unique and strange example of Italian Australian relations – the relationship between the Italian Consul General and the Australian Commonwealth Government. This chapter will consider these relations. It will outline the accepted contemporary role of consular agents and consider how and why, in the years between Italy's entry into the War in 1915 and the armistice, the role of the Consul and his relations with the Australian government became powerful enough to change laws and ultimately change the lives of Italians living in Australia.

The Italian Consul-General in Australia

Under the 1883 *Treaty of Commerce and Navigation* between Great Britain and Italy, Italians living in British territories, and therefore in Australia, had the right to appoint consular representatives and, despite the small number of Italians in Australia in this period, broad consular representation was soon established. Vice-Consuls were appointed in Melbourne and Sydney and consular agencies (nearly all run by men of non-Italian origin) were set up in Adelaide, Brisbane, Townsville, Launceston and Perth. Overseeing these offices was the Italian Consul-General. Located in Melbourne the Consul-General in Australia was also responsible for Italians in New Zealand and Pacific

Islands such as Fiji and therefore was more correctly referred to as the Consul-General for Australasia.

Historically, the role of the Italian Consul-General was an apolitical one, and the Consul played no part in the representation of Italy abroad (Papalia 2004:11). Rather, as O'Connor (1996:49) notes, this office was primarily responsible for the preparation of trade and statistical reports. However, after 1900, the role began to incorporate some limited responsibility for assisting the increasing numbers of Italian migrants abroad. Furthermore, Consuls increasingly took up humanitarian causes when the need arose, for example raising money in Australia for the victims of the Messina earthquake in 1908 (O'Connor 1996:48).

In 1911, Luigi Mercatelli, a highly respected envoy who had held the consular position in Australia from 1908 was recalled for deployment to the increasingly sensitive location of Libya. It would be 1913 before his replacement, Emilio Eles, arrived and in the interim Melbourne Vice-Consul Giovanni Ferrando, of whom more will be heard later in this chapter, acted in the role.

Little is known of Emilio Eles before his arrival in Australia. By piecing together snippets of documentation it is possible to establish that he was born in 1874 in Sinigallia, twenty-five kilometres north of Ancona on the Adriatic coast. He graduated in law in Rome and was subsequently admitted to the consular service in 1902. His first posting, 1902, was to Smyrna in Turkey (*La Revue Diplomatique* 29 June 1902:7) however, later that same year he was sent to New York as a Vice Consul. Four years later in 1906 he was transferred to Bizerte, Tunisia (*La Revue Diplomatique* 5 December 1909:7). Finally in November 1910, after being awarded a Knight of the Crown of Italy and henceforth referred to as *Cavaliere*, he is transferred to Florianopolis (Santa Catharina) in Brazil (*Almanak Administrativo Mercantile e Industrial do Rio de Janeiro* 1913:771), his last posting before arriving in Australia.

Therefore, when the *Victorian Government Gazette* (1914:81) officially announced the appointment of Emilio Eles as Consul for Italy in Australasia it would appear that this position was part of the ongoing progression on Eles' career ladder. On his arrival in Australia, the *Daily News* described him as a man "scarce past middle-age, erect, of handsome features, and a delightful conversationalist". The article continued noting Eles' gushing enthusiasm for his role, which he himself claimed to be "one of great honour for one so young". The career Consul was full of praise for Australia, and he wished to promote the "best of relations" with the country and its press (*The Daily News* 1914:3). This initial interview certainly sets the tone for Eles' subsequent exposure, both in and out of the media, and in five years in office he would gain significantly more publicity and notoriety than his predecessors.

Almost immediately Eles settled into a series of social and official events perhaps far greater than expected from a consul representing a small immigrant population and a nation allied to Germany at a time when war was considered inevitable. He spoke in public on several issues, including welcoming Australian Cadets returning from a visit to Europe, and his presence at social functions, including a dinner at Government House in Sydney as the guest of Governor and Lady Strickland, was often detailed in the press. Eles made himself known to the Australian Prime Minister (Fisher), writing to him of his grief at events such as the loss of the AE1 submarine and its crew and the great loss to the British Empire on the death of Lord Kitchener. Eles was also a frequent contributor to "letters to the editor" in the local daily newspapers.

In December 1914 Eles was called upon by the Italian Consular Agent in South Australia, Mr Paterson, to intervene on behalf of three Italian citizens in Port Pirie. With care of Italian citizens abroad now an excepted role of the Consul-General, Eles agreed to intercede. The men were charged with causing an altercation involving a razor and enquiries led Eles to believe that the Italians concerned were "hardworking, peaceful men" while the Australian participants "had bad reputations". With Great Britain at war in Europe, Eles expressed his concern for his Italian countrymen focusing on the fact that "the mob element at a place like Port Pirie would be strongly prejudiced against foreigners without discriminating between enemy subjects and those of friendly or neutral countries" (South Australian State Records: GRG24/6, 1915/35). Eles' dealings with the South Australian Premier met with what he considered to be a less than desired response and he was unable to achieve any remittance on the imposed fines.

Italy's Declaration of War with Austria-Hungary in May 1915, however, gave Eles the opportunity to promote Italy's allied role. He spoke at public meetings such as War Anniversary Day, in August 1915 at the Fitzroy Town Hall, joining those attending in singing patriotic songs and celebrating allied efforts. In a more traditional Consular role he also announced that he had begun to collect funds from his countrymen for the Italian Red Cross and he and his wife and daughter were regularly seen at fundraising events. Although perhaps more publicly visible than previous Consul-Generals in Australia, Eles was, at this time, a dedicated agent acting mostly in accord with previous consular practice.

In July 1915 however, Eles started to broaden the scope of his activities. He had already made it clear to Australian authorities that Italians could not serve in the Australian forces, but now announced in the press that although Italians eligible for military service living in Australia were not yet required to join the colours, they were required to report to the nearest Italian consular office and register their details, or else be considered deserters.

By 1916 it was apparent through his actions and associations that Eles was an enthusiastic supporter of the Australian war effort. He had established a relationship with Italian born Brigadier-General Ramaciotti who was commander of the Australian Second Military

District (New South Wales) and accompanied him on a visit to mark the arrival in Sydney of the hospital ship *Karoola*. However, in regard to Italians of military age in Australia Eles remained adamant that there was no provision in Italian military law to allow for their enlistment in local forces, rather they should remain on call to serve in Italy.

This stance was in marked contrast to that of other nations such as Canada and Great Britain, where Italian Consuls gave permission for Italians to join local expeditionary forces. It was also in contrast to the actions of other Allied Consuls in Australia, such as those from France and Russia, who gave permission for their citizens to join the Australian Imperial Forces (AIF). Given that, from the outset of war the Department of Defence and other government agencies had been peppered with inquiries from military districts and recruiting officers asking if presenting non-naturalised Italians could join the AIF, this stance caused considerable ill feeling among both Australian authorities and Italians wishing to enlist. In many circles Eles was becoming unpopular.

In fact, Eles' popularity with certain sections of the Italian immigrant population was questionable even before his wartime activities. His appointment as Consul-General was not well received by Ferrando, the man he replaced, who, as a prominent Melbourne Italian businessman with extensive local support, probably had an expectation of permanently taking on the role in which he was acting. The relationship between the two men deteriorated irretrievably in 1915 when Eles terminated Ferrando's position as Vice Consul, an action that both divided the Italian community and brought Australian authorities into what should have been a purely Consular matter (National Archives Australia: A11804, 1915/277). Ferrando complained to the Australian Governor General, claiming that he had been "harshly and unjustly treated" and that the action of the Consul was illegal, as he did not have "the power to dismiss me, nor to notify the Consular Body, until his action has been approved by the Italian

Government" (National Archives Australia: A11804, 1915/277). Eles, in response, remained unyielding in his decision to sack Ferrando and the Governor General, in seeking a resolution to the issue, wrote to the Secretary for State for Colonies, stating that Ferrando:

> who has been Vice-Consul for Italy since 1902, is a person of good repute in the community and has the confidence of the bulk of the Italian residents in Melbourne, a large number of whom, it is stated, have made representation on his behalf to the authorities in Rome (National Archives Australia: A11804, 1915/277).

The dispute was sufficiently noteworthy that it initiated the following rather "tongue in cheek" comment in *The Bulletin*:

> The little Italian community in Melbourne has a row all of its own. Its [sic] Consul, Cavaliere Emilio Eles, does his consulting in the way of a Cavaliere, and largely Ferrando, was driven from the post of hon. Vice-Consul. Whereupon the partisans of Ferrando, who is a Cavaliere, too, have petitioned Rome to hold an inquiry. Meantime the community digs back into ancestry, and seeks to prove that this one or that isn't Italiano at all, but the grandson maybe of an Austrian cavalry officer, and Eles is whipping up a counter petition and it is expected that when the Quirinal hears of the rumpus a force of Bersaglieri will at the very least be hurried to the scene (National Archives Australia: MP16/1, 1917/1196).

A force of *Bersaglieri* were not dispatched, indeed there is no evidence of any response from Italy on the matter, but when the accusations reached London, the Secretary of State for Colonies cabled the Prime Minister's office requesting that secret enquiries be made as to whether Eles had "tendencies favourable to Germany or Austria" (National Archives Australia: A11804, 1915/277).

Unlike the overtly hand in glove relationship that would soon develop between Eles and the Australian government, early dealings were far more guarded with Eles becoming the subject of a secret military intelligence investigation. Noteworthy in their initial report which indicated that the Italian Consul was, in general:

> well liked by his compatriots until his dismissal of the Vice-Consul. The latter has since endeavoured to stir up feeling against him, but the better class of opinion is in favour of the Consul, though it is thought that he was perhaps somewhat lacking in tact ... Eles stands favourably with the Consular body and his relations with the Government Departments, though slight, are quite satisfactory. It is stated that his grandfather was an Austrian (National Archives Australia: A11804, 1915/277).

This was the description of Eles' relations with the Australian government as "slight", an adjective that, as we will see, by 1917, could hardly be further from the truth.

From the Australian government perspective

Although the number of Italian immigrants in Australia in this period was comparatively small, their presence was strongly contested. Italian occupational concentrations and subsequent geographical congregations in areas such as the Queensland sugarcane fields and the Western Australian mining industry in many ways overemphasised both their number and their "threat" to Australian social and labour norms. Reporting of Italians as undesirable immigrants has been well documented by scholars (see for example Cresciani 2003, Randazzo and Cigler 1987) and will not be elaborated on here. Suffice to say that, even after the Italian declaration of war on the side of the allies, Italians in Australia remained "unwanted aliens". This status was only further amplified with Eles refusal for Italians to be allowed to enlist in the Australian Forces.

As the war progressed, and Italian volunteers (under instruction from the Consul) continued to be turned away at enlistment offices, the so-called "Italian problem" became even more of an issue for the Australian authorities. Early patriotic fervour passed and by 1916 enlistments in Australia's completely volunteer army were falling. As the need for men increased, recruitment became a key issue and despite a number of government and private initiatives, it would remain a primary concern for the duration of the war. Across Australia, especially in Queensland and Western Australia, it was thought that Italians were a key factor in the lack of volunteers. If Italians did not have to serve, and could therefore stay and take the jobs of Australian men, why would Australian men enlist?

In response to this dilemma, on 6 March 1916, the Queensland State Executive passed a resolution that "Italians in this State would be allowed to enlist with the Australian Forces or go to Italy to fight with their own army" (National Archives Australia: MP367/1, 592/4/1116). One month later, on the other side of the country, the Australian Labour Federation in Perth called for urgent attention to the problem of Italians and enlistment, and the Secretary of the War Council of Western Australia pleaded for something to be done about the Italians on the goldfields who were "taking the places of our own men who are on active service ... causing acute dissatisfaction ... detrimental to recruiting" (National Archives Australia: MP367/1, 592/4/1116).

At this time, Senator Pearce (Minister for Defence), reported that there were approximately 3,500 Italians on West Australia's goldfields, most of whom were men of military age. The Department of Defence went as far as to claim that:

> ... it would be of advantage in time to come to Italian residents in this country if they were permitted to identify themselves with their fellow citizens of Australia ... in doing so they would still be serving the interests of their own country (National Archives Australia: A1, 1916/20181).

Despite these calls, the Italian Consul refused to modify his previous decision and, in April 1916, in response to continual calls for a solution to the Italian issue, Pearce suggested that the British government should represent this matter to the government of Italy. Accordingly, on 4 May a cable was sent to the British Imperial Authorities recommending that the Italian government be approached regarding their giving permission for Italians to join the AIF. At this stage the Italian government responded that Italians could not join the AIF and further representations to the Italian government, via the Imperial Authorities, received similar answers. It is unclear why the Italian government singled out Italians in Australia when their compatriots in other nations were already in action in, for example, British and Canadian Expeditionary Forces. What was clear was that the situation was at a stalemate. However, by 1917, following heavy losses, Italy was also increasingly in need of additional men. Finally, on 13 June, the Italian government, via the Secretary of State for Colonies, asked if Italians in Australia could be sent to Italy on neutral vessels or on ships carrying Australian goods and troops to Europe (National Archives Australia: MP367/1, 592/4/1116).

Initially, the Australian response was that no ships were available, and they persisted with their own position that Italians should be allowed to join the AIF. However, by November of that year, following the Second Conscription Referendum defeat, and with no foreseeable means of recruiting Italians into the AIF, the Australian government capitulated. Believing that the removal of Italians was essential to Australian volunteerism, they agreed to aid the Consul in the round up of Italians and called on powers, under Section 2J of the Alien Restriction Order of 1915 and Section 5 of the War Precautions Act, to do so (National Archives Australia: MP367/1, 592/4/1116).

And so began the "hand in glove" relations between the Italian Consul-General Emilio Eles and the Australian government, which would see over 500 Italian men forcibly repatriated to serve in the Italian Army – repatriated despite the fact that Australia was a non-conscript nation.

Hand in glove: the Australian government and the Italian Consul-General

With the course set, the Australian government was committed in its relations with the Consul. The Acts to allow the round up and the deportation were already in place, however further assistance was readily offered. For example, in anticipation of potential Italian resistance to the order of repatriation, the Australian government used information supplied under the Alien Registration Act, 1916, to individually locate Italian residents who did not come forward. Furthermore, they offered the use of police and Australian troops to arrest and detain any such recalcitrants. The government also committed the use of troops for the supervision of Italians until they reached their proposed destination and even offered the use of AIF camps as detention centres for those Italians awaiting deportation. With the legal and logistical elements in place, the Australian government and the Italian Consul issued calls to arms in local newspapers across the country such as the following, which appeared in *The Sydney Morning Herald*:

> Mr Shallard, Consular Agent for Italy, notifies that all Italian Conscripts born in 1874 to 1899, are called compulsorily to join the Colours in Italy (*The Sydney Morning Herald* 1917:6).

To ensure a strong response to the call, the Australian government assisted the round up by passing amendments to the War Precautions Act (additional regulations 17EA), which made Italian reservists who refused to render service, and those who induced them not to comply, guilty of an offence. Notification of this amendment was duly published in state newspapers and read:

> A regulation under the War Precautions Act dealing with the call up of Italian Reservists was gazetted today. It provides that any reservist who fails to comply with the notice issued by the Consul or other representative of the King of Italy calling upon him to return to Italian territory or submit himself to a medical

examination shall be guilty of an offence. It will also be an offence for any person to advise or endeavour to persuade a reservist not to comply with the notice (*Examiner* 1918:3).

However, it was soon apparent that the response to these nation-wide advertisements was limited, and a Department of Defence paper, dated 18 January 1918, claimed that some Italians were treating the matter of compulsory deportation "as a joke, believing no compulsion can be exercised" (National Archives Australia: MP367/1, 592/4/1116). The paper concluded that more threatening notification would be required, maintaining that arrest and deportation should occur if Italian subjects failed to comply. Accordingly, on 1 February 1918, Eles issued a second formal call up notice this time threatening that those not presenting would be "considered guilty of desertion and coercitive [sic] measures prescribed by law, [would] be taken against them" (National Archives Australia: MP367/1, 592/4/295).

At the same time it was determined that the Consul, accompanied by an entourage of Australian officials, would begin to tour the country to round up those who did not come forward. The government appointed Lieutenant-Colonel James Walker as Officer Commanding Italian Reservist Repatriation and Walker, an Australian officer, acting under the instructions of Eles, commenced the first round up of reservists in Victoria. The Australian government, to assist the process, supplied railway warrants to cover train travel for Italians (National Archives Australia: MP367/1, 592/4/1145).

From Victoria, Walker and Eles proceeded to Adelaide, Port Pirie and then Broken Hill where the close relationship that had developed between the government and Eles and their mutual determination became evident with the arrest of Italians *at gunpoint*. On 22 May 1918, twenty armed Military and South Australian State Police joined by a number of New South Wales Police converged on Broken Hill to arrest Italian men of military age (South Australian State Records: GRG24/6, 1918/475). William Finlayson, the Federal Member for

Brisbane, who had witnessed the arrests while waiting for a train, reported to parliament that he had seen "a sight which caused me considerable sorrow" and went on to report that these Italians:

> had travelled all night from Broken Hill in unlighted carriages, and under military escort, being lined up on the platform, and marched off under armed escort to be deported later on for military service overseas (Commonwealth of Australia Parliamentary Debates 30 May 1918:5310).

This, as Finlayson pointed out, was an action directly contrary to the Australian rejection of compulsory military service. For the first time a member of parliament, albeit a member of the opposition, protested that "we are actually allowing a foreign consul to dictate to us a policy which is in direct opposition to the popular will, and which so far as we are able to discover, has not even the authority of the government he represents" (Commonwealth of Australia Parliamentary Debates 30 May 1918).

So far, the Australian government had amended the War Precautions Act, provided military personal, military holding camps and transport, as well as military and state police, to aid in the round up of Italians. But there was more to come! In anticipation of opposition to the forced repatriation of Italians, Eles requested censorship of all events pertaining to the round up. To prevent potential opposition and further questioning by those who might be opposed to the deportation, the Australian government readily agreed and instructed censors to prohibit any reporting or reference to opposition to the call to arms (National Archives Australia: MP367/1, 592/4/1116).

The censorship was very effective and the story was not told in the press. In fact, Michael Considine (Federal Member for Barrier) told parliament after the events in Broken Hill that the "press is well muzzled, [and] ... members of Parliament, too are well muzzled. Their *Hansard* speeches even are subject to censorship" (Commonwealth of Australia Parliamentary Debates 23 May 1918: 5077).

Censorship extended to personal letters and as the war and the round up of Italians progressed, the antipathy towards the Consul-General became far more widespread as evidenced in the censor intercepting letters where Eles is referred to as "our coward of a Consul" (National Archives Australia: PP14/2, PF/601), "a sympathiser with Austria" (National Archives Australia: A11804, 1915/277) and a treacherous man willing to send his own people to slaughter (National Archives Australia: PP14/2, PF/601). This mistrust of Eles even extended to death threats against him and Police reports from Western Australia frequently refer to the fact that "the Consul will be shot on arrival" and that "if the Italian Consul comes up here they will do for him" (National Archives Australia: A11804, 1915/277). But death threats did not come to fruition and the might of the relationship continued as Eles and the Australian government sent the first shiploads of Italians to Italy and as Eles pushed his agenda even further and began to target individuals.

The first and most important of these individuals to have been targeted for special action by the Consul was his old adversary, the ex-Vice-Consul Giovanni Ferrando. A Knight of the Crown of Italy in recognition of his services to his country as a prominent and successful migrant, businessman and consular representative, Ferrando was described by his peers as "an asset to the Italian community" in Australia (National Archives Australia: MP367/1, 592/4/1086). Despite the fact that he had already volunteered for service in Italy in 1915 and been found medically unfit, Eles was determined that he should be included in the roundup. Ferrando, initially, was equally as determined that, given his medical status and his belief in the moral and legal wrongs of the deportation, he would not report as ordered. When he did eventually report, after giving Eles a letter to forward to the Minister of War in Italy in which he argued that the Consul had "adopted a malicious attitude towards him", and that he was receiving unfair and unjustly harsh treatment (National Archives Australia: MP367/1, 592/4/1086), he was again found unfit for service.

Despite this medical report, Eles remained determined that Ferrando would be deported to serve in the Italian army, and refused to forward Ferrando's appeal to the authorities in Italy (National Archives Australia: A10075, 1918/28). Eles was no longer acting in his Consular role of representing his people but rather was operating more and more on an agenda of his own making and one which the Australian government was only too willing to support.

Eles argued that while Ferrando might not be fit for the Australian Army he certainly was fit for the Italian Army and, furthermore, his refusing to answer the call to arms was "[s]etting a bad example to his compatriots some of whom are following his lead and failing to report" (National Archives Australia: MP367/1, 592/4/1086). Eles pushed this point further and in a letter to the Department of Defence, Eles asserted that Ferrando was in fact:

> the primary cause of the dissatisfaction among my compatriots and of the misleading statements made in the House of Representatives and elsewhere, in connection with the calling up of Italians in Australia for military service in Italy, and I have no hesitation in stating that the presence of this deserter in this Country and his persistent, unpatriotic activity will continue to endanger the whole of the work which I am doing with your valuable assistance (National Archives Australia: MP367/1, 592/4/1145).

In doing so Eles certainly appears to be playing into the Australian government belief that the deportation of Italians would aid Australian recruitment. Consequently, the Minister for Defence agreed that Ferrando's deportation was necessary "with a view to the public safety and the defence of the Commonwealth" and wrote to Ferrando informing him that "in exercise of the powers conferred upon ... [him] by the *Aliens Restriction Order* 1915, I do hereby order that Giovanni Ferrando ... shall be deported from the Commonwealth" (Hayball 1918:242).

When the deportation did not occur immediately an irate Eles wrote again to the Department demanding to know why Ferrando had not yet been arrested, further evidence of the Consul's determination and the relations that had developed between the two parties.

In actuality, at this time, Ferrando was in hospital for surgery, a fact that did not deter Eles or the government. The Adjutant General, in a letter to the Commander of the 3rd Military District, wrote:

> every precaution is to be taken to ensure that Ferrando does not again escape. It is considered that the best course will be to leave him in the private hospital where he is at present until Saturday ... On that day he should be medically examined by two medical officers in the morning to ascertain if he is fit to travel, and if so, then he is to be sent to Sydney by the express on Saturday afternoon and is to be embarked with the next draft of Italians (National Archives Australia: MP367/1, 592/4/1086).

Accordingly, Ferrando was arrested at Merton Private Hospital and placed on a train from Melbourne to Sydney for immediate deportation under the order signed by the Defence Minister, Senator Pearce (National Archives Australia: A10075, 1918/28). The legality of the government's approach was immediately tested in a High Court action brought by Ferrando, tellingly against both Pearce and Eles. Ferrando challenged his arrest on a number of counts, including the claim that he was not medically fit to serve, but, in a majority judgement, the High Court dismissed his claim and validated the government's position. Ferrando was ordered to pay costs, to place himself under a £5,000 bond and to proceed to Italy by such boat as the Minister directed (National Archives Australia: MP367/1, 592/4/1086). Furthermore, he was instructed that in no way was he to hinder the call up of other Italians and that he should discontinue all court action against the Minister and the Consul (National Archives Australia: MP367/1, 592/4/1086).

Having lost this case, Ferrando then asked to be released from confinement, so that he could organise his business, and, once done, travel to Italy, intending on arrival there to submit his case directly to the Italian military authorities. As Ferrando's business was in Melbourne, the Adjutant General directed that he could return there, but was to be under escort and kept in detention at all times, the cost of which would be borne by Ferrando himself (National Archives Australia: MP367/1, 592/4/1086).

The Department of Defence remained sceptical of Ferrando's motives and, in a Minute Paper dated 30 August, declared that he was "merely trying to gain time and ... it [would be] desirable that he should be embarked at once" (National Archives Australia: MP367/1, 592/4/1086). So, not only did Ferrando have to pay the cost of his incarceration and supervision but was also responsible for the travel costs to the port of his deportation, Fremantle, where under the military escort of Captain Bush and Lieutenant Brown (Intelligence Department), he left on the steamer *HMAT Bakara* on 14 September 1918 to London (National Archives Australia: MP367/1, 592/4/1086).

Ferrando had not only been deported as a common criminal, but would on arrival in Rome, actually be discharged by the Italian Military authorities as "unfit for any military duty" and at the behest of Baron Sonnino, Italian Minister of Affairs, the King of Italy would confer upon him the honour of "*Ufficiale* of the Crown of Italy" (National Archives Australia: MP367/1, 592/4/1151). This of course suggests that Eles' actions were not fully supported by the Italian government. Perhaps as Ferrando said on his return:

> The Australian Government in applying deportation to all Italians and especially to a man like me committed the greatest blunder ever made amounting to cruelty, for which I hold answerable and for all suffering, humiliation (imprisonment) and whatever loss and expenses sustained through their action ... and certainly does not reflect credit on the Australian Government and their

British ideas of 'Fair Play' (National Archives Australia: MP367/1, 592/4/1086).

Meanwhile, relations between the Consul and the Australian government continued to push forward the deportation of Italians and the targeting of individuals. An equally extreme example of Eles' ability to manipulate Australian authorities was the treatment of a man named Cesare D'Atri who was described by the Consul as a "ringleader" of the agitation against the call up (National Archives Australia: B741, V/125). D'Atri, being a naturalised British subject did not report to the Consulate when called to arms. Eles took immediate and extreme objection and quickly set the Department of Home and Territories in motion to "make the necessary enquiries as to the validity of [D'Atri's] naturalisation in order that ... [he] may request his arrest" (National Archives Australia: B741, V/125).

This task, in itself, indicates just how much cooperation Eles was receiving from the Australian authorities. Initial enquiries indicated that the naturalisation was in fact legal, having been conferred in August 1915, after D'Atri had been resident the required two years (National Archives Australia: B741, V/125). Completely unhappy with this result, Eles made further enquiries to get D'Atri's naturalisation revoked. While the Australian authorities did not discount the idea, they did highlight the problems under the current law, saying that they:

> could hardly take steps to have his naturalisation revoked, unless proceedings were taken under the Section of the new Act (1917) which states that naturalisation can be revoked without assigning any reason (National Archives Australia: B741, V/125).

Under this 1917 Act, an offence would have to be found against the War Precautions Regulations.

D'Atri was known to be a committee member of the Sicilian Club in Melbourne. He was also known to have taken an active role at meetings at this club to protest against the action taken in regard to deporting

Italian reservists. Furthermore, he was one of those who forwarded a petition to the Minister for Defence protesting against the calling up of Italian reservists (National Archives Australia: MP367/1, 592/4/982). However, these factors were not sufficient to initiate investigation until Eles stated that D'Atri was of interest to the Ministry of Internal Affairs in Rome who apparently suspected that D'Atri was connected with the sinking of a mail boat, near the coast of Italy in March 1917, despite all evidence indicating that he was in Australia at this time (National Archives Australia: MP367/1, 592/4/982). Eles claimed that D'Atri was a man of "very bad reputation ... likely to commit any offence or act of disloyalty" (National Archives Australia: MP367/1, 592/4/982). In addition, D'Atri had, according to his Consul:

> been twice submitted to trial for fraudulent bankruptcy and about 12 years ago, he defrauded a certain number of people in his native town of Ponza for the amount of 100,000 lire (4.000st) (National Archives Australia: MP367/1, 592/4/982).

D'Atri was described as a man with "very little education but a brilliant intelligence, especially versed to plan all sorts of trickeries and frauds" (National Archives Australia: MP367/1, 592/4/982). On these claims, D'Atri was a potential threat to Australian security and was placed under investigation.

Detective Jones' report on D'Atri relied on the evidence of an unnamed informant who declared that on his arrival in Australia he "represented himself as a Captain in the Italian Navy ... [then] as a Lieutenant" (National Archives Australia: MP367/1, 592/4/982). This same informant considered D'Atri a man of mystery, an "Arabian or Turk – he speaks Italian only a little, but is said to be fluent in Arabic language. [What's more] he is said to be in possession of photographs of himself dressed as an Arabian Officer" (National Archives Australia: MP367/1, 592/4/982).

Under pressure from Eles, various other government departments worked to build a case for the Consul in regard to this naturalised British, allied Italian. Eventually, the Department of Trade and Customs found the chink when they discovered that D'Atri had in fact left the country briefly and thereby had not resided continuously in Australia for the period required by the naturalisation law. In October 1918, under interview by the officers of the Third Military District, D'Atri admitted that he had "left in March 1914 for Egypt returning again in June 1914" and was thereby out of Australia for approximately three months (National Archives Australia: MP367/1, 592/4/982).

The officers of the Third Military District strongly recommended that his Naturalisation Certificate be cancelled and in December 1918, after the War was over as it turned out, D'Atri was "denaturalised" and recommended for deportation from Australia. Much to the consternation of the Consul however, in January 1919, well after the armistice, D'Atri was still in Australia and in a letter to the Department of Defence, Eles outlined his disgust. He stated that as D'Atri:

> never reported to this Consulate ... he is a deserter, and if your Department had not discontinued the arrest of Italian Reservists, Recalcitrants and Deserters I should request his apprehension for embarkation. My Government not having repealed the order for the calling up of Italian Reservists resident in Australia, D'Atri is considered by this Office still under obligation to repatriate in order to join the colours (National Archives Australia: MP367/1, 592/4/982).

Other individuals also came under the intense scrutiny of the Consul and correspondence from Eles to the Department of Home and Territories, requesting investigation to check the claimed naturalisation of Italian immigrants, was common as he left no stone unturned in his determination to round up his compatriots.

Even those few Italians (approximately 150) who had enlisted in the AIF were not immune and Eles managed to track down two such volunteers who he claimed were not naturalised Australians and, with the full cooperation of the Australian government, have them removed from Australian service and shipped to Italy to serve in the Italian Army. (See, for example, the cases of Giovanni Cipolla and Germano Cunial, in National Archives Australia: B2455).

One final, and perhaps the most bizarre of examples to highlight the extremes to which the relationship between the Italian Consul and the Australian government had developed was the case of Antonio Soro. Despite the fact that Italian-born Soro was serving life imprisonment for the murder of schoolteacher Patricia Bickett, he was released under an agreement between Eles and the government for repatriation to Italy to serve in the Italian Army (*Barrier Daily Truth* 1918: 3). Ironically, Soro returned to Australia after the war, a free man, and there was nothing the Australian authorities could do to stop him.

Conclusion

It was certainly the case that, despite the evident dislike of the Consul within the Italian immigrant population, the concerns raised regarding Eles' allegiances and behaviour and the questions over the legitimacy of the call to the colours (at least in the eyes of those affected), the Australian government appeared to be happy to work with Eles in the deportation of the Italians. According to Mr Brennan (Member for Batman) this "somewhat officious person ... a trade agent, with no international status", had "a halo of importance, and almost sanctity surrounding" (Commonwealth of Australia Parliamentary Debates 30 May 1918: 5346) him as far as the Australian government was concerned. Brennan, speaking on behalf of the Labor Party in general, claimed that:

> the Consul-General dominates the Prime Minister. Anything he asks to be done in regard to these unfortunate Italians is done. No inquiry is made as to whether the procedure is sanctioned

by law, fair play, or anything else. Then the Consul goes to the Minister for Defence and asks for a certificate that somebody is an alien. The Minister signs a certificate that such a person is an alien regardless of the fact that his brother Minister has previously signed that the man is not an alien but a naturalized subject (Commonwealth of Australia Parliamentary Debates 30 May 1918:5349).

The significance of this close relationship between Eles and the Australian government is clear. Italians in Australia, seeking to avoid what they saw as discriminatory conscription, were not only subject to legal restrictions under the War Precautions Act, controlled by censorship, and strangled by the inability to petition or raise questions in Parliament, but also had no means of recourse through their Consul. Eles was uninterested in even hearing claims against deportation and as a result Italians in Australia:

> naturalized and unnaturalized, are quite 'full up' of their Consul-General ... who affects to stand arbitrarily between [them] ... and their Government. So 'full up' are they that, if not before the war, at any rate a considerable time ago, there was a joint and, I am informed, almost unanimous movement to rid themselves of him, as a person who does not adequately and fairly represent them for any purpose (Commonwealth of Australia Parliamentary Debates 30 May 1918:5347).

Indeed, with virtually all channels closed, it would seem that the only official avenue open to Italians was that of Labor Party Members willing to raise questions and initiate discussion in the House. Even this avenue was limited, as many questions went unanswered or, under the War Precautions Act, were sidestepped as threats to security and deemed to be not for public knowledge. Labor members such as Brennan, Considine, Blakeley, Higgs and Tudor did continue to speak out vowing to continue protesting "as long as our protests have any possible chance" (Commonwealth of Australia Parliamentary Debates

30 May 1918:5349). They also continued to be outspoken against the Consul-General, whom they believed "abrogates to himself powers and duties which he should not properly have or exercise" (Commonwealth of Australia Parliamentary Debates 30 May 1918:5349). Mr McGrath, Member for Ballarat, even questioned why Eles, as a fit young man of military age, was himself not serving his country rather than sending "unfortunate young men, many of whom cannot speak a word of Italian" (Commonwealth of Australia Parliamentary Debates 26 June 1919:5813) back to Italy.

The relationship that developed between the Italian Consul-General Emilio Eles and the Australian government during the First World War was unique. The formal role of the Consul, as noted by Mr Brennan, was "very little more ... than an agent of his government for a strictly limited number of minor purposes, and [did not even have] ... the right to himself communicate with his Government" (Commonwealth of Australia Parliamentary Debates 30 May 1918:5347). Quoting from Hall's *International Law,* Brennan went on to outline the very limited and local roles of a consul, none of which had, at this time, any international implications. Indeed, as he argued, consuls were not diplomatic representatives, they did not have diplomatic privileges and, furthermore, they did not have "anything to do with the intercourse between their home State and the State they reside[d] in" (Commonwealth of Australia Parliamentary Debates 30 May 1918:5348).

And yet Eles' powers went well beyond these boundaries. In June 1918, when Mr Blakeley, Member for Darling, visited the Consul-General in the offices especially set aside for him at Victoria Barracks, he was greeted by what he described as a "gold braided Australian official of high rank" (Commonwealth of Australia Parliamentary Debates 12 June 1918:5812) who informed him that the Consul would not see him. Being determined, he did eventually manage to talk to the man he called the "Czar of Italy" before he was forcibly ejected by the Australian official. Blakeley strongly objected on a number of counts, not the least of which was that the Consul had been "given high officials to act as his body guard in his infamous deportation" procedure (Commonwealth of Australia Parliamentary Debates 12 June 1918:5812).

Clearly, the Australian authorities worked hand in glove with the Consul during the war, apparently never questioning his authority or actions. In fact, as Considine highlights, the Italian Consul was "utilising the governmental machinery of the people of Australia for the very object against which [they] ... emphatically declared themselves" (Commonwealth of Australia Parliamentary Debates 19 April 1918:4090), namely, conscription.

Even more galling to his compatriots was the fact that Eles took to the task of rounding up and deporting them with what can only be described as vigour and passion, even to the extent of obsession. In the correspondence between Eles and the Australian authorities there is constant pressure from him to round up the Italians. Eles constantly pushed for the arrest and detention of any who ignored the call to colours. No one, in Eles' view, should have been immune to the call.

So what was the Australian government's role and motivation? Was it really a belief that Italians were hindering Australian recruitment? Were they completely under the spell of a charismatic Consul? Did they believe that the forced deportation of Italians would aid the Allied cause? Or was this a natural conclusion to the long term and well documented antipathy of the Australian authorities to an unwanted immigrant group – the swarthy, knife-wielding, mafia agents so frequently described in the twenty or more years before the war?

Even if the Australian government was not actually driving the deportation of Italians, they were at the very least willing participants in the act. Only twice did they stand up to the Consul in his quest and refuse to co-operate. In the first instance they delayed the round up of

Italians in Queensland for their own advantage, as their labour was essential to the sugar harvest (National Archives Australia: MP367/1, 592/4/1116). In the second instance, the Department of Defence argued that Italian reservist Reinaldo Massoni, a Surgical Instrument Maker, "should be allowed to remain in Australia in order that his special knowledge and skill could be made available in the interests of the treatment of wounded soldiers" (National Archives Australia: MP367/1, 592/4/1116). However, the authorities soon ceded to the desires of the Consul when he replied that:

> Italian Military Regulations do not consider temporary exemptions for men employed in Massoni's capacity and that ... no exemptions whatever can be granted to deserters (National Archives Australia: MP367/1, 592/4/1116).

It is interesting to note that Massoni was considered a deserter by his Consul as he had not presented as requested due to his occupation, therefore, despite Australian governmental protest, he was eventually sent to Italy to serve. He did return to Australia after the war and was naturalised in 1922.

Many Italians believed that Eles' actions had nothing to do with Italy, or the Italian King and government, but were rather an arrangement made between himself and the Australian government, and that this was a conspiracy between their Consul and the Australian authorities (National Archives Australia: PP14/2, PF/601). Suspicions were aroused even further when the Consul, without notifying the originators, declined to forward a telegram to the Minister for War in Italy asking if the Italian government was indeed aware of the situation in Australia (National Archives Australia: PP14/2, PF/601).

The legacy of these actions was long standing. Post war, the Italian community in Australia was still asking questions about the role that their Consul had played in their experiences. In September 1920, almost two years after the war, members of the Italian community in

Melbourne were still trying to ascertain the truth of the situation. They pleaded that it was:

> urgent that it be made clear to us whether the compulsory calling up of Italians was really approved by the Italian Government, or was it a fact that it represented nothing else but an illusion, a deception ... If there was no intrigue, let it be communicated officially to us that the calling up never existed, that it was all deceit, that the Italians who repatriated to render service were cheated ... Trusting that the little light requested by us on this subject will not be denied us (National Archives Australia: MP367/1, 592/4/1116).

Many, having obeyed their Consul for what they believed to be their country's call to arms, were, after the event, extremely indignant, angry and confused. They:

> [sacrificed their] businesses, underwent the discomforts and deprivations incidental to the necessary training and voyage, and sustained the hardships of war, only to find on our return to Australia the allegation persistently made that our sacrifice and service were really the outcome of arrangements between Cavaliere Eles the late Italian Consul General and the Federal Government of Australia (National Archives Australia: MP367/1, 592/4/1116).

What is worse, those looking to become naturalised post war were still being asked what service they gave during the war and, in the case of Italians, forms were often accompanied by letters demanding whether they had been called upon by the Italian government to enlist during the recent war, and, if eligible, why they did not go to the front? (National Archives Australia: A659, 1940/1/5335) As the newspaper *Truth* wrote in September of 1919:

> Great distress was caused by Italians in this country being called up as conscripts, and consequently, selling their belongings, and,

in many cases, leaving their families unprovided for. This matter caused much indignation among local Italians. The Consul-General (Cavaliere Eles) who issued the call to Italians has since been sent to Hong Kong. At the time of the conscription, or supposed conscription, of Italians, many wished him at Hong Kong. Thus their wish has been gratified (National Archives Australia: A659, 1940/1/5335).

Perhaps the apparent banishment of Eles to a lesser position in Hong Kong gives some evidence to the argument that this was a Consul who worked alone – a Consul who sacrificed his own countrymen for potential career gain. However, during his service in Australia Eles received recognition from the Italian government with the award of the Order of Saints Maurice and Lazarus (1915) and his promotion from Knight to Officer of the Crown of Italy (1917). Does this suggest that the Italo-Australian's faith in the innocence of their King and government in the roundup was misplaced? There is unlikely ever to be a complete answer to the questions raised in this chapter. It is however instructive to note that the experiences of Italian immigrants in Canada at the same time, under a different Consul and under a different government, were not the same. There was no round up or deportation, rather, there was a welcoming of soldiers of an allied nation into the Canadian forces.

What is clear is that Eles' attitude and behaviour had a significant impact on attitudes and behaviours of the rest of the Italian community in Australia at this time. Eles' actions towards his compatriots certainly reinforced their own perception, born out of pre-war xenophobia and racism, that they were unwanted immigrants. The Australian government's enthusiastic support for the repatriation of Italians, though possibly driven by their frustration about falling levels of volunteerism in the Australian population, did nothing to dispel this view.

Bibliography

Almanak Administrativo Mercantile e Industrial do Rio de Janeiro, 1913.

Barrier Daily Truth, Broken Hill, 30 May 1918, 'Murderer Released Deported to Italy'.

Commonwealth of Australia Parliamentary Debates, 12 June 1918, Mr Blakeley, House of Representatives, vol. IX George V LXXXV, pp 5809-15.

Commonwealth of Australia Parliamentary Debates, 19 April 1918, Mr. Considine, House of Representatives, vol. VIII & IX George V LXXXIV.

Commonwealth of Australia Parliamentary Debates, 23 May 1918, Mr. Considine, House of Representatives, vol. IX George V LXXXV.

Commonwealth of Australia Parliamentary Debates, 26 June 1919, Mr Watt, House of Representatives, vol. VIII-IX George V LXXVIII, p 10130.

Commonwealth of Australia Parliamentary Debates, 30 May 1918, Mr Brennan, House of Representatives, vol. VIII & IX George V LXXXV.

Commonwealth of Australia Parliamentary Debates, 30 May 1918, Mr. Finlayson, House of Representatives, vol. IX George V LXXXV, p 5310.

Cresciani, G., *The Italians in Australia*, Cambridge University Press, Cambridge, 2003.

Examiner, Launceston, Tasmania, 8 March 1918, 'Italian Reservists'.

Hayball, A.H. (ed.), *Commonwealth Law Reports High Court of Australia*, Charles F Maxwell, Melbourne, 1918.

La Revue Diplomatique, Politique – Colonial, Littéraire et Finaciere, France, 5 December 1909.

La Revue Diplomatique, Politique – Colonial, Littéraire et Finaciere, France, 29 June 1902.

National Archives Australia: A1, *Enrolment of Italians in Australian Expeditionary Forces*, 1916/20181, 1915-1916.

National Archives Australia: A659, *Correspondence files, class 1 (general, passports)*; 1940/1/5335, Naturalisation of French, Russian and Italian subjects of military age, 1892-1970.

National Archives Australia: A10075, *Cause Book case records (Victoria), annual single number series*; 1919/10, Ferrando, Cavalier Giovanni v Eles, Emelio, 1903-1973.

National Archives Australia: A10075, *Cause Book case records (Victoria), annual single number series*; 1918/28, Ferrando, G v Pearce, G & another, 1903-1973.

National Archives Australia: A11804, *General Correspondence of Governor-General (excluding War files)*; 1915/277, Italian Consul, Melbourne (Cavaliers E. Eles), 1912-1927.

National Archives Australia: B2455, *First Australian Imperial Force Personnel Dossiers, 1914-1920*; Various, World War One Attestation Documents, 1914-1920.

National Archives Australia: MP16/1, *World War I Intelligence section case files, annual single number series*; 1917/1196, Consul for Italy Eles, 1914-1923.

National Archives Australia: B741, *Correspondence files, single number series with 'V' Victoria prefix*; V/125, D'Atri Cesare. Victorian Railways & 55 Lonsdale St., Melb. Naturalized Italian – or Committee Italian Club – rather Turbulent, 1914-1964.

National Archives Australia: PP14/2, *Reports and personal files, single number series*; PF/601, Repatriation Italian Reservists, 1914-1920.

National Archives Australia: PP14/1, *Intelligence reports of internments, repatriations, affiliations and general investigations, multiple number series*; 4/7/507, Italian Reservists, 1915-1920.

National Archives Australia: MP367/1, *General Correspondence files*; 592/4/982, Cesare D'Arti – Revokation of Naturalization – Italian Reservist, 1917-1929.

National Archives Australia: MP367/1, *General correspondence files*; 592/4/1086, Giovanni Ferrando, 1917-1929.

National Archives Australia: MP367/1, *General correspondence files*; 592/4/1145, Italian Reservists – Giovanni Ferrando, 1917-1929.

National Archives Australia: MP367/1, *General correspondence files*; 592/4/295, Italian Reservists Mobilization, 1917-1929.

National Archives Australia: MP367/1, *General correspondence files*; 592/4/1116, Italians – Enlistment in AIF and Calling up of Italian Reservists, 1917-1929.

O'Connor, D., *No Need To Be Afraid: Italian Settlers in South Australia Between 1839 and the Second World War*, Wakefield Press, Kent Town, Adelaide, 1996.

Papalia, G., 'Imaginary Colonies: Fascist Views of Australia in Italian Diplomatic Correspondence 1922-1940' in *Eras*, Number 6, November 2004, 2004, p N.P.

Randazzo, N. & Cigler, M., *The Italians in Australia*, AE Press, Melbourne, 1987.

South Australian State Records: GRG24/6, *Chief Secretary's Office*; 1915/35, Correspondence files.

South Australian State Records: GRG24/6, *Correspondence files ('CSO' files)*; 1918/475, Report Sergeant D Reiley, City Watch House Adelaide to Sub Inspector Beare Adelaide, 1842-1984.

The Daily News, Perth, 24 February 1914, 'Foreign Consuls'.

The Sydney Morning Herald, Sydney, 20 December 1917, 'Italians to Join Colours'.

Victorian Government Gazette, 14 January 1914.

5
Mussolini's Australian Campaign of 1935-1936

Gerardo Papalia

Introduction

Italy's foreign policy during the Fascist era was consistently expansionist. To increase its effectiveness the Italian government engaged in 'parallel diplomacy'. This involved conducting relations with other countries on two different levels. One level was what we would consider customary diplomatic processes. The other consisted in more or less covert interference in the internal political, economic and social process of other countries, that extended to the indoctrination and manipulation of Italian migrants, conducted either by special operatives or by diplomatic personnel acting in an unofficial capacity.

For this period, in Australia substantial research has been conducted on how the Italian government indoctrinated and manipulated the local Italian migrant community. Here the ground-breaking work was Gianfranco Cresciani's *Fascism, Anti-Fascism and Italians in Australia 1922-1945,* published in 1979. Since then, however, research on other forms of "parallel diplomacy" in Australia has been scarce. In particular, very little use has been made of the Italian diplomatic archives with few exceptions. This significant collection of documents has largely been neglected by scholars.

This chapter intends to partly redress this gap by uncovering some of the most significant contents of these archives. They reveal an unprecedented scenario of espionage, interference in Australia's internal political processes, covert deals with local politicians, manipulation of mainstream media and the establishment of economic lobby groups. They show that Italian diplomatic activity in Australia during the Fascist era was much more extensive and profound than previously recognised, with examples of "parallel diplomacy" similar to those encountered in other countries.

In Australia these activities appear to be concentrated in the years 1935-36, that coincide with the Italian invasion and occupation of Ethiopia. This act of aggression provoked the British government into taking a leading role by advocating the application of economic sanctions against Italy through the League of Nations. Australia also applied sanctions, both as a dominion of the British Empire and as a member of the League of Nations. Italy's response was to redouble its parallel diplomatic efforts to "break the sanctionist front".

Australia's position was of particular interest to the Italian government because its withdrawal from sanctions would have represented a grave blow both to British and League of Nations solidarity. Moreover, Australia was the most vulnerable of the dominions because of its strategic exposure to Japanese expansionism and its reliance on the British fleet for protection. The British navy needed freedom of access through the Mediterranean in order to defend Australia effectively, and this could not be guaranteed if there was a conflict with Italy.

Italian-Ethiopian War Turning Point

Mussolini's decision to invade Ethiopia in 1935 derived from his recognition that the rise in German power, after Hitler's accession to Chancellor in 1933, would inevitably condition any attempt by Italy to independently expand its sphere of influence within continental Europe. What remained was scope for expansion in the Mediterranean and Africa, a policy that would ultimately involve armed conflict with Great Britain. In terms of world diplomacy the Italian-Ethiopian campaign heralded the convergence of interests between Italy, Germany's Third Reich and Imperial Japan, which would later consolidate into the Axis alliance.

When Italian forces crossed Ethiopia's borders in early October 1935, there was an outcry among world public opinion. Particularly in Great Britain, this reaction was informed by strong support for "collective security" under the guarantee of the League of Nations, an organisation founded in the aftermath of World War I with the precise intent to end international aggression. The British government, in response to its public opinion, took the lead at the League of Nations to censure the Italian government. The League condemned the invasion and imposed economic sanctions on Italy.

Australia's situation

Alone of all the dominions, Australia had already been dragged into the dispute well before sanctions were imposed in November 1935. Already by mid-1935 tensions between Great Britain and Italy had reached breaking point. In late August the British government decided to send its 144-vessel Home Fleet into the Mediterranean as a show of force. The Italian government retaliated by sending sufficient forces to its colony of Libya to threaten British control of the Suez Canal. The British Admiralty called upon the Australian government to send two of its most powerful and modern battleships, light cruiser *H.M.A.S. Sydney* and heavy cruiser *H.M.A.S. Australia*, to join its Home Fleet. Australia's United Australia Party cabinet, under the prime ministership of Joseph Lyons, agreed immediately without informing the public or parliament.

Any conflict between Italy and Great Britain would have severed the Mediterranean and Suez route, the most important lifeline guaranteeing Australia's defence against any Japanese attack, for at the time Australia relied almost entirely on the British Fleet. Despite these risks, the Australian government acquiesced to British policy on Italy because, as pointed out by Stanley Melbourne Bruce, Australia's High Commissioner in London and its representative at the League of Nations, a defection at this stage "... would weaken undoubtedly impression created in Italy by unanimity of support, from within and without the Empire, of British policy and would lead to relaxation of pressure on Mussolini to moderate his course ...". On 18 November 1935 Australia applied sanctions against Italy but with great reluctance and only after strenuously arguing against them in London through Bruce.

Italian espionage in Australia

The Italian government was fully informed regarding the defence vulnerabilities of the Commonwealth. Throughout the Fascist era, its consuls kept a close watch on even minimal developments in Australian and Empire defence strategy, planning and upgrading of the armed forces. They carefully read Australian newspaper reports and government documents to glean information regarding ship movements, improvements to coastal installations and any deficiencies in defence preparedness. Exchanges of warships and personnel with British forces were noted, as was weapons systems compatibility.

In one of the most significant reports regarding Australian defence, an intercepted United States' press report forwarded to Rome in 1930, Italian Consul General Antonio Grossardi made the following statement: "Australia is one of the most isolated regions of the Empire, it has a small widespread population and is thus in a situation of the greatest danger. Its present armaments are inadequate in respect of its all but enviable conditions." In a subsequent report on Australian politics Grossardi attributed Australia's defence problems to the White Australia policy, which he defined as "an unilateral Monroe Doctrine", that created enmity among the Asian nations, particularly Japan. It was for this reason, he argued, that Australia had to depend so heavily on British naval power.

Espionage was also carried out by Italian naval personnel on board a visiting Italian warship, the *Diaz*, which came to Australia to celebrate the Melbourne Centenary. The ship's captain sent a number of reports in late 1934 and early 1935 from various stops on its way to and from Australia, including information regarding the naval bases at Singapore and at the port of Fremantle. The extent of Australian defence coordination with British forces was also carefully noted, particularly in the years 1933-1935.

In a report dated November 1935, the Italian Consul in Melbourne, Enrico Anzilotti, reviewed Australia's defence. In it he affirmed that Australia's strategic situation was the most precarious among the Dominions (excepting New Zealand) because of the long distance from Britain's Mediterranean bases and the country's proximity to densely populated nations like China and Japan. Australia's vulnerability meant its continuing dependence on the British Navy. The risk of Japanese aggression was the most worrying threat to Australia because it could only be countered if the British fleet was not militarily engaged in the Mediterranean at the same time.

Anzilotti's view would be reinforced by the opinion of Consul General Paolo Vita-Finzi who arrived in Australia on 22 November 1935. The following is his succinct comment in a report to his superiors: "...[Australia] under the tacit menace of Japanese expansion, without any appreciable army and fleet of its own ... has no other shield except that of the British Imperial fleet." It was on the basis of this information that the Italian government realised that an opportunity existed to pressure Australia either into abandoning sanctions outright, or at the very least to weaken British Empire resolve to contrast Italian objectives.

The first diplomatic exchanges between Italy and Australia

The Italian-Ethiopian dispute triggered an intensification of the activities of Italian consuls in Australia. The diplomatic archives reveal how Anzilotti, and particularly Paolo Vita-Finzi, played a vital role in reporting on events in Australia but also in launching 'parallel diplomacy' in support of Italian government policy.

The salient characteristic of diplomatic relations between Italy and Australia in this period was the Italian government's insistence on dealing directly with its Australian counterpart. This was unusual because at the time the Australian government had no international representatives in the world outside the British Empire and relied on the British Foreign Service. On a purely formal level, this was reflected in the fact that Italian diplomatic representation in Australia was not ambassadorial, but consular, whose main task was to look after the needs of the local Italian migrant population. Nevertheless, for the duration of the Italian-Ethiopian dispute, the role the Italian government assigned to its Consuls went beyond mere consular representation and acquired the functions and form if not the status of full diplomatic representation. This is an indication of the importance invested by the Italian government in maintaining direct contact with the Australian government.

The Italian government operated under the calculated and deliberate premise that Australia was to all intents and purposes an independent country. This had been the assumption informing all Italian diplomatic correspondence of the Fascist era starting with Grossardi, who had deemed Australia's connection with the "Mother Country" to be contingent and not eternal. There were also substantive reasons of opportunity for this stance. Firstly, it offered the Italian government the opportunity to engage directly with Australia without the mediation of the British. Hence, it was both divisive, seen in empire terms, but at the same time astute because it assumed that Australia's and Great Britain's interests did not necessarily coincide. Secondly, it placed Australia in the uncomfortable position of having to directly account for its policy decisions without being able to hide behind the League of Nations or the dictates of British policy.

As tensions between Italy and Great Britain reached a peak in August 1935, the Italian government moved to sound out the Australian government's position. It instructed Anzilotti, as the acting Consul *de carriere*, to consign its aide memoire explaining its position on the Italian-Ethiopian dispute to Prime Minister Lyons. This was handed to Lyons personally by Buoninsegni Vitali, the acting Consul General in Sydney. The aide memoire outlined the reasons behind Italy's policy towards Ethiopia as a response to the threat it posed to the Italian colonies of Eritrea and Somaliland and its refusal to abolish the slave trade. These arguments were subsequently printed in the *Labour Daily* in a statement released by Vitali.

Anzilotti's report back to Rome on 3 September relates Lyons' reactions as being "favourably impressed", adding that Italy had "a good case" that should be taken to the League. Lyons reassured Vitali that he would instruct Bruce to consult the Italian documentation held by the Italian Delegation at the League of Nations headquarters in Geneva. Lyons expressed "... his sympathy for Italy and profound esteem for the Duce ...". Anzilotti concluded: "I gained the impression that he is contrary to sanctions and generally any action which could involve Australia in the Italian-Abyssinian conflict."

The Australian government was indeed scrambling to mitigate British policy towards Italy. On 11 September Bruce gave a speech before the League Assembly which in his own words: "... deliberately refrained from clarifying [Australia's] position." Lyons subsequent "long awaited" statement to Parliament on 23 September regarding Australian policy on sanctions stated that : "... the policy of the Commonwealth government was one of close cooperation with the United Kingdom government for continual efforts to settle the dispute by peaceful means and for the maintenance of the principles of the League." This speech moved the British High Commissioner in Canberra to inquire as to the solidity of the Australian government's commitment. It thus comes as no surprise that the same opinion could have been shared by Italian consular representatives. Vitali's subsequent report to Rome indicated his belief that "the Federal government had not yet made a decision".

When sanctions began on 18 November, Italy's consular representatives in Australia were informed of this event by their Ministry and not directly by the Australian government, which maintained its rigid adherence to protocol, and refused to conduct any direct diplomatic exchange with them. Despite this setback, the Italian government insisted in its attempts to directly engage with the Australian government: Anzilotti sent a message to the Minister for External Affairs George Pearce on 12 November. The letter appears to be part of a standard text letter protesting against the application of sanctions. It makes reference to conclusions of the famous 'Memorandum' presented by the Italian government to the League in Geneva. This portrayed the situation in Ethiopia in such terms as to justify the Italian decision to invade the country. Moreover, it claimed that sanctions had been applied hurriedly and without consultation, and that they had not been adopted in previous international disputes that were more serious.

The letter, however, did not simply proffer a complaint. It also issued a quite explicit warning as to what the Italian government intended to do:

> No one will contest the right and the necessity for the Italian government to take steps in order to defend and to assure the very existence of its people.
>
> The Italian government will thus be compelled to take economic and financial steps which may cause substantial deviation of the present traffic and trade in order to be able to secure what the life of the nation requires.
>
> The prohibition of all the Italian exports more than an economic measure, is a real act of hostility which amply justified the inevitable counter-measures that will be adopted.

The letter ended with the following comment:

> ... the Italian government, whilst it has taken all the necessary precautions with a view to prevent the present situation from creating dangerous complications, believes to be its duty to direct the attention of the governments of the States Members of the League of Nations upon the responsibilities implied by the impending measures, as well as upon the gravity of their consequences.

The letter left vague the issue of what these "counter-measures" would be. As we shall see later, they implied military action. On 22 November Pearce responded directly to Anzilotti by stating:

> ... the present unfortunate dispute was not one between Italy and any individual member of the League, but an issue between Italy and every state member of the League. As such, the Commonwealth government is of the firm opinion that there is no cause for ill-feeling between the Australian and Italian people, who have ever been actuated by deep feelings of mutual regard and esteem, and it would not care to contemplate any resentment could persist between our peoples after the dispute has been settled.

Pearce closed the message by stating that he hoped that the dispute could be settled acceptably for all parties (CRS A2908/1 Item J18 P1).

On 29 January 1936 Vita-Finzi sent an official letter to the Commonwealth government. This appeared to be a standard protest also sent to other countries much like its November predecessor. In the letter, the Italian government lamented the recently stipulated military arrangements between the British, French and other governments in the League. It reaffirmed its desire not to take any action which would lead to its "colonial" conflict assuming a European dimension. Despite the milder tone of this message, the Australian government decided to contact the British government for advice on how to respond. It advised the Commonwealth to take no action. Once again, the Australian government refused to respond directly to the Italian government preferring to shelter behind the aegis of the League and indirectly, but substantially, British policy.

Political opposition to sanctions within Australia

In Australia, the parliamentary exchanges between government and opposition highlighted the crucial aspects of the sanctions policy with its mingling of strategic and economic considerations. Not surprisingly, they were carefully scoured by the consuls for any information that they could exploit to weaken the Australian government's resolve on sanctions. The Consuls would be quick to follow the first signs of opposition to Commonwealth policy.

At the time the federal ALP strongly opposed sanctions. The staunchest opposition came from the Catholic leaning ALP right, which saw support for the ideal 'collective security' embodied in the League as an emanation of the Communist International. Following Lyons speech announcing Australian support for British policy, ALP leader Frank Forde moved to adopt the policy of "non-participation". In contrast, John Albert Beasley, who was the federal parliamentary leader of the staunchly Catholic Lang Labor faction of NSW called for a motion that Parliament formally declare its neutrality and requested the immediate recall of *HMAS Australia* from the Mediterranean Fleet as part of a policy of "absolute isolation and strict neutrality". On October 9, Curtin, soon to become the next leader of the Federal Labor Party, tempered the extreme neutralist stance of the Lang faction by espousing "non-participation" on the basis that that the sanctions bill was "warlike". Ultimately, the ALP as a whole would officially adopt " non-participation" as its policy.

However, this did not deter the Lang Labor faction. On 11 October Beasley proposed an amendment to the Ministerial statement presented by Lyons to Parliament on 23 September. In it he called for the withdrawal of all Australian vessels from the Mediterranean and the declaration of the formal neutrality of Australia. The motion was defeated, but received 19 ALP ayes including those of Curtin and Forde, as well as those of Beasley, Frank Brennan, Jock Garden, Edward John Ward, Darby Riordan and Sol Rosevear, all of whom belonged to the Lang faction.

The debate on sanctions, in particular Lang Labor's call for neutrality, was noted by Anzilotti and reported to Rome. On 14 October Anzilotti reported Curtin's statement that the sanctions were unjust because they were coercive and imposed on the Italian people suffering for actions it was not responsible for. Curtin added that Italian migrants would have to be protected against violence and economic reprisals.

The Italian documents also detail the position taken by state Labor parties, particularly in NSW, Victoria and Western Australia. The most copious and interesting regards the NSW Labor party, dominated by ex-premier Jack Lang who also could count on the support of his faction in the federal parliament. Vitali reported on Lang's call for neutrality, the withdrawal of Australian ships from Mediterranean and the recall of Bruce from the League, ostensibly to avoid the temptation of adhering to the sanctions policy. Vitali added that Lang had much public support even outside his party. Lang's statements were circulated throughout the Italian diplomatic service.

The war between Italy and Ethiopia began to turn in Italy's favour in April 1936. This further spurred Vita-Finzi to scour parliamentary debates for any indication of government policy changes or potential sources of support for Italian government objectives. He informed Rome about the Federal Parliamentary debates of March and early April 1936 when Ward and Herbert Peter Lazzarini of the federal Lang Labor faction asked why the government was persisting with the sanctions when they had failed to bring about an end to the war. Lazzarini asked for comment from the Prime Minister regarding reports that high explosives and poison gas manufactured in Great Britain were being exported to Italy.

Favourable Press Opinion

The information and intelligence gathering activities by the consuls also extended to the combing of press reports. In a report dated 23 March, Vita-Finzi mentions both *The Labour Daily* and *The Bulletin* as being the only main papers which had taken a line favourable to Italy. In particular he stated that "this office [i.e. the Consulate General] has always kept up contact" with *The Labour Daily* defining it as an "unexpected ally" for having continuously denounced the risk of war associated with sanctions. This was not surprising considering that the newspaper was the mouthpiece for Lang Labor. Vita-Finzi added that this paper willingly published news and photographs from the Italian Ministry of the Press and Propaganda, which were normally boycotted by other papers. Even before Vita-Finzi's arrival, *The Labour Daily* had attracted the attention of the consuls for its support of the anti-sanctions campaign. Generally speaking, the paper consistently reported information from Italian sources, or which gave the Italian viewpoint.

Vita-Finzi's letter on 23 March also mentions *The Bulletin*, defined as "independent and authoritative", which had taken a line against "the lies of the popular press serving British interests". He considered the magazine as being of particular value for the fact that it was currently read in the "best" intellectual and social circles of Australia. Vita-Finzi's assessment derived from the magazine's editorial policy of uncompromising opposition to sanctions on the grounds that they did not serve British or Australia's interests. Already in August 1935, *The Bulletin*'s position was for keeping Australia outside of a conflict which it deemed posed no threat at all to British interests in the region. In contrast, participation in sanctions, it sustained, was fraught with dangers particularly commercial ones. Australia was the only Dominion whose naval forces were committed in the Mediterranean. *The Bulletin* argued that any participation in sanctions should only be with hard and fast guarantees of backing from other powers.

As the war progressed, *The Bulletin* criticised the bias of the cable news on issues like the reported use of gas by Italian forces, which it doubted. Ethiopia, too, was depicted as hardly being a civilised country, whose economy was based on slavery. On this latter point, evidence was marshalled from an eminent Australian surgeon and war veteran, Tommaso Fiaschi, whose son Piero was an Australian war hero. In January *The Bulletin* again mentioned trade, passing rueful comment on news that synthetic wool had made such technical progress that it had good chances of substituting Australian wool exports to Germany, Italy and Japan.

The Australian Committee for propaganda in favour of Italy and *Letters from Rome.*

In the early months of 1936 Vita-Finzi began to organise an anti-sanctions lobby. In late February he could already present to his superiors in Rome the newly constituted 'Australian Committee for propaganda in favour of Italy' based in Sydney. Its membership counted people of some public resonance like the ex-NSW Attorney General, Davis Hall, the well known industrialist Earnest Wunderlick, Pier Fiaschi and a certain Mr. Fitzpatrick noted for his charitable and social activities. The objective of this committee was to "rebut hostile propaganda against Italy and to bring into light its rights in this controversy." The first meeting was held at the Consulate-General.

In early 1936, the Italian Consulate of Sydney and the local *fascio* published a collection of letters written by Dr. Herbert M. Moran for the Australian public with the express aim of contrasting what the author considered the distortions of British propaganda. Moran was a well known sportsman, renowned surgeon and war hero of Irish-Australian extraction. As an opinion leader he played an important role in support of the Italian position throughout the conflict. He shared many characteristics with other pro-Italian propagandists throughout the world. The title of the book was *Letters from Rome.* In it, Moran extolled the "civilising mission" of Italy in Ethiopia and expressed his fears regarding the strategic consequences of sanctions on Italy in its role as a shield against Bolshevism and Nazism. His book had a print run of 4,000 copies.

On February 5, a favourable review of Moran's book, was printed in *The Bulletin*'s editorial page under the title: "An Australian in Rome." *The Bulletin*'s review centred on the main thrust of the publication, where the author criticised the factious attitude of the Australian and British press regarding the Italian-Ethiopian dispute. It highlighted the contrasts between what it considered to be British press propaganda and Italian "reality" as depicted by Moran. The Italian people were described as standing by the Fascist regime and being roused to its support by the sanctions. In response to reports of Italian "atrocities" it was stated that Red Cross inquiry had recommended no action be taken. The review was so effective in its support for Italy that Vita-Finzi decided to have it reprinted and distributed by the Consulate General.

Coordinated Press Campaign against sanctions.

The subsequent initiatives taken in Australia by Italian Consular personnel in April-May 1936 should be appraised in the diplomatic context of the period, which saw the Italian government's attempt to establish an accommodation with its British counterpart from a position of strength, following decisive Italian victories against Ethiopian forces. Given this international scenario, it is easy to understand the heightened impact any news regarding any changes on the Australian government's position would have had on Italian policy makers. There was also the problem of sanctions that, in spite of their inability to stop the war, were beginning to weigh heavily on the Italian economy.

On 21 April Vita-Finzi asked his government for authorisation to begin a "press campaign by some papers" for the lifting of sanctions.

As we shall see, he was referring in particular to *The Labour Daily* and *The Bulletin*. The potential of press criticism of government policy on sanctions was readily appreciated by Vita-Finzi, who had worked as a journalist before entering the diplomatic service. The proposal by Vita-Finzi to begin a press campaign did not originate in a vacuum, nor did it represent a break with tradition. It represented a vital part of the Italian parallel diplomatic style, of which there were many examples in other countries.

The Italian government, evidently feeling the urgency of this conjuncture, authorised Vita-Finzi to begin his press campaign the very next day by telegram. On 22 April Vita-Finzi informed Rome that he had begun his press campaign. On 24 April he telegraphed his Ministry that both *The Labour Daily* and *The Bulletin* had begun a campaign against sanctions.

On 22 April, *The Labour Daily* in an editorial regarding the looming trade war ("Trade Diversion") with Japan and the United States, emphasised the opportunity presented by regaining the Italian market previously valued at an average of £2 million per annum to Australian exporters. Two days later, it reported the debate in the Senate regarding wool, where it was argued by Senate Opposition leader Joe Collings that artificial substitutes for wool posed a real threat to Australian exports, particularly in Japan, Germany and Italy. Regarding Italy, it considered inevitable that the country should resort to substitutes. At the time over half Australia's exports were made up of wool.

Vita-Finzi took the opportunity provided by these press reports to pressure the Australian government in regard to trade. An encounter between Henry Gullett, Minister for Trade Treaties and Vita-Finzi was reported in the Australian press as taking place on 27 April. This may have been no coincidence, given that Gullett had been defined by Grossardi "an excellent friend of Italy". Such a history of confidence in Gullett may explain why the meeting was probably not "official" in that no direct report exists in the Italian documentation and was later denied by the Australian government.

However, the encounter was reported in *The Labour Daily* and *The Bulletin*. The *Labor Daily*'s report was printed the day after the supposed encounter, and included an interview with Vita-Finzi, confirming that its reporters had very close contact with the Consul-General. The article related that the meeting between Vita-Finzi and Gullett had discussed trade relations between Italy and Australia and that a parliamentary statement might ensue in the House of Representatives. The paper reported Vita-Finzi as claiming that the effect of sanctions would "ultimately react more adversely on Australia than on Italy." Due to sanctions, Australia had already accumulated an unfavourable balance of £200,000. Finally, Vita-Finzi affirmed that following the cessation of hostilities any return to trade between Italy and other countries would be prioritised according to three criteria: (1) with those countries which had not enforced sanctions; (2) with those that had technically enforced sanctions but had not ceased to trade with Italy; (3) with those which had enforced sanctions.

In his telegram of 21 April Vita-Finzi had also asked his government for approval to announce to the local newspapers that an incentive would be provided to the Australian government by offering it most favoured nation status if it decided to abandon sanctions. Vita-Finzi said that the campaign would certainly have "moral" if not practical effects. The proposal was in line with the main objectives of Italian foreign policy of the time, to convince sanctionist countries to apply sanctions in a "friendly" manner by highlighting the grave consequences which they could have in the future. Vita-Finzi had evidently surmised that Australia could still represent a weak link in the chain of British Empire's unity of action.

Ultimately Rome decided not to offer favoured nation status if Australia abandoned sanctions. This decision was taken at the highest level: the Italian government's Inter-Ministerial Commission for

Sanctions on 28 April 1936. At this meeting, it was affirmed that Prime Minister Mussolini had issued a directive that "energetic action [be taken] by diplomatic representatives to persuade some States to abandon sanctions". The best way of doing this was to make some exceptions to the recently adopted policy of autarchy by offering concessions to those countries that would benefit most from the re-establishment of trade. The potential existed for the Australian government to be influenced by such a policy because: "Australia is quite worried at seeing Great Britain concentrate most of its attention and military forces in the Mediterranean and Africa, leaving the Australian continent undefended or almost, in the face of a possible southward expansion by the Japanese." In the end Australia was not chosen because Italy "could well do without the wool and hides that Australia provided before the sanctions", especially considering that Australia did not appear interested in opening up its markets to "important" Italian products.

Vita-Finzi could confirm to his Ministry on 30 April that *The Labour Daily*, a newspaper "with which I am continuing to maintain contact", had published articles claiming the sanctions had failed and that the Lyons government could no longer justify keeping the cruisers *Australia* and *Sydney* in the Mediterranean. One of its reported newspaper articles contained the following sentence: "Apparently, the government has not yet had time to consider the position in the Pacific." In addition, Vita-Finzi affirmed *The Labour Daily* had advocated withdrawal from sanctions to make up for lost exports.

The Bulletin had already published articles favourable to Italy, as we have seen. The magazine was recognised by Vita-Finzi as representing powerful farming (and wool) interests describing it as an: "authoritative organ, widespread among intellectuals and especially among the owners of large farms". A *Bulletin* representative assured the Consul General that it would be publishing articles against the sanctions on 29 April and 6 May. As promised to Vita-Finzi, *The Bulletin*'s issue of 29 April contained an important leader titled 'Britain's Appalling Policy' together with a letter from Moran titled 'With the Italian Armies', plus a small comment on the loss of exports estimated at £355,000. The editorial lambasted Eden for being ridiculous and provocative in causing "the permanent alienation of an old friend now increasingly strong in the Red Sea". Other brief columns in the same issue contrasted a comment by Pearce that all League members were still cooperating in applying sanctions with reports that Ecuador had already decided to abandon them (4 April), and Argentina about to follow suit. Argentina was Australia's global competitor in the wool trade. In the meantime, it was affirmed, Australia had sustained substantial losses in exports. The pulling out of sanctions by Ecuador had already been reported in early April by *The Labour Daily*.

In a dispatch dated 1 May, the Consul General reported the above articles of the 29th and stated that the agreement with *The Bulletin* to stage a "joint" campaign to have sanctions lifted was continuing. On 6 May, in an editorial titled 'Leaguers demand War', the magazine pointed out the inconsistencies in the League's policy towards Italy compared to its sidestepping of similar international crises, notably the Japan-China dispute.

As had happened with "An Australian in Rome", some of *The Bulletin*'s articles represented excellent material for propaganda. Vita-Finzi lost no time in making copies of "Britain's Appalling Policy" as well as Moran's letter (both published on 29 April) for use as pamphlets to be distributed by "people in the trust" of the Consulate General. The diplomatic documents contain clippings from *The Bulletin* of these articles and in particular copies of the reprints made by the Consulate General. Vita-Finzi added in his report of 9 May, containing the clippings, that the magazine had: "... readily agreed to our request to accentuate the uselessness of sanctions as a means to obtaining peace and the damage they have done to Australian commerce, as can be surmised from the following brief articles." He announced that the next issue would dedicate more space to this topic.

Ethiopia's capital Addis Abada fell to Italian forces on 5 May. However, this did not mark the end of sanctions nor Vita-Finzi's press campaign to have the sanctions lifted. As he had anticipated in his reports to Rome, *The Bulletin*'s very next issue dated 13 May contained a long article titled "Sanctions, Hailé Selassié and War" which began by reporting the alleged conversation between Gullett and Vita-Finzi on the resumption of trade, and contrasted it with a statement by Pearce that sanctions were succeeding. *The Bulletin* concluded that the government had been "misinformed on almost every phase of the Italo-Abyssinian quarrel". Then the article went on to describe Italian forces entering Addis Abada as liberators for the city. These reports in *The Bulletin* and *The Labour Daily* came at a time when the rest of the press was also changing its position regarding sanctions and thus contributed to creating a cumulative effect on public opinion. Later in June, *The Sun*, *The Herald* and *The Age* would join the *The Labour Daily* and *The Bulletin* in calling for trade with Italy to be resumed as soon as possible.

Covert Agreement with ALP politicians.

In parallel with his press campaign, Vita-Finzi also worked with Labor politicians. On 19 April the Italian government had received a report from its ambassador in London, Dino Grandi, indicating that the Australian government was about to withdraw from sanctions. Grandi concluded that the Australian government believed that collective security was an empty expression. Bruce's speech to the League Council on 20 April, in which he openly stated his long held view that the League was not sufficiently universal for its sanctions to deter international aggression, served to further confirm this impression.

The Italian government acted swiftly on the basis of this news. On 20 April it sent a telegram to Vita-Finzi asking for further information, accompanied with the following instructions:

> The moment appears suitable for you to point out in Australia how British policy in the Mediterranean has led it over recent months to recall numerous vessels from other seas weakening British forces in the Far East, and consequently diminishing the ability to defend Australia. You could also conveniently emphasise the danger which European complications could present for Australia given that everything appears to indicate that Japan would take advantage in fulfilling its expansionist objectives.

Having hinted at this argument in its messages to the Australian government of November and January, here the Italian government was now openly deploying the defence strategy argument.

Vita-Finzi immediately relayed these observations to the Australian government. On 2 May he informed Rome as to its response: "The Australian government in effect appears to be worried by the continuous expansion of Japan, but it is embarrassed in regard to changing its policy because of the delicate Australian situation with Bruce being President of the League Council ..." Vita-Finzi, realising the opportunities that such political uncertainty appeared to offer, added: "This Consulate General will however seek to apply indirect pressure via the Labor Opposition and the influential farmers' group regarding the renewal of the export trade ...". This latter measure would soon become the Lanital campaign.

Vita-Finzi also responded to this request from his superiors by negotiating an agreement with Labor politicians. On 22 April Vita-Finzi informed his superiors of his conversations with Beasley, whom he defined as an "influential personality of the Federal parliamentary Opposition." Vita-Finzi secured Beasley's agreement, as leader of the federal Lang ALP faction, to ask the Australian government in parliament to recall Australia's warships from the Mediterranean. The outcomes of this agreement would soon be seen. On 29 April Lang Labor parliamentarians questioned the government on this very issue.

Ward asked the government why the *HMAS Australia* and *HMAS Sydney* were still with the Home fleet and when they would return to Australia. Rosevear, a fellow member of the parliamentary Lang Faction, then interjected by citing newspaper reports that the *HMAS Australia* was in Malta and the *HMAS Sydney* in Alexandria. Ward's questions were reported to Rome the very next day by Vita-Finzi, who reassured his superiors that Opposition attacks would continue.

On the same day in parliament, Lazzarini asked whether Gullett had indeed met with the Italian Consul General and whether Australia had suffered more than Italy by the application of sanctions. The government denied any such meeting ever taking place. The following day Lazzarini accused the government of falsehood in replies given to his questions regarding the usefulness of sanctions, for its insistence that they were "having a constant and cumulative effect". He based his accusation on Bruce's speech to the League of Nations Council on 20 April. He followed up with a quote from Pearce's speech to Parliament of 24 April, in which he had admitted that the sanctions had not been "sufficiently drastic or rapid" to halt the Italian invasion. Lazzarini drew the conclusion that the government had not only given misleading but also false answers to his questions. He affirmed: "Both statements are direct admissions that sanctions against Italy have not achieved their object".

As with the press, the fall of Addis Ababa did not signal the end of the political campaign. On 6 May, Vita Finzi reported on parliamentary debates, in which Labour parliamentarians were asking the government when it would withdraw sanctions. Vita-Finzi did not limit his anti-sanctions campaign to Federal institutions, but also involved the States. On 6 May, Alam Chegi, MLC for the NSW parliament and President of the Maronite Lebanese Association of Australia, proposed a motion calling for the abolition of sanctions, the return of peaceful relations among nations and the revitalisation of the Stresa Front. Chegi was also a member of the "Friends of Italy

Committee." For his efforts Rome authorised Vita-Finzi to officially thank Chegi on behalf of the Italian government.

On 8 May it was Beasley's turn to question the government in Parliament regarding the withdrawal of the Australian warships from the Mediterranean. Vita-Finzi attributed this initiative in his report to Rome as Beasley "maintaining his promise" to him. Once again, the government response to this question was negative. Beasley also asked when trade with Italy could be expected to resume.

On 11 May Vita-Finzi notified the Commonwealth by *Note Verbale* that Italy claimed full sovereignty of Ethiopia and that the King of Italy had taken on the title of the Emperor of Ethiopia. Vita-Finzi renewed those "considerations" proffered to Pearce a few days earlier regarding the possible impact of European complications on Australia's precarious strategic position vis-à-vis Japan. Parkhill received these views and the *Note Verbale*, but in response refused to go beyond generic expressions of hope that relations between European countries would improve. Vita-Finzi concluded that the Commonwealth government would probably respond after having studied London and the League's attitude. A telegram to Rome, sent on the same day by Anzilotti, relayed press reports that the Dominion representatives, gathered in London, had insisted with the British government that sanctions be lifted.

On 12 May Vita Finzi sent to Rome his conclusions on the political situation in Australia: "Highly improbable that the Australian government could follow an independent policy from that of Great Britain, but its seems certain that it will seek to exert a moderating influence." Vita-Finzi was not far from the truth: in the course of discussions with British government representatives just after the fall of Addis Ababa, Bruce forcefully and consistently argued that sanctions had to be abandoned. By mid-June, Keith Officer of the London branch of the Department of External Affairs in London, was gloomily reporting back to Canberra that war with Italy would be a likely prospect if the sanctions continued. Moreover, British prestige had been badly shaken in the Eastern Mediterranean by Italy's defiance of sanctions. The prospects were grim: "... the aid of France could not be depended on and Japan and/or Germany might take advantage of the situation ...".

The Lanital campaign

Following up on his telegram of 2 May, Vita-Finzi informed Rome on 7 May that he had prepared an Anti-Sanctionist Manifesto which he had distributed among political, industrial and commercial circles. The telegram was followed up by a letter on 16 June, attached to a copy of the 'Manifesto'. It contained about one hundred signatures from people who had been approached by "people in the trust" of the Consulate General, who took pains not to be seen as the "direct inspirer" of the 'Manifesto', despite having drafted the Manifesto and circulated it to all Commonwealth ministers, senators and MHRs, many state politicians, the newspapers and prominent professionals. Vita-Finzi added that another manifesto was in preparation with over two hundred more signatures if the government continued with the sanctions. Parallel to this initiative, another anti-sanctionist petition containing five hundred signatures, which had already been presented to Lyons, was being circulated in the State of Victoria by the observant Catholic Labor MLC, Esmond L. Kiernan.

The 'Manifesto' was couched in a language to make it appear inspired by concerned Australians. It made a case for the resumption of normal trade with Italy, given that the Italian-Ethiopian conflict had ended. It then went on to point out that Australia had enjoyed a favourable balance of trade with Italy averaging £3 million a year between 1930 and 1935, in a proportion of 5.5 to 1 to Australia's favour, whereas in the first three months of sanctions it had accumulated an unfavourable balance of over £80,000 or 3 to 1. The 'Manifesto' then mentioned the new Commonwealth tariff intended to divert trade away from those countries that did not buy Australian goods, arguing that Italy could again be an ideal trading partner as it had been "one of our best customers". It added the issue of Australia's trading competitors, of which much had been made in the *Labour Daily* and *The Bulletin* reports: "The fact that Australia has ceased to trade with Italy has enabled other nations to take advantage of this and reap a rich harvest; and this will have a serious effect on the future disposal of our commodities in Italy." The 'Manifesto' ended by urging the re-establishment of "friendship and trade" with Italy. An attached list of signatures contained names of people indicating both their position in society and their company affiliations. As would be expected, the vast majority belonged to the farming sector and exporting interests. None had obviously Italian names. The 'Manifesto' was reported word for word in *The Labour Daily* under the title "Australia's Loss". Then the paper gave a list of the most significant signatories. As with the Kiernan petition, it was sent on to the Prime Minister.

On 1 June, *The Labour Daily* began to publish material, undoubtedly derived from Italian sources, as part of its campaign for the removal of sanctions. The editorial of the day, titled "Japan Retaliates" argued that nationalism in Japan would lead to the search for wool substitutes in Germany and Italy. Regarding Italy, the editor had this to say: "Owing to Australia joining in the application of sanctions against Italy, the Italian government has encouraged research for a satisfactory wool substitute, and now claims that it has achieved success with a synthetic wool produced from casein." The very next day another article gave figures which showed how little Italian exports to Australia had suffered whereas Australian exports there had been "cut most drastically". On 4 June the *Labour Daily* published four front page photographs under the title "Wool from Milk" with the following caption: "Italy's reply to sanctions resulted in the manufacture of 'Lanital', a substitute for wool, made from casein, which is being used for underclothing, topcoats and suitings". This was accompanied by an in-depth article titled "New Italian Wool Substitute Impresses Experts" reporting the judgement of Australian wool experts on samples of 'Lanital'.

Vita-Finzi was quick to report this campaign by *The Labour Daily* to his superiors, boasting how it had dedicated an editorial, a column and even a road billboard to 'Lanital' on the basis of "samples and news provided by this Consulate General and Chamber of Commerce." Its effect was described as "throwing into alarm wool producers who had already been hit by Japanese customs retaliation". (This was Japan's response to Australia's application of "Trade diversion" which discriminated against Japanese products in favour of British ones). It added that the wool producers, who were afraid of losing the Italian market, were among the best propagandists against sanctions. *The Labour Daily* was not the only source of propaganda regarding the wool substitute, Moran in his *Letters from Rome* also praised this product. Important Australian visitors to Italy were even shown the product.

In synchronisation with *The Labour Daily*'s appeal to export interests in its campaign against sanctions, *The Bulletin* on 10 June also reported the grave losses to Australia exports caused by the sanctions policy. Then on 1 July an editorial titled "The Tragic Trade War", lamented the imposition of a Japanese retaliatory tariff on all major Australian products with a government licence required for wool and wheat imports. The export crisis provoked by the trade diversion policies of the Australian government were placed in the context of declining exports to other European countries. Sanctions had thus contributed to aggravate an already difficult trading situation for Australia. To make matters worse, it appeared British industry was likely to renew its import agreements with Argentina. Not surprisingly, wool growers were up in arms. On 15 July, the day sanctions were lifted, *The Bulletin* surmised that the British Empire had borne the brunt of the war by loss of trade and employment. As if this was not enough, the political aftermath included an Austro-German-Italian agreement which "looks very much like an alliance". In the following issue, *The Bulletin* estimated the impact of sanctions against Italy and bitterly remarked: "No other Dominion had to bear such an expense, and to the extent that it exceeded average upkeep the British government should foot the bill. But no doubt it will be passed on to the Australian taxpayer as another instalment of the "tune-in-to-Britain" policy.

The sanctions are lifted

On 18 June Chamberlain declared to the Commons that the British government would recommend the sanctions be abrogated at Geneva. Italy's consuls in Australia learnt this news from press reports. The *Sydney Morning Herald* reported that Lyons had instructed Bruce to pressure Baldwin to lift sanctions because Australia was "fearful of losing the Italian market". Thus the efficacy of Vita-Finzi's initiatives to have the wool growers pressure the government was confirmed.

Lyons made an official announcement before the House of Representatives on 18 June, that the Commonwealth intended to lift the sanctions on 15 July. No official communication was made to the Italian consuls in Australia. The Commonwealth government continued in the fiction of referring the issue to the League of Nations, as if relations with Italy had only been incidentally affected. When Vita-Finzi informed Rome Australia had lifted sanctions, he affirmed that: "The Australian government appears to desire to increase trade with Italy given the difficulties created by new Australian tariffs in Japan and United States." Many years later, in his autobiography, Vita-Finzi would recall that a ship full of wool left for Italy on 9 July, even before sanctions had been removed. On the same day as Vita-Finzi sent his telegram, on 16 July, the British government withdrew its Home Fleet, and with it Australia's vessels, from the Mediterranean.

The war's aftermath and Australian appeasement.

The Italian-Ethiopian war represented a watershed in public relations between Italy and Australia, even from the point of view of the Italian diplomatic service at the time. Whereas, before the war, the Fascist regime had generally benefited from a relatively positive mainstream press, afterwards it attracted increasing criticism. It was also a watershed in foreign policy terms. In the years following the dispute, the Commonwealth government made it a priority to encourage the British government to continue with a policy of "appeasement" towards Italy. Lyons welcomed the Anglo-Italian Agreement of April 1938. The fleeting détente between Italy and Great Britain that this pact represented culminated in the recognition by Great Britain, together with Australia, of Italian *de jure* dominion over Ethiopia on 23 November 1938.

As was cabled at the time by Lyons to the British government: "Commonwealth government strongly of the opinion that, as a contribution to peace, Anglo-Italian agreement should be brought into operation forthwith and *de jure* recognition accorded to Italian Empire in Abyssinia ... in present condition of world, a peaceful and friendly Mediterranean is in our opinion essential." This policy of appeasement was associated with a strengthening of Empire defences. In many respects appeasement was the most natural policy option for Australia. At least in the short term it freed the British navy from any potential entanglement with Italian forces in the Mediterranean, enabling it to rescue Australia in case of Japanese aggression.

Conclusion

Italy's invasion of Ethiopia represented a turning point in Italian policy towards Australia. From the moment the Commonwealth followed the British lead in imposing sanctions, the Italian government applied "parallel diplomacy" in an attempt to break its resolve, as it did with other sanctions imposing countries. The Italian government, on the basis of the wealth of intelligence provided by the meticulous work of its consuls and military personnel, was fully aware of Australia's defence vulnerabilities. It knew that any tension between it and the British government would negatively impact on the latter's ability to defend Australia against Japanese aggression. The Italian government used this knowledge to pressure Australia to withdraw from sanctions. Had it succeeded it would have broken both the "sanctionist front" and the British Empire's unity of resolve, representing a substantial diplomatic coup.

Throughout the crisis the Italian government insisted on engaging directly with its Australian counterpart without British mediation. In so doing it sought to exploit what it knew to be the underlying incompatibilities between Australia's strategic and commercial interests and those of Great Britain. It ordered its diplomats in Australia to organise cultural and trade lobbies, coordinate press campaigns with leading Australian newspapers and negotiate agreements with Labor politicians to pressure the Australian government on both federal and state levels.

The Italian government's policy towards Australia was the most effective under the circumstances. One can affirm this because throughout the crisis the Australian government sought to dissuade the British from persisting in their pro-sanctions policy. The Italian government's lack of success in inducing the Australian government to break away from British policy and abandon sanctions was not due to a mistaken strategy. Rather, its immediate failure was due to the abiding strength of the bond between Australia and Great Britain in spite of their differences. However, in terms of the subsequent adoption of the policy of appeasement by Great Britain, which was warmly welcomed by the Australian government, it was extremely successful. Neither Great Britain nor Australia would take any real action to oppose Italy's interests until Italy itself took up arms against both on 10 June 1940.

Bibliography

Primary Sources

I – ARCHIVAL

National Archives of Australia, Canberra

First Lyons Ministry. Jan. 1935-Dec. 1935. Cabinet Papers. CRSA 6006/5, Microfilm Roll 9.

Correspondence Files. Dept. External Affairs (II) Central Office. CRS A461/18.

Dept. External Affairs (II) Correspondence Files, Alphabetical Series. CRS A981/1.

Correspondence Files, Alphabetical Series. Dept. External Affairs, London Office. CRS A2937/1.

Correspondence Files, Single Number Series with Alphabetical Prefix. Australian High Commissioner, United Kingdon, London. CRS A2908/1.

Correspondence Files, Multiple Number series. 'The Shedden Collection' [Records collected by Sir Frederick Shedden during his career with the Department of defence and in researching the history of Australian defence Policy], Dept. of defence, Central Administration. CRS A5954/1.

National Library of Australia

Original Correspondence Dominion Office (D.O. 35) Microform, 1926-1960. (Public Record Office, London D.O. 35).

Confidential Print Dominions Office (D.O. 114) Microform, 1924-1951.

'Diaries of Jay Pierrepoint Moffat U.S. Consul General to Australia 1935-1937' Microfilm: MFM G 7251.

Italian Historical Society- COASIT., Melbourne: I.H.S.

Italian Diplomatic Archives, Australia Political Series, (Affari Politici) 1919-1945. Microfilm, Reels: 8-17. Document Numbers from: 4408-8252.

II – Printed Primary Sources

(i) Official Publications

Commonwealth of Australia, Parliamentary Debates: CPD vol No. 147, 150: 1935-1936

Commonwealth of Australia, Votes and Proceedings of the House of Representatives, No. 50. 1935.

(ii) Other Published Documents

Moran, H.M. 1935, *Letters from Rome. An Australian's view of the Italo-Abyssinian Question*, Angus and Robertson, Sydney.

(iii) Newspapers

Il Giornale Italiano, (Sydney) 1933, 1935-1936, 1937.

The Age, (Melbourne) 1935-1936

The Bulletin,(Sydney) 1935-1936

The Labour Daily, (Sydney) 1935-1936

The Sydney Morning Herald, 1935-1936

Secondary Sources

I – BOOKS

(i) Autobiographies, Biographies and Memoirs

Vita-Finzi, P. 1989, *Giorni lontani, Appunti e ricordi*, Il Mulino, Bologna.

(ii) Other Books

Andrews, G.M. 1970, *Isolationism and Appeasement in Australia*, Australian National Press, Canberra.

Baer, G.W. 1967, *The Coming of the Italian-Ethiopian War*, Harvard University Press, Cambridge Massachusetts.

Bridge, C. (ed.) 1991, *From Munich to Vietnam. Australia's Relations* with *Great Britain and the United States since the 1930's*, Melbourne University Press, Carlton.

Cresciani, G. 1980, *Fascism, Anti-fascism and Italians in Australia. 1922-1945*, Australian National Press, Canberra.

De Felice, R. 1975 (1974), *Mussolini il duce. I. Gli anni del consenso, 1929-1936*, Einaudi Editore, Turin.

Del Boca, A. 1986 (1979), *Gli italiani in Africa Orientale. La conquista dell'Impero*. 2 vols, Laterza, Bari.

Hudson, W.J. 1980, *Australia and the League of Nations*, Sydney University Press.

Lamb, R. 1998, *Mussolini e gli Inglesi*, Corbaccio Editore, Milano (Original edition: Mussolini and the British).

Mori, R. *Mussolini e la conquista dell'Etiopia*, Le Monnier, Florence, 1978.

Procacci, G. 1984, *Dalla parte dell'Etiopia*, Feltrinelli, Milan.

Quartararo, R. 1980, *Roma tra Londra e Berlino, La politica estera fascista dal 1930 al 1940*. Bonacci Editore, Rome.

Rumi, G. 1974, *L'imperialismo fascista*. Mursia Editore.

Santoro, S. 1991, *La politica estera di una media potenza. L'Italia dall'Unità ad oggi*. Il Mulino, Bologna.

II – Essays and Articles

Ferguson, E. A., Fry, T.P., Holmes, J.G., Murray Smith, A., 'Australian Foreign Policy – Formation and Expression of Australian Opinion.': in *Australian Policies, Political and Strategic*, Australian Institute of International Affairs. Australian Supplementary Papers, Series D, 1938.

Pesman Cooper, R. 1989, 'An Australian in Mussolini's Italy: Herbert Michael Moran' in *Overland* vol. 115: 44-53.

Twomey, P., 'Munich', in Bridge, C. (ed.) 1991, *From Munich to Vietnam. Australia's Relations with Great Britain and the United States since the 1930's*, Melbourne University Press, Carlton: 12-37.

6
Australia-Italy: A Not So "Special" Trade Relationship

Bruno Mascitelli

Introduction

Australia and Italy are both developed and modern economies with complementary economic strengths and shared common economic values. Both economies enjoy membership of international economic bodies such as the OECD, World Trade Organisation and acknowledge each other for their regional positioning. Both countries were impacted by the 2008-10 global financial crises (GFC) but in very different ways. Italy, as the world's eighth largest economy, was hit especially hard by the global financial crisis and, more recently, by the Eurozone sovereignty crisis. Not surprisingly, the size of the Italian economy is smaller today than what it was in 2008 in real terms and in some respects there has been a noticeable decline in Italian consumption (DFAT Fact Sheet 2012). Since 2011 Italy has also been the focus of great political instability with "technical" and improvised coalitions seeking to bring calm, stability and growth to the economy. On many occasions Italy has expressed envy that Australia has such a stable political environment and that it was able to avoid the worst of the financial crisis and maintain a growth economy. Australia enjoyed an on average three per cent growth in its economy over the past 20 years. Moreover, Australia's ability to avoid recession during the GFC was exceptional by Western economy standards and public debt, despite all the bungling of the stimulus packages of the Labor Rudd government, was minuscule in comparison to the 130 per cent public debt to GDP which burdens the Italian economy.

Since 2010 Italy-Australia trade has been quite volatile. Surprisingly, this had less to do with the Italian economic crisis and more with the decline and shift of Australian exports to Italy. While the Italian economy has registered negative growth, Italian exports to Australia have remained on the whole quite positive in this short three year period. From a standpoint of Italian export destinations, Australia stood in 26th position, registering a small one per cent of Italy's total exports. Italy's number one export destination is, and has been for decades, Germany, followed by France and then the United States. Its most significant import sources were Germany with 14.5 per cent followed by France (8.2 per cent) and then China (6.5 per cent). Australia was in 60th position with 0.2 per cent. In 2011 Italy was Australia's fifth-largest export market in the European Union (EU) compared to it being the second largest export market in the 1990s. Italy however remains the third-largest source of EU imports after Germany and the United Kingdom.

Over the decades the bilateral trade relationship between Australia and Italy has been substantially low key and of limited importance in the overall global commercial setting. The substance of this relationship has been generally framed within the context of normal international transactions in the global market and therefore driven by the demand and supply mechanism. Its impact on the respective economies although real, was limited and had little or no strategic importance. The ranking of each of the two countries in each other's export and import priority of recent was low and of little importance. It was, so speak, a relationship of being "business as usual".

Most literature on the trade relationship between these two countries has often sought to highlight the most minimal improvements in the trade figures. Scholars of this area have made too much of slight changes and movements when the real long term trend was of limited effect. There are some underlying assumptions that motivated scholars in this area to believe that trade would lead in an upward direction. On the one hand it was assumed that Australia's primary products exports (especially wool) would provide long term, sustained growth in a market (like Italy) that appreciated Australian wool. This would be the likely scenario if other factors had remained unchanged, but they did not. China burst onto the scene and Australia found itself with an oversupply of wool. The conditions were again different for minerals like coal and iron ore. The argument was that Italy had few energy resources and Australia had iron ore essential for steel producing economies. But Italy cut its steel capacity and the primary materials for this industry were no longer sought after. Another key assumption was that because Australia was the home to a large number of Italo-Australians, there would be high demand for imported Italian products as well as locally produced 'Italian' goods in Australia, both factors positively impacting bilateral trade.

The aim of this chapter is to unravel some of these persistent assumptions and expectations about trade between Italy and Australia and provide the reader with evidence-based reality on the state of economic and trade relations between Italy and Australia. This chapter does not seek to play down whatever the relationship is but to provide a reality check that may diverge from popular myths which have been allowed to remain unchallenged. This "special" trading relationship never eventuated. Italy and Australia, despite the large Italian immigrant community, developed a "normal" trading relationship and the role of the immigrant community in terms of its impact on trade has been greatly exaggerated as will be demonstrated. The chapter will start by tracing the history of the trade relationship, especially after Italians made Australia their new home.

Personal histories to institutional roles. Quantifying Italian–Australian trade

Italian-Australian trade is made up of pioneering personal histories alongside the broader macro-economic activity in the early days of relations between these two countries. As Joseph Gentilli (1973) notes, the earliest pioneering Italians in Australia were quite colourful individuals. The earliest recorded data of Italian immigrants in pre-Federation Australia shows a very small community with the largest group settled in the colony of Victoria. Blainey reminds us:

> Italians had been quietly living in Victoria for almost a century before the post-war flood arrived ... One in every nine immigrants to Australia between 1947 and 1974 was Italian, and an even higher proportion came to Victoria. Public opinion ultimately classed them as fine immigrants, and a survey of the Italians who had returned home – and so were more likely to be unenthusiastic – concluded that most of the old Australians were not unfriendly (Blainey 1984:202-203).

In order to support this small but growing Italian community, the Italian government established in Melbourne the first Italian Consulate in Australia in 1864 (Gentilli 1973).

Even though their numbers were small, there were some notable Italian pioneers that brought commercial acumen to shape the developing urban economies of pre-Federation Australia. Most prominent were the Florentine trio of friends Ettore Checchi and Carlo Cattani – both engineers – and physicist Pietro Baracchi. From the time of their immigration in 1874 they quickly became prominent in the economic and social life of their adopted city, Melbourne. Baracchi became the director of the city's Observatory for Meteorology and Astronomy and Cattani was Chief Engineer, and then Director of the Ministry of Public Works of Victoria. An astute urban planner, his landscape and engineering shaped the bayside suburb of St.

Kilda. Checchi became an accomplished hydro-engineer and was instrumental in preparing the pre-feasibility for irrigation systems in the Murray River basin, which later became central to the regional economies of three Australian states (Gentilli 1973:194).

During the 1930s and 1940s important individuals stood out within the community for their trading activities with Italy, and this was boosted with the increase in Italians arriving after 1947. The reach and popularity of community channels like print media (*Il Globo* was established in 1959) increased, as too did other associations that engendered social connectivity and advocacy, such as the very first examples of community or citizens aid/advice bureaus and welfare organisations (i.e. *Patronati e Mutuo Soccorso*). One leading Italian who made his mark in the 1930s and 1940s and who played a major role in establishing the Melbourne branch of the Italian Welfare Association (*Comitato Assistenza Italiano* – COASIT) was Gualtiero Vaccari. While Vaccari's role in Australian society attracts controversial readings, he became known, with his wife, as an Italian benefactor and social entrepreneur in Melbourne. Originally from a merchant family from Ferrara, he migrated to Australia in 1912, and after a time supporting the Italian Consulate in Melbourne in 1921, he founded G. Vaccari & Co. His skills in trade saw him become a well-known agent for Italian companies importing products as synthetic fibres, ball and roller bearings, and cotton goods. According to Vaccari's biographer "by the mid-1930s, G. Vaccari & Co. controlled more than half of the total Italian imports into the State of Victoria" (Easdown 2006: 32). As his business grew, by 1962 it became a fully diversified business located in La Trobe Street, supplying industrial equipment, especially to the automotive sector.

But at the macro level, as observed by Steele:

> ... trade between the two countries [Italy and Australia]...had picked up after the First World War when, in 1919, the Italian shipping line Lloyd Sabaudo instituted bimonthly services with

Australia, and soon afterwards increased the service to 15 a year. During the 1920s Italy enthusiastically bought raw materials from Australia and exported manufactures – at a ratio of five to one in Australia's favour (Steele 2008).

Before Federation, Australia's approach on the whole towards trade was to ensure a better outcome for mother England. The 1883 Anglo-Italian Treaty of Commerce and Navigation did just that. At the Imperial Conference in 1923 the Australian Prime Minister at the time declared that "the whole basis of our trading policy is to try and ensure, as far as we can, the Australian market for the British manufacturer" (Steele 2008).

Trade between Italy and the Oceania region was quite limited up to 1948. To put this pre-war level of Oceania trade in context using 1925 as our example year, and comparing Oceania level of trade to those for the Americas, in 1925 there was €651,000 in imports from Oceania and €68,000 in exports, while the data relating to America shows €4.6 million in imports and €2 million in exports. This stronger trade growth is of course proportionate to the larger growing economies in both the United States and in South America.

When Australia became a signatory to the 1932 Ottawa Agreement, Italy amongst other countries, felt the protectionist effect of this agreement as it provided preferential treatment to countries of the British Empire. Soon after Italy complained that it was facing unfair treatment concerning its products entering Australia. As a result, the purchase of wool by Italy was significantly reduced and Australian exports to Italy were to face a similar fate, declining from £4.6 million to £1 million. The outbreak of the war in 1940 put an end to any continuation of the Anglo-Italian Treaty. A new era would only re-emerge at the conclusion of the war.

Table 6.1: Australian trade with Italy 1950–2012 (in $A 000's)

	1950-51	1960-61	1970-71	1980-81	1990-91	2000-01	2011-12
Exports	98,020	95,450	70,897	383,252	923,174	2,101,101	833,635
Imports	33,310	31,558	86,089	426,320	1,390,348	3,258,245	5,351,459
Total	131,330	127,008	156,986	809,572	2,313,522	5,359,346	6,185,094

Source: Adapted by the author from Dept. of Foreign Affairs and Trade, Composition of Trade Australia, Dept. of Foreign Affairs and Trade, Market Information and Analysis Unit, 2002 and 2011-12.

As is evident from Table 6.1, Australian exports to Italy between 1950 and 2012 increased ninefold. These increases were a mixed bag between lows such as in 2011-12 with Australian exports declining to $A833 million, to highs such as 2001 of $A2.1 billion in exports to Italy. At the same time Italian exports to Australia between 1950 and 2012 increased by 160 times, growing from $A33.3 million to $A5.3 billion. Moreover, trade between Italy and Australia contracted for both exports and imports during the period in which migration of Italians to Australia peaked. These strong Italian export figures were a product of a fast growing economy in the aftermath of the Second World War's "economic miracle", as Italy was catapulted to the fifth largest economy in 1987. It should also be remembered that between 1950 and 2000 global trade increased by 27 times. This impressive global trade increase was largely due to strong performances from emerging economies and declining barriers to trade. Returning to our two nations, total trade in 2011-12 between Italy and Australia reached a total of $A6.1 billion of which 80 per cent was provided by Italy.

Italian migration to Australia was at its height between the 1950s and 1960s when hundreds of thousands of Italian migrants, as part of the larger Australian migration program for the post-war economic development, arrived. During the period 1947-1976, a total of 280,570 Italians settled in Australia (Castles 1992). The bulk of migrants from Italy were unskilled and found employment in line with this. Since the end of Italian migration in the 1970s, Italian-born Australians have continued to decline, while the Australians born of Italian ancestry have steadily increased. The 2011 Census recorded 185,402 Italian-born people in Australia, a fall of 6.9 per cent from the 2006 Census. The 2011 distribution by state and territory showed Victoria had the largest number with 76,909 followed by New South Wales with 51,626, South Australia 20,708 and Western Australia 19,477.

There is a common perception that there is a connection between the migration period of Italians to Australia and the trade patterns between Italy and Australia. The following section will explore this hypothesis.

The effect of Italian immigration on Italian-Australian trade

Has post-war large-scale migration from Italy to Australia had an impact on the bilateral trade between Italy and Australia? Some respond instinctively, indicating that the connection is a natural consequence. Battiston and Mascitelli (2007) showed in their study that, while this may have been the case in other scenarios, such as the Bolivian case study of Bacarreza and Ehrlich (2006), there was little evidence suggesting this to be the case with trade between Italy and Australia.

Another feature of the Battiston & Mascitelli study (2007) was that though most Italians in Australia (either Italy born or of Italian ancestry) resided in Victoria (over 40 per cent), a trade correlation between Victoria and Italy was not evident. The State-by-State trade with Italy data evidenced in Table 6.2 suggest that there is a tenuous relationship between the concentrated presence of Italians and strong trade with Italy. Table 6.2 indicates that both Western Australia and Queensland, which have relatively smaller Italian concentrations than Victoria and NSW, have stronger exports to Italy. What is evidently at play here is the fact that Western Australia and Queensland are mineral and resources states that are more strategic to Italian energy needs. In addition NSW, which has one of the strongest levels of Italian imports, does not have the greatest number of Italians within its boundaries. Therefore the assertion that Italian migration plays a role in promoting Australian Italian trade seems tenuous.

Table 6.2: Italy trade with Australian States 2007-2008

	NSW	Vic	Qld	SA	WA
Exports ($m) to Italy	418	218	481	31	240
Exports to Italy (%)	28.7	15	33	2	18
Imports from Italy	2,079	1,664	535	192	403
Imports from Italy (%)	42.05	34	10.9	3.9	8.2
Total State pop.	6,311,168	4,612,097	3,585,639	1,458,912	1,832,008
% of Aust. Pop.	33	25	19	8	10
Italy born (2006)	55,170	82,850	14,000	22,930	1,040
% of Italians in Australia	27.7	41.6	7.0	11.3	10.5

Source: Adapted by the author from A. Lawrence, paper presented at the 4th ACIS Conference, Brisbane, 2007, unpublished; from the Department of Foreign Affairs and Trade, Composition of Trade 2007-08, Canberra, Commonwealth of Australia 2007-08; The Department of Immigration and Citizenship, Community Information Summary, 2009: http:www.immi.gov.13

Another peculiarity in relation to trade between Italy and Australia is revealed by the data in Table 6.3 of comparable Australian trade figures with Italy, the United Kingdom, France and Germany from 1950-1951 to 2011-12. The trade figures indicate that trade between Italy and Australia grew by 18 times. Yet during the same period, Australia-France trade increased 17 times, and trade growth between Germany and Australia increased 90 times. Yet, Australians with a French and German background are much fewer in numbers than those of Italian background.

Table 6.3: Australian trade with selected countries 1950/51-2004/05 (in 000's)

	1950/51	1960/61	1970/71	1980/81	1990/91	2000/01	2011/12
UK	1,354,972	1,144,244	1,381,015	2,273,173	5,098,790	10,966,939	14,927354
Italy	131,330	127,008	156,686	809,572	2,313,522	5,359,346	6,185,094
France	212,468	135,588	177,256	668,923	2,007,028	3,555,949	4,952,038
Germany	84,928	188,900	447,343	1,567,421	4,170,442	7,666,082	13,281049

Source: Department of Foreign Affairs and Trade, Composition of Trade 2002, 2011/12.

It's the economy stupid!

What is most evident from Table 6.3 is that the expansion of trade, insofar as Australia and some of its key European allies were concerned, was more associated with economic growth than with the presence of immigrants from that country. It was a relationship of supply and demand – if there was a demand for the product then there was an attempt to supply it. Australia was a supplier of primary products to markets where there was a need such as the UK, Germany, France and of course Italy. What became more evident in later decades, with the smaller levels of Italian migration, was that newly arrived Italians were better skilled and educated, who possessed business skills and wanted to create bridges with their country of origin. Facilitators for Italian-Australian trade in the 1950s and 1960s did not exist but by the late 1970s and 1980s Australia saw the establishment of Italian Chambers of Commerce and Industry throughout the Commonwealth (except for Sydney where it had been established since 1922).

While history tells us that much of this Italy-Australia relationship is about supply and demand, neither of the two nations made much attempt to make their respective markets "special". Companies and the respective governments made scant connections and rarely sought to emphasise each other's markets. In many respects this *laissez faire* approach was purely in tune with strategic interests. The relationship was essentially one that functioned within the context of normal international transactions in the global market and therefore driven by demand and supply mechanisms.

The global role of the Italian Chambers of Commerce Abroad

Italy has its *Istituto di Commercio Estero* (ICE) or *Invitalia,* that works as the export facilitator of the government for Italian companies. ICE has been present in Australia since 1945. Their staff numbers in Australia have varied over the years. Having previously been based in Melbourne, they moved to Sydney in the 1980s, where they currently operate an office with six staff, including the Trade Commissioner sent from Rome. In their most recent review, undertaken in June 2011, they reported that there are 113 Italian companies with an Australian market presence (ICE website 2013).

The establishment of Italian Chambers of Commerce Abroad (Assocamerestere) over more than a century ago represented the attempt by Italian industry to globalise and engage with international markets. Their success was measured by their ability to provide the international structures for Italian business and to resource the brokering of information and intelligence to support trade and economic development. They serve as a locus of influence, recognition and connectivity for their members, most of whom are of Italian ethnicity and background.

The constitution of these chambers abroad, from the oldest to the more recent ones, was brokered by Italians abroad, influenced at times by social and historical conditions. For example, the constitution of the oldest intercontinental chambers took usually place in perfect synchronisation with the first waves of large-scale migration to Montevideo (1883), Buenos Aires (1884), New York (1887), San Paolo (1902) and Chicago (1907) (Assocamerestero 2011). Many of the entrepreneurs who founded these chambers were self-made men who sought to carve economic influence and achieve success in new countries, usually without being offered access to local circles or loci of influence or wealth. The formation of the chambers hence served as a social forum for entrepreneurs as well as for their community-minded founding fathers.

The legitimacy and recognition that an office-bearing position in a chamber offers to Italian entrepreneurs has some genuine resonance. This is because Italian Chambers abroad receive funding from the Italian Ministry of Economic Development (or its various iterations over the decades) to promote trade. Hence office-bearers and chamber operational staff have real accountability and portfolio responsibilities to promote bilateral trade, and report directly to Assocamerestero in Rome. This role differs from other ethnic chamber groups that essentially have community and networking outcomes or social aims. The chambers also have a certain amount of political influence and draw their membership base from a cross-section of economically successful ethnic or national identities.

Italian Chambers of Commerce and Industry in Australia

The Italian Chambers of Commerce have had a tangible presence in Australia for decades with recognised Chambers in Sydney, Melbourne, Adelaide, Brisbane and Perth. The first presence of an Italian Chamber of Commerce and Industry was formed in Sydney in 1922, making it one of the oldest Italian Chambers outside Italy. Most interesting, it was constituted at a time when there were just over 2,000 Italian migrants in New South Wales. The founding of the Italian Chamber in Sydney seems to be a result of fortuitous circumstances, with a number of distinguished migrants, recently arrived (mainly from central and northern Italy), with strong professional skills (including excellent English) and with common desires and aspirations. Among these individuals was Antonio Baccarini, who held a science degree, was fluent in English and exhibited a typical, southern Italian popular cleverness (he was born in Avellino in Campania). His contacts and connections back in Italy and the UK soon saw him become prominent in business circles and he is cited as a founder in 1922 of the Sydney Chamber (Cresciani 1979a). In 1923 he bought an interest in an import and export firm, W. Plant & Co. Ltd, with which he became associated in the following decades. Most notably, he became a prominent exponent of Italian fascist proclamations and policies. Pro-Mussolini political allegiances and sympathies with *il Fascio* were common among other prominent members of the Italian business community. Like other entrepreneurs, Baccarini used his economic recognition for community and philanthropic pursuits. He was the founder of the local Dante Alighieri Art and Literary Society, and was its president in 1927-35 (Cresciani 1979b).

Baccarini and other arrivals in Sydney in the 1920s were ably mentored and supported by the wealth and prestige of the Chamber and its structures and especially by the very able Maffio Rossi. The son of a silk merchant from Lombardy, Rossi, an accountant (who had furthered his career in London), decided to set sail for Australia and arrived in 1880. By 1883, in association with his friend Francesco Villa, he opened a drapery and linen store in Ivanhoe, NSW, and soon expanded to Hillston. Following his move to Sydney in 1898, Rossi soon acquired the necessary experience in Australian retail and enterprise practices, and started importing Italian manufactured goods on a much larger scale. In 1906 he established the Australian Commercial Co. Ltd that soon became the largest importer of Italian marble and maintained this position of virtual monopoly until World War Two. Among other products Rossi imported were Borsalino hats, buttons, shoes, olive oil and vermouth. In 1922 he was appointed foundation president of the Sydney Chamber and held this role for ten years. Rossi also had the honour of being the first known Australian investor to buy out an Italian business in Italy. On a trip to Italy in 1929, he bought a factory manufacturing textile trim at Intra on Lake Maggiore, and brought to Australia the plant, its thirty factory workers, its technical manager and formed the Hatbands & Trimmings Manufacturing Co. Ltd (Cresciani 1988).

Archival information on members of the Italian community in Sydney in the 1920s includes detailed biographical data on the Honorary Secretary General of the Chamber in Sydney, F.M. Bianchi. A pugnacious patriot and military man originally from Ancona, he settled in Australia (via India) in 1928 after a decorated army career. He became the editor of *Il Giornale Italiano* and founder of the printing house Cosmopolitan Publishing Co, as well as the official representative for the famous beer brand *Nastro Azzurro*. His partner in the printing business was Franco Battistessa. Both had Fascist allegiances. The two – like many Italian economic pioneers who arrived in Australia in the 1920s – had a military background, and the inherent nationalism underlying Fascism was for them obviously *de rigueur*, and would later become quite perilous as wartime hostilities commenced in 1940.

Other prominent members of the Chamber in its first twenty years were the Melocco Brothers – Pietro Galliano and Antonio. Born in Udine, they were highly skilled artisans, mosaic artists and marble workers who had learnt their trade in New York, Paris and their native Friuli. The 1920s were a boom time for the Meloccos, whose work was included in many prominent Sydney buildings. Incorporated in 1927, the Melocco Bros Pty Ltd employed up to two hundred people and prospered up to the 1960s. Among the many techniques they introduced to Australia was the use of ready mix cement, terrazzo and scagliola (faux-marble). It is estimated that the Meloccos undertook about 90 per cent of the marble, scagliola and terrazzo work in Sydney between 1910 and 1965. An interesting note also marked their rich life: Peter, in spite of his wealth and influence, was interned in 1940 during wartime hostilities like many Italian men, as an enemy of the State. It is alleged this was partly because of his membership of the Chamber and its Fascist links (Kevin 2005).

Earliest archival material regarding the Italian Chamber in Sydney also includes some reference to the Chamber's publication of the *Italian Bulletin of Commerce* that was widely distributed through Italian offices and through various Ministry offices in Italy. The Sydney Chamber moderated its political stance after 1948, as Italian migration increased, bringing to these shores Italians with diverse political views. As the Australian economy grew and as Italy and Australia resumed relations, greater commercial and social initiatives spread out across the community. The Sydney Chamber began to expand its activities through delegates to other states and increased its influence through greater membership. Readers can examine the profiles of the five Italian Chambers (Sydney, Melbourne, Perth, Adelaide and Brisbane) in the appendices.

Australia puts a footprint in Italy's economic heart, Milano

The first Australian government commercial presence was in 1951 in Rome, with staff working within the Embassy. At the time wool sales to Italy dominated exports, although some diversification occurred after the 1960s. As Schedvin noted (2008), working from Rome or from Milan was a question government agencies needed to deal with:

> Milan as the centre of Italian commerce and manufacturing was more appropriate than Rome as a location. Rome was largely a policy post with responsibility for the Food and Agricultural Organization (FAO) and issues concerning agricultural policy. It was not well placed to interface with the large number of small firms clustered in the Italian north-west (Schedvin 2008: 246).

In the early years of Australia's official presence in Italy, Australian officials were repeatedly invited to Italian trade exhibitions such as the Fiera del Levante in Bari in 1954, and to fairs in Padua and Parma. Minister McGuire attended the 1955 Fiera del Levante in Bari and was at that fair again in 1956, reporting after his visit: "I still yearn to show a Holden car, if only to counter the view of Australia as populated entirely by sheep, kangaroos and Bondi-beachers" (Steele 2008). These were irregular Australian trade activities and promotion, that took a qualitative leap with the establishment of the trade-based Consulate General in Milan in the late 1960s.

Following President Saragat's visit to Australia in late 1967, Australia decided to establish a Consulate General in Milan that would play a predominantly trade role. The Consulate came into being in March 1968 with Dudley Fagg, Commissioner in Rome since 1966. He was put in charge of opening Milan's legation, assumed the role of Consul General (Trade Commissioner) for the remainder of that year, and in 1969 was succeeded by Arthur Jamieson (see Table 6.4). Commissioner Fagg, according to Schedvin (2008), "... had been recruited from the private sector, and had been a member of the trade commissioner service since 1960, having served in Trinidad and Bombay as well as Rome" (2008: 246). At the time, the functioning export facilitation body for the Australian government was the Trade Commissioner Service, which in 1985 was re-named the Australian Trade Commission (Austrade). Given Milan's commercial dominance in Italy, the Australian government saw its presence as a better place to work with the business community, while the Embassy in Rome would play a broader diplomatic and consular role throughout Italy.

Table 6.4 – Milan Consulate General (Trade post) – 1968 onwards

Consul General /Senior Trade Commissioner	Period of responsibility
Dudley Fagg	March 1968
Arthur Jamieson	January 1969
Robert Scott	May 1973
Desmond McSweeney	December 1976
Bruce Conduit	April 1980
Thomas Walton	May 1983
Philip Brandon	1985
Alex Karas	1987
John McFarlane	1989/90
Barry Hain	1990
Gerard Lanzarone	1993
Rod Morehouse	1997
Michael Tindall	2000
Tim Gauci	2005
Simone Desmarchelier	2010

Source: The author

Over the years the Austrade office fluctuated in staff numbers and areas of responsibility. In 2013 there were about six staff including the trade commissioner, who also acts as Consul-General. The numbers of staff (Australian based inclusive) are half of what they were in the early 1990s and one-third the number of the 1980s. Investment attraction was not promoted in any structured way until the mid-1990s, though it currently is an ongoing activity of the office. Its overall strategy and direction is provided by investment officers based in Paris, in conjunction with the head office in Sydney. Austrade's website cites that the Milan office's services are primarily focused on attracting foreign direct investment into Australia and promoting the

Australian education sector. Other areas highlighted include biotech/ cleantech and renewables, pharmaceuticals, services and education.

Italian-Australian relations in the 21st century

The current documentation of the trade relationship between Australia and Italy is primarily that of government submissions, superficial country analysis and the occasional research/legal profile of the two countries for fiscal and export promotion. There is little academic scrutiny and the media is very scant in its appraisal of Australian-Italian economic relations, and at times prone to stereotyping. The lack of documentation is surprising, given that at times Australia performed well, primarily in sales of wool to Italy (during the 1980s and 1990s) and especially as Italy for a short period assumed the role of second largest export market for Australian products in Europe after the UK. In the academic sphere very little material has been published that makes any substantial reference to Italian-Australian trade relations. Most of the literature addresses other themes in this relationship, including language, migration and cultural relationships. The local Italian Australian press has been vocal and outspoken about the lack of momentum in the area of Italian-Australian trade. In March 2001, Melbourne's *Il Globo* ridiculed the "joke" of immobility in the area of trade between Italy and Australia after repeated committees, bodies and commissions had been established to tackle this lack of progress (Randazzo 2001).

Table 6.5 – Italian Exports to Australia in 2012. Top six products

Product	2008	2009	2010	2011	2012
Medicaments	321,604	394,460	475,653	618,573	665,050
Organo-inorganic compounds	270,805	333,174	454,176,	433,607	456,204
Pumps	88,034	292,997	87,233	72,304	209,567
Taps cocks and valves	115,449	106,858	84,850	83,119	150,154
Rotating electrical plants and parts	35,491	26,887	28,611	31,714	128,848
Heating & cooling equipment & parts	114,844	135,826	107,947	131,506	122,120
Total Italian exports to Australia	5,334,435	4,888,228	4,897,185	5,027,166	5,351,459
Trade surplus with Australia	+3,646,653	+3,875,884	+3,763,028	+3,768,922	+4,517,824

Source: DFAT Composition of Trade, 2012, p. 205, http://www.dfat.gov.au/publications/stats-pubs/cot-fy-2011-12.pdf

As can be discerned from Table 6.5, documenting Italian exports to Australia between 2008 and 2012, Italy is primarily a provider of medical and manufactured equipment. Over these and previous years Italy's strong performance in exporting value-added items has been its key feature. Moreover, it has managed to increase its sales or at least maintain some level of consistency in its provision of these products.

Table 6.6 – Australian Exports to Italy in 2012. Top six products

Product	2008	2009	2010	2011	2012
Coal	586,678	250,757	393,654	434,641	308,072
Wool and other animal hair	251,911	86,616	133,396	199,671	151,404
Confidential items	292,073	198,364	176,558	180,973	61,703
Wheat	21,411	81,989	50,293	72,901	83,480
Leather	75,636	53,493	61,238	59,507	47,691
Beef	20,073	10,279	21,321	22,567	23,123
Total Australian exports to Italy	1,687,782	1,012,344	1,134,157	1,258,244	833,635
Trade deficit with Italy	-3,646,653	-3,875,884	-3,763,028	-3,768,922	-4,517,824

Source: DFAT Composition of Trade, 2012, p. 205 http://www.dfat.gov.au/publications/stats-pubs/cot-fy-2011-12.pdf

Table 6.6, on the other hand, documents Australian exports to Italy between 2008 and 2012. Australia is mainly a primary products exporter to this market and the two top products have declined considerably from 2008 to 2012. This has in part been a result of greater choice available to the Italian market for coal and wool, as well as trading variations such as exchange rates.

Trade between Italy and Australia over the recent past has seen a growing trade surplus on the Italian side as can be seen from Table 6.6. This is partially due to the strengthening of the value of Italian exports to Australia but also to the decline in value of Australian exports to Italy. The exact reasons for these two trends have not been documented, but anecdotal evidence suggests that Australian exports in the Italian market meet greater competition for coal, wool and other primary products. On the stronger Italian export side, Italy has been able to maintain a strong presence in manufactured items that meet Australian economic needs.

Italian and Italian-Australian companies in Australia

Italian investment in Australia is relatively small, reflecting Italy's generally low Foreign Direct Investment (FDI) in countries outside Italy. Most of Italy's FDI is directed within the EU and the Mediterranean area. Over the decades numerous Italian companies have engaged with the Australian market, including activities which went from simply exporting, setting up a representative office or in more significant cases establishing a fully established company presence. FIAT for example started engaging with the Australian market as far back as 1922 (Totaro 2012). Other firms such as IVECO, Olivetti, Ferrero (confectionery) and Pirelli have had some form of operations in Australia but not all have managed to survive. Other firms, such as ENI, Alfa Romeo and Alitalia, until the 1980s and 1990s state owned and managed, had a presence in Australia but were closed as a result of decisions made in Italy. Until the French Lactalis takeover, Parmalat (dairy product manufacturers) was one of the most consistent Italian investments in Australia. Other Italian investments included the Luxottica (eyewear) buyout of OPSM, Ansaldo STS (railway signalling and infrastructure), Permasteelisa (construction, aluminium, glass), and Amplifon (hearing aids). ENI, the Italian energy producer, was active in offshore gas and oil exploration in Australia, often in partnership with other companies. In November 2011, SAIPEM, part of the ENI Group, won a €1.3 billion offshore gas pipeline project in Australia. Over the decades, several Italian banks established a presence in Australia with representative offices. These included *Banca Nazionale del Lavoro*, *Banca Commerciale*, *Banca di Roma* and *Monte dei Paschi di Siena*. In 2013, only one of these banks continues to maintain a presence in Australia.

The successful investment of IVECO tells a more positive story as does the return of FIAT and its various divisions such as Alfa Romeo and Ferrari. The return of FIAT auto, with the FIAT 500 and the Punto, has revitalised the Italian motor car presence in the Australian market from a sales standpoint. The commercial vehicles brand IVECO, part of the substantial FIAT Industrial Division, was a significant investment in Australia with its wholly owned plant. IVECO, based in Dandenong, Victoria, was commissioned in 1952, trading under the International Harvester brand. Since then, it has produced more than 225,000 truck and bus chassis. The Dandenong plant represents a major investment in the local truck and bus industry and employed more than 600 Australians in 2013 and many more through its supply chain. Annual reports show that IVECO recorded sales of €955 million in Australia in 2012, up from €825 million in 2011. On the other end of the spectrum, Ferrari Australasia does well in the Australian market recording sales in 2011 of 150 Ferraris from a yearly production in Italy of 7,000 vehicles.

In the energy/utilities and renewables sector, a substantial project that required a major investment by an Italian company was the work that Pirelli Cavi e Sistemi (now Prysmian) undertook between 2002 and 2006. On behalf of Basslink Pty Ltd and in partnership with Siemens, Pirelli's knowhow and infrastructure were instrumental in building what is the second longest undersea high-voltage cable in the world, from Tasmania's power network to the southeast Australian electricity grid. The engineering feat required three trips from Prysmian's ship *Giulio Verne* from Naples to Melbourne and Tasmania, to carry 295km of cable. Prysmian are still very active in Australia with its cable business and were recently awarded an NBN Co Limited contract for the supply of fibre optic cables for the development of the new national broadband network. The total value of the contract, which has been secured by Prysmian Telecom Cables & Systems Australia (100 per cent owned by Prysmian), is €223 million (A$per centillion) over five years (Prysmian website 2013). Italian technical knowhow in civic engineering and in building and construction has been an important contribution to Australia's economic development. The Italo-Australian companies Electric Power Transmission, Transfield and Tenix have been significant players in this regard.

Firm internationalisation in Italy and Australia

Given Italy's small and medium sized company economy, its ability and success in internationalising its firms has been exceptional. For 2011 alone, 205,000 firms undertook export activity. These businesses are typically family-owned SMEs, and make up the lion's share of Italy's industrial architecture. Analysis indicates that up until the late 1990s the dynamic part of the Italian economy was small-scale family firms, frequently located in the central regions of Emilia-Romagna, Tuscany and the Marche region and these firms facilitated Italy's strong economic growth, compared to Germany, for example in the 1980s (Fukuyama 1995: 93).

In a comparative context between Australia and Italy, as demonstrated in Figure 6.1, the percentage of Australian SMEs that export is only 4 per cent compared to Italy's 49 per cent. The Australian economy is less a SME economy and much of the value of its exports is located in the "big end of town", meaning the large multinational companies in the minerals sector of the economy. Although the mining industry in Australia only represents one per cent of the total number of the exporters, it contributes $134 billion (54 per cent) of the total value of goods exports. The mining industry also had the highest average value of exports per exporter ($234 million). In Italy the industry sectors with the highest percentage of exporting businesses earning more than €50 million were, by way of comparison, in refined petroleum products, pharmaceutical, medical, chemical and botanical products and transport vehicles.

Investment: a lopsided relationship

Over a number of years Australia has invested in Italy at almost double the level of what Italy invests in Australia. Based on 2012 data, Australia invested $A3.2 billion in Italy, compared with Italy's investment of $A1.7 billion (DFAT Fact Sheets 2013). On the whole, major Australian investments in Italy include Po Valley Energy, which owns a number of onshore and offshore gas exploration and production licences, and owns and operates two gas treatment plants in Italy. Bovis Lend Lease participates in major Italian and European infrastructure projects *via* its Milan headquarters. Cochlear, Chep, Aconex, Australian Wool Innovation, Berrigner Blass, Nufarm, Dyesol, Solahart and Vix-ERG are other Australian businesses with a direct presence in Italy, while NewsCorp wholly owns Italy's leading satellite TV company and SKY Italia.

Australian investments in Italy for those companies that have been able to find specific niches have proven quite successful. An example was Macquarie Group's profitable investment in Rome's Leonardo Da Vinci (Fiumicino) Airport. Having paid €480 million for a 44.7 per cent stake in Rome's airport in March 2003, Macquarie Airports received €1237 million in cash sale in June 2007, producing a substantial profit (Mayne 2007). Over the last decade energy/utilities and renewables have made important contributions to Italian-Australian bilateral trade.

Why low levels of Italian investment in Australia?

Total stock of FDI from Italian companies in Australia in 2012 was very low, A$1,752 million, while foreign direct investment was low at $A618 million. This is overshadowed by the $A20 billion in investment stock from France, the $A25 billion investment stock from Canada, not to mention the $A555 billion investment stock from the United States. Italy's investment in Australia is so low it is added in the "other sources" category, as can be seen from Table 6.7. It would be expected that given Italy's exceptionally strong export market share in certain products in Australia as well as Asia, that this could have been the catalyst for establishing investment infrastructure to take advantage of this market share. This by and large has not occurred. A weakness in the Italian approach is the inability to see investment in Australia as a long-term commercial venture.

Table 6.7 – Stock of Foreign Direct Investment in Australia by Country, 2011[1]

Country	Total stock of investment $ million	Share of total foreign investment %	Foreign direct investment (FDI) $ million	Share of total FDI %
USA	555,868	27.4	122,379	24.1
UK	470,846	23.2	69,747	13.7
Japan	123,410	6.1	52,334	10.3
Singapore	48,709	2.4	19,966	3.9
Netherlands	43,706	2.2	32,870	6.5
Switzerland	42,281	2.1	23,005	4.5
Hong Kong SAR	39,416	1.9	6,714	1.3
New Zealand	29,707	1.5	5,980	1.2
Canada	25,048	1.2	17,326	3.4
Luxembourg	23,542	1.2	2,344	0.5
Germany	22,491	1.1	14,333	2.8
France	20,036	1.0	6,777	1.3
China (Mainland)	19,047	0.9	13,354	2.6
International capital markets2	46,355	2.3	0	0.0
Total Unspecified	322,874	15.9	31,296	6.2
Other sources	196,696	9.7	88,935	17.5
Total all sources	**2,030,032**	**100.0**	**507,360**	**100.0**

Footnotes: As at 31 December 2011; 2: Excludes international capital markets unspecified, which is not available but has been included in "Other Sources" for total stock of investment.

Source: NSW government (ABS Cat. No. 5352.0, 2011).

Equally important within the mindset of Italian investors is a "close-to-home attitude". According to a former Australian Investment Commissioner in Milan in the late 1990s, Italian industries were inclined to invest closer to Italy in order to maintain their administrative control and were less inclined to delegate control to foreign subsidiaries. Neither country has ongoing dedicated in-country investment facilitators. The inability of investment facilitators to adequately match and complement Australian and Italian industry sectors has been pivotal. In some quarters of the Italian economy, there is still the perception that Australia is a location of high labour costs, language barriers, and an investment location offering limited return to initial investment relative to emerging economies. A study by the research institute Prometeia-Comit into the five-year trend facing fifty industrial sectors in Italy showed that Italian investment was strongest in areas where high value-added costs existed. These include areas such as industrial production and transport, but Australia does not fit into this sector's profile. In fields such as fashion, home furnishings and mechanical production Italian companies are less inclined to invest abroad. When they do, as in the case of fashion, they are inclined to invest in Europe including in Eastern Europe and more recently in China where labour costs are lower (*Il Sole 24 Ore* 1998).

Investing in Italy. The Australian perception

In 2001 a study was undertaken about the motives and perception of Australian companies to investing in Europe and more specifically in Italy. The spread of companies surveyed covered Australia and eight separate sectors and concluded with 93 valid responses. It included publicly listed companies as well as smaller and medium sized organisations that had a common focus and interest of investment in Europe, but not currently undertaking investment in Italy. The research identified many companies that were trading in Italy and Europe but not necessarily investing there. Some companies were neither trading nor investing in Europe but had expressed interest in doing so (Mascitelli 2001).

The responses in this survey highlighted some of Italy's recurring strengths, including that it was part of the EU, that it had close proximity to large markets and was itself a large market. They also acknowledged that Italy had a high standard of living, had a large pool of skilled labour and was a country capable of purchasing goods and paying for them. Italy was appreciated for its traditionally friendly people, welcoming tourist attractions and for being a fun loving location. Many referred to it as a "good place to have a holiday". In cultural and tourist terms it was very much appreciated and revered. The cost of labour received frequent mention as being low and competitive. This was especially in comparison to France and Germany.

The inability to communicate and have a dialogue with Italians due to language difficulty was also a frequent response. The common response was that "Italians don't speak English". Many companies felt that Italian market entry was neither easy nor transparent and that Italy was not an easy country with which to do business. There was some apprehension over the poor banking system and especially much comment on Italy's corruption and the perception of criminality that discouraged investors from risking their capital. Some companies indicated there had been a historic concern with the instability of its political and economic system. Other weaknesses, to of a lesser extent, included the distance from Australia, the very bureaucratic nature of the Italian business system and the fact that the Italian government does very little to promote business.

Conclusion

The common perception held by the Italian community in Australia was the urban myth that trade between these two countries was strategic, that it was strong and that it was a product of Italian migration. These views remained substantially unchallenged for decades and became an accepted state of affairs. In specific periods over the last decades, Italian Australian trade has stood out. It was vibrant, growing and even significant. But these were moments that were not long-lived. These two nations had their trade strategy locked in different geo-political entities. For Italy, it was the European Union. For Australia, it was its geographical proximity to Asia which became the key.

The kind of Italian immigration towards Australia in the 1950s and 1960s did not contribute to enhancing trade relations between the two countries. Australia and Italy found a relationship where Australia needed migrants to build its economy, while Italy, during the 1950s, needed to shed people in order to recover economically. Surprisingly, decades after this mass immigration the two countries failed to exploit, in trade terms, the presence of the established Italian community.

The only relatively strong trade relationship between the two nations has by and large occurred due to market factors. It has developed outside specific efforts by the two governments and, as we have seen, only in very small part due to the Italian community's role in Australia. It will in the future be driven by the same objectives that drove it in the past: business opportunities.

Bibliography

Assocameraestero, 2011, *Le Camere di Commercio Italiane all'Estero Natura, caratteristiche e funzioni*, Assocameraestero, 2011, http://www.assocamerestero.it/camere/, accessed 1 October 2013.

Austrade Milan website, http://www.austrade.gov.au/DealerLocator/LocatorDetailsPage.aspx?back=1&storeID=68, accessed 3 October 2013.

Bacarreza G. and L. Ehrlich, 2006, 'The impact of migration on foreign trade: a developing country approach', Munich Personal RePEc Archive (MPRA), Paper no. 1090, Munich, 2006 http://mpra.ub.uni-muenchen.de/1090/, viewed on 9 December 2007.

Battiston S. and B. Mascitelli, 2007, 'Migration, ethnic concentration and international trade growth: the case of Italians in Australia', *People and Place*, Vol. 15, issue 4, 2007.

Blainey G., 1984, *Our Side of the Country: A Story of Victoria*, Methuen Haynes Publishing, Melbourne.

Castles S., 1992, 'Italian migration and settlement since 1945', in S. Castles,

C. Alcorso, G. Rando, and E. Vasta, *Australia's Italians – Culture and Community in a Changing Society*, Allen & Unwin, St. Leonards, NSW, 1992, pp. 42-3.

COASIT, Committee for Assistance to Italian migrants, http://www.COASIT. asn.au/index.-php?option=com_content&view=frontpage&Itemid=1, accessed 13 May 2013.

Collins J., K. Gibson, C. Alcorso, S. Castles and D. Tait, 1995, *A Shop Full of Dreams: Ethnic Small Business in Australia,* Pluto Press, NSW.

Collins, J., 1992, 'Cappuccino capitalism: Italian immigrants and Australian business', in S. Castles, C. Alcorso, G. Rando, and E. Vasta, *Australia's Italians – Culture and Community in a Changing Society*, Allen & Unwin, St. Leonards, NSW, 1992, pp. 73-84.

Cresciani G., 1988, 'Maffio Rossi', *Australian Dictionary of Biography*, National Centre of Biography, Australian National University, http://adb.anu.edu.au/biography/rossi-maffio-8275, accessed 2 October 2013.

Cresciani G., 1979a, 'Baccarini, Antonio', *Australian Dictionary of Biography*, National Centre of Biography, Australian National University, http://adb.anu.edu.au/-biography/baccarini-antonio-5086/text8487, accessed 2 October 2013.

Cresciani G., 1979b, *Fascismo, antifascismo e gli italiani in Australia 1922-1945*, Bonacci Editore Roma.

DFAT 2012, Composition of Trade, 2012, http://www.dfat.gov.au/publications/stats-pubs/cot-fy-2011-12.pdf, accessed 24 September 2013.

DFAT Fact Sheets, 2012, Italy Fact Sheets, department of Foreign Affairs and Trade, http://www.dfat.gov.au/geo/fs/ital.pdf, accessed 3 October 2013.

Easdown G., 2006, *Gualtiero Vaccari: A Man of Quality*, Wilkinson Publishing Pty Ltd, Melbourne.

Fukuyama F., 1995, 'Social Capital and the Global Economy', *Foreign Affairs*, Vol. 74, No. 5 (Sep.-Oct. 1995), pp. 89-103.

Gentilli, J., 1973, 'Italiani d'Australia ieri ed oggi', *Il Veltro* XVII 2-3, pp. 191-204. From the Elda Vaccari collection – Victoria University Library, item P/C9300908 available online http://library.vu.edu.au/search-/c?SEARCH=p%2Fc9300908, accessed 15 May 2013.

Il Sole 24 Ore, 1998, Trasporti e Largo Consumo guidano gli investimenti italiani all'estero, 3 July 1998.

ICE 2013, Istituto per il commercio con l'estero, http://www.ice.gov.it/, accessed 1 October 2013.

Kevin C., 2005, 'Melocco Brothers – Galliano, Pietro, Anthony, *Australian Dictionary of Biography*, National Centre of Biography, Australian National University, http://adb.anu.edu.au/biographies/search/?scope=all&query=-melocco&rs=&.x=40&.y=15, accessed 2 October 2013.

Mascitelli B., 2001, 'Analysis of Australian Investment in Europe', Prepared for Sviluppo Italia, undertaken by Swinburne University of Technology, December 2001, Melbourne.

Mayne S., 2007, 'Rome Airport pay-day delivers humble pie for Macquarie critics', June 18, 2007, http://www.crikey.com.au/2007/06/18/rome-airport-pay-day-delivers-humble-pie-for-macquarie-critics/ accessed 27 September 2013.

NSW government, 'Investment and stock of foreign investment in Australia', 2011, http://www.business.nsw.gov.au/invest-in-nsw/about-nsw/trade-and-investment/stock-of-foreign-direct-investment-in-australia-by-country

Pomfret R., 1995, Ed. *Australia's Trade Policies*, Oxford University Press, Melbourne.

Prysmian 2013, Taken from the www.prysmiangroup.com website, http://australia.prysmiangroup.com/en/index.html, accessed 3 October 2013.

Randazzo N., 2001, *Basta con le favole sull'interscambio italo-australiano!*, Il Globo, 12 March 2001.

Rossetto G., 1989, 'Trade between Italy and Australia', in C. Bettoni and J. Lo Bianco, *Understanding Italy: Language, Culture, Commerce – An Australian Perspective*, The University of Sydney and the Frederick May Foundation for Italian Studies, Sydney 1989, pp. 25-29.

Schedvin B., 2008, 'Emissaries of trade: A history of the Trade Commissioner Service', Austrade, Department of Foreign Affairs and Trade, Canberra.

Steele R., 2008, '20th-century diplomatic and trade relations', Chapter. 2, *Australians in Italy, Contemporary Lives and Impressions,* Edited by Bill Kent, Ros Pesman & Cynthia Troup, http://books.publishing.monash. edu/apps/bookworm/view/Australians-+in+Italy/52/xhtml/title.html, accessed 1 October 2013.

Totaro P., 2012, Personal email communication from Paolo Totaro, who was an employee of FIAT in the 1960s. Email dated 4 September 2012.

Appendices

Italian Chambers of Commerce and Industry – Sydney

Name	Established	Members	Agreements
Italian Chamber of Commerce and Industry in Australia (Sydney) Inc.	1922	388	Chambers of Bergamo, Parma, Trapani Export desks of Padova, Brescia and Catanzaro Promex; Probrixia; Promocatanzaro Fiera Milano Fiere di Parma SSICA Parma Consorzio Prosciutto di Parma Consorzio Parma Couture Regione Calabria Bologna Fiere FederUnacoma NSW Dept. of State & Regional Development Universitá Bocconi Milano Universitá IULM University of Sydney

Italian Chambers of Commerce across Australia – Melbourne

Name	Established	Members	Agreements
Italian Chamber of Commerce and Industry in Australia (Melbourne) Inc.	1985	330	Friuli Venezia Giulia Region Investment-Desk Centro Estero della Regione del Veneto Verona Fiere (Australian representative) Invitalia (Italian investment agency) Northern Territory Chamber of Commerce Tasmania Chamber of Commerce All-Energy Australia William Angliss Institute (Hospitality sector)

Italian Chambers of Commerce and Industry Australia – Brisbane

Name	Established	Members	Agreements
Italian Chamber of Commerce and Industry in Australia (Queensland) Inc.	1989	112	Queensland government City of Brisbane Trade and Investment Queensland Lord Mayors Multicultural Round Table Università Commerciale Luigi Bocconi Milano Università Ca Foscari Venezia Politecnico delle Marche Ancona Scuole Scienze Aziendali Firenze Bond University Australia Queensland University of Technology Griffith University

Italian Chambers of Commerce and Industry Australia –Perth

Name	Established	Members	Agreements
Italian Chamber of Commerce and Industry in Australia Inc. – (Perth) Inc.	1990	180	Chambers of Commerce and Industry W.A. International Business Council of W. A. Universita' Bocconi Milano Department of State Development, Western Australia IULM Milano (University) Chamber of Ravenna

Italian Chambers of Commerce across Australia – Adelaide

Name	Established	Members	Agreements
Italian Chamber of Commerce and Industry in Australia (Adelaide) Inc.	1972	353	SA government PUGLIA Desk API Milano Promos Milano Promec Modena Fiere di Parma Fiera del Levante Sprint Puglia Universita' Bocconi Universita' delle Scienze Gastronomiche Brindisi Desk – Australia Reggio Calabria Desk – Australia Napoli Desk – Australia

7
Exploitation, Emigration and Anarchism: The Case of Isidoro Alessandro Bertazzon

Gianfranco Cresciani

During the second half of the 19th century, communism was not the only spectre haunting Europe, as alleged by Karl Marx and Friedrich Engels in their *Manifest der Kommunistischen Partei* of 1848. Another, more immediate, violent and elusive threat menaced conservative as well as liberal governments of the time: that of anarchism. The Paris Commune motivated its sympathisers in many countries to take up the black flag of anarchism and conspire for the destruction of the established order. Some 4,000 communards were deported to the penal colony of New Caledonia and some of them, following their amnesty in 1879, passing through New South Wales before returning to France, brought anarchist ideas to Australia. The young Francesco Sceusa, who had met Errico Malatesta and other leading anarchists in Naples during his student days, after coming in contact with these communards, unsuccessfully tried to set up an anarchist network in Sydney.[1] The first Anarchist Club was founded in Melbourne on 1 May 1886.[2] Incidentally, among the deportees to the Isle of Pines was an Italian anarchist, Amilcare Cipriani, who had taken part in the Commune with the rank of colonel, in charge of the defence of Place Vendôme, where he was seriously injured. Cipriani returned to Paris in 1880.[3]

On 24 June 1894 an Italian anarchist, Sante Caserio, assassinated the French president, Marie-François Sadi Carnot, in what was the culmination of a series of anarchist attacks in France and elsewhere, many by Italians. The European community felt threatened. At the International Revolutionary Congress in London in 1881 the Russian anarchist, Prince Pyotr Alexeivich Kropotkin, had called for violent action, "propaganda through deeds", and the first symbolic acts of violence had in fact been committed a few years earlier. There were seven attempts on Queen Victoria's life during her reign. However, the 1890s were different. It was the decade of the bomb: dynamite was the new weapon and kings, presidents, ministers and official buildings were the targets. In France, the attacks began in 1892. The French anarchist François Ravachol, who was celebrated in folksongs and legend, became the living symbol of hatred for society's power structure. As would be the case during Fascism, Nazism and the Italian students' revolt in 1968, many intellectuals and young people from wealthy families flirted with violence. Attacks had been launched at the same time in several countries, encouraging the idea that a powerful anarchist Black International organisation was at work. The ruling classes, haunted by the spectre of terrorism, could not understand, or understood too well, the reasons for the hatred and each act of violence increased their fear of revolt from below. Perhaps, the reason could be found in the fact that, to quote Australian historian Richard Bosworth's aphorism, "all ruling elites are rapacious, but some are more rapacious than others". Workers were seen as potential criminals and anarchists as mad dogs to be destroyed at all costs. The anarchist threat acquired mythic proportions.

The first proposal for international cooperation to quell anarchism came from Italy, which was regarded as the breeding ground of international terrorism and was therefore anxious to restore its tarnished reputation. This tradition of violence had its origin in the traditional, total alienation of Italy's peasant population from its ruling class, exploitative, bourgeois and spiteful of the "lesser breed". The predictable response by these "wretched of the earth", following simmering resentment or open acts of defiance ruthlessly put down, was emigration, banditry or empathy with the mafia. Italians had been implicated in a number of attempts on heads of state and Italian immigrants had a bad name across Europe. Their large communities, regularly swelled by an influx of seasonal workers, were widely resented. The International Conference for the Social Defence Against Anarchists was held in Rome between 24 November and 21 December 1898, following the assassination on 10 September 1898 of Empress Elisabeth of Austria by Italian migrant Luigi Lucheni, on the promenade of Lake Geneva. Fifty-four delegates attended from 21 different countries. Every participating government agreed to set up special structures for the surveillance of those suspected of anarchism, defined "as any act that used violent means to destroy the organisation of society". Other resolutions drafted in the final protocol included the introduction of legislation to prohibit the illegitimate possession and use of explosives, membership in anarchist networks, the distribution of anarchist propaganda and the rendering of assistance to anarchists. It was also agreed that governments should try to limit press coverage of anarchist activities, and that the death penalty should be mandatory punishment for all assassinations of heads of state.

However, there was no international anarchist network, no conspiracy and no plot. There was no central command, only individuals acting independently in small cells, linked only by their hatred of the status quo under which large sections of society were marginalised. Anarchists argued that they had taken up arms in a legitimate fight for justice and that their acts were merely in self-defence for an oppressed section of society. Anarchist cells claimed to be the vanguard of a stateless proletariat, although some people did realise they were only tiny and isolated groups. Prince Kropotkin once confided to Errico Malatesta that he feared they were the only two people in the world who believed that revolution was imminent.[4] It is interesting to note that many of the leading anarchists had not a working class background, although advocating the redemption of the masses from social servitude. Kropotkin was a wealthy aristocrat, William Golding the son of a Calvinist minister, Pierre-Joseph Proudhon was once described by Karl Marx as a petit-bourgeois, Michael Bakunin's father was a member of the provincial nobility, Carlo Cafiero was a wealthy Neapolitan landowner and Saverio Merlino an intellectual. Their anarchism was a reaction against the plight of those whom British social historian and libertarian socialist GDH Cole called the "common people".

Italy had already taken action four years before the International Conference to screen potential enemies of the state. The creation of a register of people considered dangerous to public order and security dates back to the prime ministership of Francesco Crispi. On 25 May 1894, an office was set up within the Directorate-General of Public Security of the Ministry of the Interior, with the task of maintaining and updating a register of political opponents. Anarchists, republicans, socialists as well as vagrants were the subject of extensive surveillance that fed data to the archive of personal files. In 1925 this section of the Ministry assumed the name of Central Political Records Information System (*Casellario Politico Centrale* – CPC). The archive consists of 152,589 personal files with documentation mainly between 1894 and 1945. The files contain notes, reports and minutes of interrogation, police measures and often a brief biography of people under surveillance. During the Fascist period, police monitoring included not only opponents but also people defined generically as being fascist, and ethnic minorities, especially those in Venezia Giulia. The archive also contains printed material (newspapers, flyers, posters, brochures) and photographs, as well as documents seized by the police because considered subversive or having an anti-government bias. Also, there is a rich iconographic documentation, consisting of approximately 120,000 photographs taken in most cases by police.[5] Surveillance, begun in Italy, continued in the country of emigration.

Abroad, information on alleged *sovversivi* (subversives) was collected and fed to the CPC, through the *Prefetti* (Prefects), by diplomatic and consular officials, who availed themselves of the assistance of pliant foreign governments and police authorities, of members of the party in power and of a network of *fiduciari* (informers), mainly local Italian migrants, who were in the pay of liberal and fascist officials or who spied out of ideological or political conviction, or of self-interest.

Among the Italian regions where anarchism spread at the time of the growth of capitalism was the Veneto. The region's enduring conditions of poverty and destitution were admirably described, despite his own dubious flirtation with Fascism, by Italian writer Luigi Meneghello, born in the small village of Malo, near Schio, in his novel *Libera Nos a Malo*, (Deliver Us from Evil), where the name of the village is the same as the word 'evil' in one of the lines of the Latin version of the Lord's Prayer.[6] From the early 1800s, Schio and Piovene, two small country centres in a predominantly agrarian area, saw the rapid expansion of Lanificio Rossi, considered by many to be "the Italian Manchester", a textile concern that rapidly became one of Italy's largest industrial monopolies. In 1898, the year when its founder Alessandro Rossi died, Lanifico Rossi employed 5,000 people, its factories covered an area of 160,000 square metres and its turnover exceeded 20 million lire, an enormous amount for that time.[7] Its labour force was in part formed by local peasants, part-time labourers living near to starvation, but who in times of economic crisis could fall back for sustenance on the produce of their fields. The majority of its textile workers came from the periphery of the Veneto, having been politicised by the gap between rich and poor, and escaping from hunger, destitution, unemployment and repression at the hands of latifundia owners and the police. They harboured revolutionary, republican and anarchist ideas and were motivated by smouldering hatred of landlords and priests, although anarchism could often become a sort of replacement religion for them. Unlike their local fellow workers, they could not accept salary reductions or dismissal, as for them this meant an impossible return to their birthplace, or emigration. In February 1891 their militancy brought on a confrontation with Lane Rossi's management, when the latter wanted to reduce their pay by 30 per cent. At the time they were earning 1,35 lire for a 12-hour day's work, enough to only buy a kilo of bread, a litre of wine and two hundred grams of flour, not enough to feed a person. In 1883, in Schio, 15 per cent of deaths were caused by pellagra, an illness caused by a deficiency of vitamin PP, affecting people who were predominantly eating wheat products, like bread or *polenta* (maize), the cheapest staple diet for the working class. The following year, 28.5 per cent of deaths in Schio were caused by tuberculosis, owing to unhealthy working conditions.

Lane Rossi's employees decided to strike and fight against the proposed wage cut. The strike lasted four days and ended with the defeat of the employees. Alessandro Rossi jettisoned workers whom he considered *sovversivi* or, as he called them, *zavorra* (ballast). The following months a steady flow of people decided to emigrate and flee from what Italian historian Saverio Merli called, with manifest exaggeration, "an industrial *ergastolo* (life imprisonment)". 12 per cent of Schio's population and six per cent of the surrounding areas, totalling 3,213 people, left the province. Ten years after, in October 1901, another industrial dispute ended similarly. Giovanni Rossi, son of Alessandro, summarily dismissed dozens of "subversive" young male workers and employed 13-year-old girls to take their place. Again, the only avenue left to the despondent, dismissed workers was to emigrate, venting their spleen by crying *Viva l'America e morte ai signori* (Long live America and death to the wealthy). In the United States, some would be lucky and become rich, as well as conservative, capitalist and even racist. Schio's local newspaper *El Visentin,* in an article of dire sentimentality of 25 January 1902 entitled "Forgotten Victims", reported the arrival at Ellis Island of these destitute youth: "Not one of them had previously set foot outside their world, and came to America with a broken heart for having left behind their loving families, their fiancées, their village, their friends, but were brave and hopeful, persuaded of having done their duty and trusting in a better future. Their last farewell had been for their former factory colleagues on the production chain (*compagni di catena*); their last thought was for the young, whom they counselled to hold out, and try again [to strike] when there would be full employment". The person who welcomed them at their arrival in New York was Arturo Meunier, another exile from Schio, who directed the newcomers to the nearby Italian settlements of Paterson and West Hoboken in New Jersey, where they soon found employment in the local textile factories.[8] The reason why peasants from the Veneto chose to emigrate rather than to rebel, like their counterparts in Catalonia and Andalusia, was in part due to the pervasive influence of the Catholic Church and the century-old clerical rule of the Habsburg monarchy, that stifled any attempt to organise as well as to rise. *Jacquerie* was foreign to the mindset of "religious" *contadini* in the Veneto.

The fact that anarchism was popular among the workers of Lane Rossi at Schio and Possagno was not coincidental. Landlords and industrial barons were identified with the state and its agencies, and the abolition of the former must unavoidably lead to the abolition of the latter. Some of the best names of Italian anarchism came from the Veneto region. Pietro Tresso was born in 1893 at Magré, near Schio, and would become one of the most outspoken anarchists on the international scene. Tresso, tortured by the Gestapo in 1943 because he was a member of the French *maquis*, soon after was murdered, apparently by Stalin's executioners.[9] Another prominent anarchist was Emilio Castellani, born in Venice in 1851, who emigrated to the United States in 1889-1892, at the time when quite a few of textile workers from Schio took refuge in Paterson. Castellani died in Venice in 1921.[10]

During the last ten years of the 19th century Paterson's Italian population exceeded 30,000, half of them employed in the silk industry. It was a hotbed of anarchism. Between 1894 until its banning in 1908, *La Questione Sociale*, a weekly that would reach a peak distribution of 15,000 copies, read in most mining centres and Italian settlements in the United States, was printed there. It was followed by another paper, *Era Nuova* (A New Era), published in 1908-1916. Prominent anarchists visited Paterson, Saverio Merlino in 1892, Pietro Gori in 1895 and Errico Malatesta in 1899. Anarchist Gaetano Bresci was one of the founders of *La Questione Sociale*. He left Paterson to return to Italy and murder on 29 July 1900 Umberto 1, King of Italy, in Brescia. Perhaps the most influential anarchist in the United States, a proponent of insurrectionary anarchism, of "propaganda through deeds", advocating violence against institutions, including assassination of "tyrants" and "enemies of the people" and leader of the anti-organisation current of anarchism was Luigi Galleani. Born in Vercelli, Piedmont, in 1861, he became an anarchist while studying law at the University of Turin. Wanted by police, he fled to France and Switzerland, where he worked with noted geographer and fellow anarchist Élisée Reclus. Upon his return to Italy in 1894, he was arrested and sentenced to five years in prison and *domicilio coatto* (internal exile) on Pantelleria. In 1900 he escaped from this island and fled to Egypt and in 1901 emigrated to the USA, settled in Paterson and became the editor of *La Questione Sociale*. In 1903 he founded and edited the weekly *Cronaca Sovversiva* (Subversive Chronicle) that would last until March 1919, the year in which he was deported to Italy. This journal had a peak print run of 5,000 copies that were distributed to anarchist circles and affiliates throughout the States. Galleani, an extremely effective and charismatic speaker, travelled widely, inciting his audiences to direct action and armed resistance. Years later, Vladimir Ilyich Lenin characterised this brand of anarchic terrorism as an "infantile disorder". Carlo Buda, brother of bomb maker Mario Buda, said of him: "You heard Galleani speak, and you were ready to shoot the first policeman you saw".[11] His followers began their bombing attacks in 1914, the same year that Galleani published his pamphlet *Faccia a faccia con il nemico* (Face to Face with the Enemy). He also spoke at the Circolo di Studi Sociali in Seattle, a meeting place for migrants from the Veneto.

The United States, or "Merica", as the mostly illiterate migrants called the New Eldorado, attracted many textile workers from Schio, Possagno and the surrounding areas, well after the Lane Rossi industrial dispute of 1901. Hunger and hatred for the *signori* compelled them, be they anarchist or of other political persuasion, to desperately go at an early age in search of fortune across the ocean. Isidoro Alessandro Bertazzon was one of them. He was born on 12 May 1891 in the hamlet of Pieve di Soligo, in the province of Treviso to Luigi and Angela Collet, one of their seven children, the others being brothers Angelo, Pietro and Girolamo and sisters Luigia, Anna and Giuseppina. Little is known about his parents, although an anarchist streak must have run through the mother's extended family, as an Angelo Antonio Collet, born in 1876 at Pieve di Soligo and emigrating to Switzerland to find work as a bricklayer, had a file opened on him in the CPC because he was "anti-fascist".[12] Not much is known about Isidoro's youth, with the exception of an understandably negative biographical note drafted by the *Prefetto* of Treviso in 1929, stating that Bertazzon "has a bad reputation among the locals because of his openly stated subversive theories. He attended only the primary school, but had a quick and alert intellect. During his stay in Pieve di Soligo he worked as a labourer – showing commitment to work and family. He behaved with indifference towards the authorities and never belonged to workers' organisations nor benefit associations, nor held political or administrative positions. He never held lectures or speeches, nor collaborated to newspapers. He had no criminal record. While residing in the fatherland he fanatically professed anarchist beliefs and assiduously committed himself to propaganda, without noticeable results, because he was not known to the masses ... [he is an] avid reader of anarchist books and pamphlets".[13]

At the beginning of the 20th century, employment opportunities in the Veneto for a professed young anarchist were dim if not non-existent, and Isidoro Bertazzon joined the long queue of people crowding migrant ships bound for "Merica". On 3 December 1907 he boarded in Genoa the cargo steamer *SS Liguria,* on his way to Quebec City, in the Province of Quebec, Canada, after he probably learned of local employment opportunities from previously emigrated *paesani* (townspeople). The ship's manifest attests that the vessel arrived at Ellis Island on 23 December 1907. Bertazzon was travelling together with four other *paesani* from Pieve di Soligo and two from Erto e Casso, in the province of Udine, all in transit for Quebec. They declared their occupation to be "workmen" and were able to read and write. Isidoro was the youngest of the group, being 16 years of age, while the two brothers from Udine, Giuseppe and Pietro Filippin, were 24 and married. The other four, Carlo Fattor, aged 23, Leonardo Belli, aged 21, Antonio Favero, aged 22 and Pietro Frare, aged 17, were all single. Being born in Northern Italy, these young men were *persona grata* to the American authorities. In 1899, the US Bureau of Immigration, alarmed by the large influx to the United States of "emotive, impulsive, very imaginative and devoid of practical sense". Southern Italian peasants, began registering the racial "look" of immigrants, distinguishing Northern Italian "Celts" from their Southern counterparts, who were classified as "Iberian". On the passenger manifest of the *SS Liguria,* under the heading "Race of People", Bertazzon and his companions were registered as being from the "North".[14]

Information on Bertazzon's life and activities between 1907 and 1917, following his arrival in New York, is not available. However, there is evidence that during this time he moved from Canada to the United States, and that in the meantime his father Luigi died at Pieve di Soligo.[15]

At the beginning of the 20th century the United States was gripped by fear of anarchist violence. On 6 September 1901, Leon Czolgosz, an American of Polish background, influenced by Russian anarchists Emma Goldman and Alexander Berkman, assassinated President William McKinley in Buffalo. As a result, in 1903 Congress approved the Anarchist Exclusion Act that for the first time barred entry to the USA on grounds of political opinion. Between 1903 and 1914 the law had a limited impact, excluding only 15 anarchists. The legislation was amended in 1918, allowing the deportation of resident immigrants. Also, in 1917 Congress passed the Selective Service Act, aimed at favouring the drafting of alien immigrants, and the Espionage Act and the Sedition Act, repressive measures punishing anti-war supporters. Among these were the anarchists and the Industrial Workers of the World (IWW or Wobblies), an organisation founded in Chicago on 24 June 1905, with a goal to promote workers' solidarity in the revolutionary struggle to overthrow the employing class. Incidentally, one of its members was the Italian migrant Carlo Tresca, who in 1913 was a leader of the Paterson strike by Italian silk workers agitating for the eight-hour working day, and whom a fascist hired killer would murder in 1943. In September 1917, Department of Justice agents made simultaneous raids on forty-eight IWW meeting halls across the country, arresting 165 of its leaders. Unlike the anarchists, the IWW did not advocate armed struggle and the use of dynamite, favouring instead the workers' full participation in managing and owning their workplaces through "industrial democracy". During this "Red Scare" period of 1917-1920, approximately 10,000 people were arrested, and some 3,500, presumed to be anarchist, were held in detention. Most were later released. Of the proven anarchists, only 556 were eventually deported.[16] Government records document major disruption in people's lives, deprivation of freedom, loss of livelihood and lives put on hold.

America's entry into the war in Europe in April 1917 further fuelled the country's fears of labour agitation and political radicalism. Seattle, in the State of Washington, was one of the centres of political militancy. During the First World War, ship construction became Seattle's most important industry. Throughout the war, Seattle shipyards produced 26.5 per cent of all ships built by the Emergency Fleet Corporation, a Federal government body entrusted with expediting war production. More than 35,000 workers were employed in the metal and wooden shipyards and allied trades. Seattle was also an important mining centre and one of the key terminals of the strategically important Great Northern Railway Company. The city hosted a sizeable Italian community, large enough to support its own newspaper, *La Gazzetta Italiana*, a conservative weekly that began publishing in 1910 until 16 June 1961, and was the Masonic mouthpiece of the Order of the Sons of Italy in America, Grand Lodge of Washington, Oregon and Idaho.

To openly voice anti-militarist, anti-nationalist or anti-war ideas in Seattle became increasingly dangerous. "Spontaneous" groups of vigilantes, whose primary task was the elimination of the IWW, were illegally formed with the tacit approval and support of the authorities. On 5 March 1917, when some 300 IWW members gathered in Everett, near Seattle, in support of striking shingle mill workers, some 200 hostile local police and citizen deputies confronted them. The gunfire that ensued left seven people killed and 50 wounded, among IWW members and deputies. Seventy-four Wobblies were arrested and charged with murder, but on 5 May 1917 the charges were dropped. No charges were ever made against the citizen deputies who murdered five Wobblies.[17] In June 1917, several hundred sailors stationed in Bremerton, Washington, were given special leave to wreck the IWW hall in Seattle. "Seditious" newspapers were targeted and closed. The President of the Immigration Commission, in speaking about left-wing immigrants to cheering members of the House of Representatives, declared that "Freedom of the Press is ours, not theirs, freedom of speech is ours, not theirs".[18] On 22 February 1918, Federal agents raided the anarchist premises at Lynn, near Boston, where Galleani's

Cronaca Sovversiva was printed, closed the paper and issued warrants for the arrest and deportation of one hundred of Gallleani's supporters.[19]

It is in this climate of dissent, strikes, violence and anarchist activity in the Seattle of 1917 that the threads of Isidoro Bertazzon's life can be taken up again. It is not known when he moved to this city and from where; it is however certain that he lived there for a while. Vincenzo Zaccagnini, an anarchist comrade, declared in December 1917 that "I had not seen Berteson (sic) for several months".[20] At that time Bertazzon was employed by the Great Northern Rail Company, cleaning coaches together with fellow anarchists Bartolomeo Massullo and Titino Dentino. In 1928, Australia's Criminal Investigation Branch, commenting on his occupation and probably referring to his duties at the Rail Company, reported that Bertazzon "is a plasterer by trade, but was previously an engine-driver".[21]

For a number of years, Italian anarchists and comrades of other nationalities met in the hall of a little Japanese church located at 821 Weller Street, Seattle, but in 1917, because of an increase in the audience, they moved to larger premises at 1009 Weller Street, in the back rooms on the ground floor of a lodging house called The Beacon. They named these premises Circolo di Studi Sociali. As Annibale Scialdo, a regular visitor, testified in his broken English, "I was there reading, and had a comfortable place to sit down, a good place to go, like men who have no house, no joy of family, no children".[22] Another Italian, Costantino D'Ascenco, under questioning described the venue as "a place where a fellow could go – women, children, men, everybody, where we could go and read books. Sometimes we used to go there and get warm by the fire".[23] This was confirmed by Battista Querio, who said that the Circolo was "a little place where you can go and read if you want to. There was a stove in there and books and a fellow could go in there and study and pass the time away".[24] The Circolo was also the venue where prominent anarchists delivered lectures. Pietro Sandretti confirmed the presence of Luigi

Galleani: "at one time there was a fellow by the name of Gallani (sic): he was making propaganda against the priest".[25] Annibale Scialdo, while questioned, confirmed that "I have heard Emma Goldman in this city" and that he was in correspondence with her and fellow anarchist Alexander Berkman.[26]

The Circolo regularly received copies of Galleani's *Cronaca Sovversiva*, in batches of 105 copies that were delivered to a Japanese fruit stand at 801 Charles Street and to an Italian grocery store in Seattle, to avoid detection from postal authorities. Vincenzo Zaccagnini, Bartolomeo Massullo and Bertazzon were among the couriers who picked up the packages from the two sites and distributed them to the newspaper's subscribers. Massullo and Bertazzon were living in the same boarding house at 1319, Tenth Avenue, Seattle.[27] Bertazzon, in order to avoid detection, also used Zaccagnini's address as a post box for his correspondence.[28] The Circolo di Studi Sociali collected money for several anarchist causes and mailed the proceedings to anarchist recipients in the USA and abroad.

Bertazzon attracted the attention of Italian consular representatives in New York, apparently for his statements in opposition to the war. The first entry in his file at Rome's CPC is dated 4 September 1917, because Italian Military Censors had intercepted a letter by Bertazzon posted in Seattle to La Spezia's anarchist newspaper *Il Libertario*, remitting US $12 in support, as the Military Censor stated, of "the anarchist idea and wishing that the day of awakening would come soon". The editor of *Il Libertario* was Pasquale Binazzi, who in 1895 had been arrested in Italy, together with Luigi Galleani, for having established a "subversive" organisation. The Italian Consul in Seattle, Paolo Brenna, sent a translation of Bertazzon's letter to Henry White, US Immigration Commissioner. Soon after, according to a report by the Italian Consul-General in New York dated 13 May 1918, White instructed the Police Department in Washington State to arrest Bertazzon.

Seattle Police sent undercover agents to attend one of the meetings held at the Circolo di Studi Sociali, to ascertain the content of their discussions. According to their report, the anarchists issued a call for a volunteer to go to Washington and assassinate President Wilson. On 12 November 1917, federal authorities arrested Bartolomeo Massullo, reputed to be the ringleader of the anarchists frequenting the Circolo. Massullo was a peasant from Bagnoli del Trigno, near Campobasso in the Abruzzi region, on whom the Italian Direzione Generale di Pubblica Sicurezza held a surveillance file because, as the Prefect of Campobasso wrote, "before emigrating, he maintained a dubious behaviour (*condotta equivoca*) and ... expressed subversive ideas". In 1913 Massullo emigrated to the United States on board the *MV America*, leaving behind wife Michelina Di Tosto and their three children. He settled in Seattle on 17 November 1913, and was unable to find work during the winter months. Massullo was then employed digging the foundations of Seattle's new Court House, labouring on the Lake Washington Canal, working on the Northern Pacific tracks and cleaning couches for that railway company. In 1914 he began frequenting the Circolo di Studi Sociali and contributed to its expenses, and in 1915 subscribed to *Cronaca Sovversiva*, that was distributed together with a copy of La Spezia's *Il Libertario*. During his interrogation by Immigration officers, Massullo admitted that Bertazzon had asked him to pick up a package containing 105 copies of *Cronaca Sovversiva* that had been couriered, in order to avoid postal scrutiny, from Lynn, Massachussetts, to a grocery shop at 801 Charles Street, Seattle, managed by a Japanese, Wichi Toyoji. Massullo's task was then to take the package to the Circolo, where, according to him, Bertazzon distributed the copies of the paper to its subscribers. Massullo confirmed that Isidoro Bertazzon was the man in charge of collecting funds and subscriptions for the paper. In May 1917, Bertazzon, already in Seattle for "nearly a year", according to a conversation he had had with Massullo, was living at 12th and Weller Street, but had no fixed address, in fact he used his comrade's home as a mailing box: "his mail comes to my house", Massullo said, " because he told me I haven't got no stated place". Bertazzon also left at Massullo's residence a suitcase containing anarchist literature, which was impounded by Immigration authorities. Massullo, who had not attended even primary school, declared to his interrogators "I kind of believe they are right, those anarchists, but I don't understand it. I don't understand what they are talking about", broke down under questioning and wrote down for Inspector Thomas Fisher the names and addresses of comrades attending the Circolo di Studi Sociali. Despite his collaboration, he was found guilty, as the Warrant for his arrest stated, "of advocating or teaching anarchy, or the overthrow by force or violence of the government of the United States, or of all forms of law, or the assassination of public officials". In March 1919 an order for his deportation was issued, but Massullo appealed, in vain. On 10 July 1919 he was put on board the *MV America* in New York and arrived in Naples on 24 July. After a few years spent in his birthplace, Bagnoli del Trigno, in 1923 Massullo emigrated to Canada and from there again entered the United States. In 1932 he was in San Francisco, and in 1935 moved to Hayward, California. After his deportation in 1919, he never engaged in political activities, although the fascist authorities kept him under surveillance until 1941. In July 1934 Massullo's name was expunged from the list of "subversives" abroad, deemed *attentatori* or capable of committing terrorist acts, but in July 1939 he was still listed in the Rubrica di Frontiera as a person to be arrested, *sia per la pericolosità del soggetto sia perchè irreperibile* (because he is a dangerous person and because he cannot be found).[29]

While Massullo was being interrogated, one night, between 4 and 5 a.m., Inspector Fisher and detective Bianchi, an Italian-speaking officer, surreptitiously entered the Circolo's premises. According to the *Seattle Daily Times*, "the place was minutely inspected, and information which later caused the names and addresses of the anarchists to fall into the government's hand was obtained". The move against Italian anarchists in Seattle was also prompted by the fact that on 24 November 1917 a large black powder bomb, constructed by Mario Buda, exploded at a Milwaukee police station, killing nine policemen and a female civilian, the worst incident of terrorist violence in the United States up to that time. The *Seattle Daily Times* reported that patrons of Seattle's Circolo di Studi Sociali might have been involved.[30]

In the afternoon and night of Sunday 25 November 1917, Immigration Commissioner Henry White and 35 heavily armed officers moved to arrest twenty-seven Italian anarchists in Seattle. The *Seattle Daily Times* revealed that one escaped arrest: "Gaining his feet at the bottom of the cliff, Inspector Fisher, although painfully injured, exchanged shots with one of the anarchists. The man, a moment before, had broken away from Fisher when placed under arrest at the anarchist headquarters, 1009 Weller St., and sought to make his escape by leaping over the embankment. The anarchist was arrested by Fisher as he was about to enter headquarters of the gang, which the federal agent had turned into a trap. Fisher started to search the man when the latter struck the officer a back blow with his elbow and made a dash for liberty. The embankment is just east of headquarters, and over this went the fleeing anarchist, with the federal man in hot pursuit. The anarchist, evidently familiar with the ground, slid down the cliff, while Fisher, at the edge of the embankment, stepped off into space and went hurtling down the hill. When Fisher reached the bottom, the anarchist was making his way up a hill on the other side of a gully, and the two men exchanged four shots. None of them took effect, so far as is known. The man succeeded in making his escape in the darkness".[31]

The twenty-six anarchists arrested at the Circolo di Studi Sociali in Weller Street and subsequently interrogated by federal Immigration officers were Giuseppe Bertolotti, Ottavio Bonanni, Giuseppe Bravi, Federico Catalini, Giovanni Cavierno, Costantino D'Ascenco, Titino

Dentino, Luigi Ercolini, Nicola Farro, Carmelo Filippini, Leo Fontana, Emilio Ghelfi, Attilio Ghilardi, Silvio Ghilardi, Francesco Goggi, Enrico Guiditti, Giovanni Matterioli, Giovanni Morgando, Antonio Pomato, Battista Querio, Domenico Querio, Luigi Ramole, Achille Ricci, Pietro Sandretto, Annibale Scialdo and Vincenzo Zaccagnini.

According to a version of the events given by the Italian Consul in Seattle, Paolo Brenna, to Tritoni, Italian Consul-General in New York, police officer Joe Bianchi apprehended Bertazzon, who asked Bianchi to be allowed to say good-bye to his family. Having naively been granted leave, Bertazzon went instead to warn his Italian anarchist comrades to go underground and he himself disappeared, evading arrest. Bianchi, peeved at having been tricked by Bertazzon, went with a number of his colleagues, armed with rifles, to Seattle's quarter of Youngstown, where at that time most Italians lived, and arrested some sixty of them. The local newspapers prominently reported the news, under the heading, "United States Police catches Reds", and published a photo of White and Massullo and, next to them, to his utmost annoyance, a photo of the Italian Consul with the caption "Chevalier Paolo Brenna, Royal Italian Consul who denounced Italian anarchists".[32] Some 31 Italians were detained and questioned by officers of the Department of Immigration, to give reason why they should not be deported. Copies of the transcripts of these interrogations were given by Henry White to the Italian Consul-General in New York, and are now in Bertazzon's CPC file. Most Italians, almost illiterate, were in trouble because they had subscribed to *Cronaca Sovversiva*. The collector of subscriptions and the distributor of anarchist literature probably was – according to the Consul-General – Isidoro Bertazzon. His opinion was corroborated when the premises of Achille Ricci were searched and, in the words of Ricci's Attorney, "quite a number of newspapers are marked 'J. Bertassen' (sic)". Another indicted person, Giovanni Cavierno, testified that "there was a fellow soliciting for subscriptions", and that "this man made a little speech in the lodge Hall [i.e. the Circolo di

Studi Sociali]". Bertazzon's primary role in fostering anarchism in Seattle was confirmed by Consul Brenna in his report to Tritoni, in which he stated that

> the main culprit in this painful episode, Isidoro Bertazzon, avoided American justice and still is a fugitive to it. He was employed by the Empire Investment Company in Portland, Oregon [after working for the Great Northern Rail Company], but no longer can be traced there ... Bertazzon's letter has unearthed the existence of a veritable hotbed of anarchist infection and defeatism in this country ... while the main culprit absconded justice, many unfortunate fellow countrymen, unfortunate rather than guilty, have been embroiled in this affair and suffered harsh terms of imprisonment ... only to be released after having paid a bond, and under constant threat of being deported to the old country.[33]

Officers of the Department of Immigration were so biased that association with known radicals, knowledge of IWW songs and possession of anarchist literature assumed immigrants' guilt. Evidence of specific actions was not necessary to secure warrants for their arrest. Detainees were not shown the warrant, issued on grounds that the accused "has been found advocating or teaching anarchy, or the overthrow by force or violence of the government of the United States or of all forms of law, or the assassination of public officials; and that he was a person likely to become a public charge at the time of his entry into the United States". Also, following their arrest, as Giovanni Morgando stated under oath, they were denied access to legal representation. When, on 30 November 1917, attorneys for Giovanni Cavierno asked Henry White for access to their client, five days after he had been arrested, they were told "by Mr White that on account of there being so many arrests made they had no chance to see this particular man, and that [they] could not be allowed to see him until the government officials had had a chance to examine him".[34] In blatant disregard for Amendment VIII of the American Constitution's Bill of Rights, which ruled that "excessive bail shall not be required, nor excessive fines imposed, nor cruel and unusual punishments inflicted", a bond of $5,000 was imposed on each one of the indicted anarchists, an impossible sum for them to raise.

Immigration authorities were keen to find Isidoro Bertazzon's whereabouts and surreptitiously tried to extract, albeit unsuccessfully, this piece of information from his comrades. The latter never "knew" or "remembered" the name of the person soliciting for subscriptions to *Cronaca Sovversiva*. Titino Dentino admitted knowing Bertazzon, of meeting him only once, four months before he was arrested, when Bertazzon came to his home together with Massullo, "because they were working together". When asked whether he was aware that Bertazzon was an anarchist, he replied, "Maybe he is". Dentino, when questioned where Bertazzon was, replied, "I was working with Berteson (sic) and Paglia. They quit about June [1917] sometime". "Where is Berteson now?" "I don't know; I have not seen him for a long time, because he left here. He came to see me once after that, you see; that was about a month after he quit".[35] Also Vincenzo Zaccagnini declared that he had not seen Bertazzon "for several months", denied that he was living at his home, although admitted that Bertazzon "used to get the paper at my house ... he used to come to my house for the letters".[36] The anarchist from Pieve di Soligo was not betrayed by his friends, with the possible exception, under duress, by Massullo.

Department of Immigration inspectors interrogating the arrested anarchists did not hide their hostility towards them. Giuseppe Bertolotti, a miner from Cle Elum, near Seattle, was quizzed about being an atheist and on his belief in evolution. He bitterly objected to his imprisonment: "I came to this country", he said, "I took out about from four to six tons of coal daily, and as a reward I was arrested in the mine without having committed any crime, and I think it is unjust".[37] Nicola Farro, despite his home having been searched, was asked: "Ever made any bombs? Did you ever have any nitroglycerine? Did you ever have any powder? Did you ever take any powder or explosives for anybody anyplace?" He answered in the negative, adding that "I don't even know what [nitroglycerine] is".[38] Some anarchists even made fun of the interrogator's questions. Giovanni Morgando had the following exchange with Inspector T.W. Lynch concerning his subscription and donations to *Cronaca Sovversiva*:

> "Mr Lynch: Do you always give up money when anyone asks you for it?
>
> A. To those who need it. For the poor people.
>
> Mr Lynch: Do you usually buy things that you do not want?
>
> A. No, I do not buy it when I do not need it.
>
> Mr Lynch: If you buy a thing it is to be presumed it is something that you need.
>
> A. I don't know. Sometimes I do not dare to say no".[39]

Federico Catalini also protested his innocence when accused of being an anarchist because anarchist literature was found in his possession: "I never harm anyone, and the books, I have so many of different kinds. They accuse me of being an anarchist because I read those books. They could call me a priest because I have been reading a lot of books about a priest".[40] Perhaps the most outrageous questioning was that made to Costantino D'Ascenco, who was living with a widow who had had four children from a deceased husband and who bore two of D'Ascenco's children. The exchange went as follows:

> "Q. You mean you are not married, just living with her?
>
> A. Yes.
>
> Q. Why didn't you marry the woman?
>
> A. At the time that we got married I was broke and she was broke and she had a big family and we didn't have money enough to spend for the marriage.

Q. Don't you know that you are violating a state law by living with that woman?

A. I don't know that I violate the state law.

Q. You know that you are violating a moral law? You know that you are not married, and that is morally wrong?

A. I can marry her any time.

Q. But don't you know that that is wrong morally?

A. I don't know that.

Q. Have you any moral sense?

A. No answer".

In his defence, D'Ascenco stated: "I want you people to make an investigation and find out that I am all right because I have been paying all my bills and supporting my family of six children and I don't owe a cent in town and I have been supporting eight of us and I would like to go back to work because we haven't much money to go ahead with".[41] On the other hand, what most incensed the arresting Immigration Inspector Thomas Fisher was the response given by Vittorio Zaccagnini's son to a question put to him by Constable Bianchi: "On the night Massula (sic) was arrested, while Mr Bianchi and I were waiting for Massulo (sic) to come home, Bianchi took your oldest boy on his knee, and asked him if he would like to be a police officer, and the boy replied: 'No, I belong to the revolution'."[42]

The boy's statement was leaked by Immigration and police officers to the *Seattle Daily Times*, along with information of Bertazzon's $12 remittance to *Il Libertario*, Italian Consul Paolo Brenna's role in the affair and details of the raid on Weller Street and other parts of the city. Not only did the paper publish these details, it also magnified anarchist activities to incredible proportions. Thus, "the Circola (sic) Studi Sociali has an estimated membership in the United States of approximately 200,000". Also, "according to information gained by federal officials in Seattle, the flood of gold sent to the main headquarters of the anarchists in Italy from the society in the United States is disbursed from Spezia (sic), with revolutionists connected with a newspaper in that city in control. The newspaper, an anarchist publication, is known as *Il Libertario*". Further, the *Times* alleged that "the anarchists plotted the death of King Victor [Emmanuel] and the overthrow of the Italian government in the most approved Russian revolutionary style". The paper called the patrons of Circolo di Studi Sociali "this band, a secret society of direct-actionists and bomb-throwers with murder and assassination as the cardinal principles of its creed".[43] Despite the *Times'* sensational headlines, having assessed the transcripts of the interrogation of Seattle's Italian anarchists, Consul-General Tritoni drastically played down the security threat posed by them. In a memorandum to Rome, he assured his Minister that of the 31 people arrested only 13 were *sospetti anarchici* (suspected of being anarchists). Seattle's Consul Brenna endorsed his opinion. He believed that the arrested Italians were "ignorant, almost illiterate people, only in part guilty of anarchy and defeatism. Many are discontented deserters, and I would be most embarrassed if I would have to describe them as dangerous anarchists".[44]

The sweeping raids and arrests did not deter some of Seattle's Italian anarchists. Almost immediately, a no better defined Anarchist Group Volontà distributed a leaflet in Italian and English, titled "Down with Democratic Inquisition", in which its authors lamented that "a few days ago, several men paid by our democratic government entered our hall, although the place was closed at the time. They entered like common thieves, breaking down the door. Everything found in the hall was seized, pamphlets and books of anarchist propaganda and scientific works were carried away ... Suppression of our press, stealing of our books and propaganda, accusation of being German spies, violation of our domiciles, jail sentences, tortures; all of these things will be as futile now as they have been in the past".

By now, the "Red Scare" was in full swing. In February 1919 the

New York Times reported that "Seattle radicals, advocates of Anarchy and Bolshevism" were among the fifty-seven men and one woman transferred to Ellis Island under armed escort, pending deportation. Among them were five Italians: Santo Angelo Accetura, Pasquale Alfiero, Fortunato Scordo, Antonio Santucci and Alberto Guerra.[45] On 24 June 1919, Luigi Galleani, together with Raffaele Schiavina and Irma and Giobbe Sanchini, were deported to Italy on board the *MV Duca degli Abruzzi*. Italian historian Leonardo Bettini claims "a similar fate was reserved at the same time for Ugo Balzano from Cleveland, Ohio, and Isidoro Bertazzon from Seattle, Washington".[46] However, Bettini's assertion cannot be corroborated and is in contradiction with the fact that Bertazzon was still in the United States in August 1920, as hereunder documented. The largest single deportation of anarchists took place on 21 December 1919, when the *USS Buford,* an Army transport nicknamed by the Press "the Soviet Ark", embarked 249 "radicals", including Emma Goldman and Alexander Berkman, under the armed escort of 62 Marines. Pistols were distributed to the crew. Its final destination was unknown as it sailed under sealed orders. Eventually the *USS Buford* discharged its unwanted human cargo in Hanko, Finland. Upon arrival on 17 January 1920, the Finnish authorities transported the deportees to the frontier with the Soviet Union.[47] The "Red Scare" had repercussions in Australian government circles and public opinion, too. The Department of Home and Territories advised the Secretary of the Attorney-General's Department that the Anarchists Exclusion Act "may affect Australia inasmuch as the closing of the United States to such persons may divert them to this country". This fear was also expressed by the Council of the Municipality of Hamilton, NSW, who wrote to the Acting Prime Minister stating that "seven thousands Bolshevik anarchists are to be deported from the United States and ... these men should not be allowed to come to Australia".[48]

Bertazzon remained in hiding, avoiding arrest for a long time. In

February 1918, Consul-General Tritoni advised Rome that *Isidoro Bertazzon risulta essere stato arrestato a Seattle*, but it must have been a false alarm since on 13 May and again on 10 July 1918 he reported that "until now Bertazzon could not be traced".[49] No mention of the escapee is made in Italian files until 8 June 1920, when Tritoni cabled Rome that Bertazzon *chiede passaporto per recarsi Regno Stop perchè tempo fa richiese passaporto sotto altro nome* (is asking for a passport as he wants to return to Italy Stop some time ago he used a false name to obtain a passport). On 6 August 1920 New York's Acting Vice-Consul reiterated his request for instructions from Rome whether he could issue a passport "to the subversive Bertazzon, who is asking for it continuously". Rome gave consent on 8 September 1920. It therefore seems that the American authorities failed to raise charges of anarchism against Bertazzon. In an email message to the author, the Assistant Archivist of the King County Archives, Seattle, stated: "I did check our Prosecuting Attorney's criminal dockets for 1917-1919. That office was bringing charges of criminal anarchy during that period, but I did not note Mr. Bertazzon's name among the defendants". Also, the US Citizenship and Immigration Services (USCIS) History Office advised the author that no file on Bertazzon's alleged deportation was being held among its records. "My guess", USCIS' historian wrote, "is that he was able to travel to Canada on his own and left from there to go to Italy".[50] On 21 July 1927 mention is made about his movements in his CPC file, when it was reported "Bertazzon repatriated from Canada at the beginning of 1921, and emigrated to Australia in August 1922". During his stay at Pieve di Soligo, according to Treviso's *Prefetto*, "he tried to raise money and subscriptions to resurrect Venezia Giulia's anarchist newspaper *Germinal*, previously edited in Trieste, with not much success because he was under strict surveillance by the *Carabinieri*".[51] However, despite being closely watched, he was able to meet other fellow anarchists in Venice. A photo of the time portrays him together with seven *sovversivi* in a Venetian *calle* (alley).

Under constant police harassment, unable to find employment in Italy or to return to the United States, which on 19 May 1921 had severely restricted Italian immigration by approving the Immigration Restriction Act, Isidoro Bertazzon chose Australia. He left Genoa on board the *MV Carignano* and arrived in Melbourne on 17 September 1922. His was a wise decision, because in January 1923 the police searched his mother's home in Pieve di Soligo, and found evidence that Isidoro was subscribing to Palermo's anarchist newspaper *Vespro Anarchico* (Anarchist Vesper) and corresponded with anarchist cells in Bologna, Palermo and Tortona. In 1927 his name would be included, under number 4932, in the Bollettino delle Ricerche, with instructions to Border Police to arrest Bertazzon in case of his return to Italy.[52] Incredibly, on 2 August 1922, a few days before embarking for Melbourne, Angelo Signoretto, Mayor of Pieve di Soligo, issued Isidoro Bertazzon, *bracciante* (labourer), with a Certificate of Good Moral, Civic and Political Conduct in order for him to seek employment. Obviously, the Mayor was not aware of Bertazzon's previous stormy "subversive" past, or did not care about it, or perhaps was sympathetic to the anarchist cause.

From 4 September 1917, the date of the first entry in his bulky file at the CPC, until the last entry of 21 February 1939, Isidoro Bertazzon, whether he be in Italy, the United States or Australia, was under unrelenting surveillance from Italian diplomats, Fascist Party officers, *fiduciari* and fellow travellers with the regime, as well as pliant police officers, bureaucrats and politicians. The covers of his CPC file bear an array of stamps and annotations that detail Bertazzon's ideas and activities as judged by the regime's spies. He was deemed to be an "Anarchist", living "Abroad-Australia", "Dangerous", "Index-carded", "*Attentatore*" (liable to make a bomb attack), "To be arrested", his name having been entered in the "Rubrica di Frontiera" (Border Register) and in the "Bollettino delle Ricerche" (Search Bulletin). Incongrously, the entry of Bertazzon's occupation described him as a *manovale – editore* (labourer – editor).

Bertazzon's arrival in Melbourne coincided with the ones by other anarchists from the Veneto region and other parts of Italy, fleeing fascist squadrism's onslaught. Among the dozens of political refugees were Francesco Carmagnola, born in San Vito di Leguzzano (Vicenza), who arrived on 13 May 1922 on board the *MV San Rossore*, Girolamo Bonaguro, from Caltrano (Vicenza), in June 1922 with the *MV Moncalieri*, Giacomo Pastega, born in Possagno (Treviso) on 4 August 1923 on the *MV Orvieto*, Francesco Fantin, from San Vito di Leguzzano, Valentino Ciotti and Mirko Da Cortà from Pieve di Cadore in January 1925 on board the *MV Moncalieri*, and Angelo Cunial from Possagno in 1926. Of the people index-carded in the CPC as anarchists, Giacomo Pastega shared, with Bertazzon, the doubtful honour of being classed as an *attentatore*. Another anarchist, Gaetano Panizzon from Magrè di Schio, who arrived in Melbourne in January 1922 and settled in Geelong, is deemed to have been among the anarchists involved on 23 March 1921 in the bombing of the Diana Theatre in Milan, resulting in 21 deaths and 80 injured. He is cited as a person involved in the supply of the explosives by one the ringleaders, Giuseppe Mariani, in his memoirs titled *Memorie di un ex-terrorista*, published in Torino in 1953. What is uncertain is whether he was aware of Mariani's terrorist purposes. There is no mention of Panizzon's involvement in the attack in his CPC file.[53]

By trade a terrazzo, marble and concrete worker, Bertazzon found work for a few months labouring in Melbourne. He sponsored his older brother Girolamo, born on 2 June 1888, and his family to come to Australia. Girolamo Bertazzon, wife Angela, née D'Agostini, daughter Chiara and son Luigi embarked from Naples on the *MV Ormuz* and arrived at Fremantle, Western Australia, on 3 May 1923.[54] For eighteen months they and Isidoro lived in rural Victoria, among other places for eight months in Cobden, near Geelong, at the Tandarook Homestead. At the end of 1924 or early 1925, Isidoro, Girolamo and his family moved to Melbourne and settled at 131 Station Street, Carlton, in a house described by a later occupant as a "renovated home [that] had a large backyard and back lane, an outside toilet and a tin bath. It also had a wood chip hot water service. [It] had a gas stove in the kitchen that was operated by inserting a one penny coin in the metal control box under the front veranda".[55] According to Consul-General Grossardi, who had Bertazzon under surveillance (*fin dal suo primo arrivo in Australia non ho mancato di tenerlo sotto stretta sorveglianza*), the Bertazzons were also managing the premises as a boarding house. In a despicable and scurrilous report to the Ministero dell'Interno, the Italian diplomat claimed "Bertazzon is working, when he feels it, as a terrazzo worker. When he is not working, he is living off his brother's and sister-in-law's back, a woman of easy virtue who is managing a pension at her address and with whom, it is alleged, Bertazzon is also maintaining an illicit relationship". In the same report, Grossardi confirmed that Bertazzon had been politically active since his arrival in Melbourne: "... he does not waste any opportunity to carry out petty propaganda against the Regime among boarders and workmates".[56] This activity, in Grossardi's opinion, had to be stopped: "As it is absolutely forbidden by the local, strict laws, to go and look for him at home or on the job, some Fascists are keeping under watch a Greek club frequented by Bertazzon, hoping to find him and give him a good beating ... so far he has eluded them, but it is a matter of time and patience and he will not be able to escape a well-earned punishment".[57]

The murder in Rome on 10 June 1924 of socialist Deputy Giacomo Matteotti, the consolidation of the Fascist dictatorship after Mussolini's speech of 3 January 1925 and the establishment in Australia of Fascist Branches in Melbourne on 17 October 1925 and 31 October 1926.[58] spurred the regime's enemies to action. Moreover, international opprobrium for the death sentence upheld by the US Supreme Court against Italian anarchist migrants Bartolomeo Sacco and Nicola Vanzetti, who would be executed on 22 August 1927, was a clarion call to Italian anarchists in Australia to organise and fight the representatives and the supporters of fascism in this country. Melbourne, Sydney, Ingham (Qld) and Broken Hill, in New South Wales, were the centres where most anarchists had settled and found employment, and it was in these places that in 1926 the first organisations were established.[59] One of the driving forces of the anarchist movement during the 1920s was Francesco Carmagnola. Some years later, the Australian Security Service drafted this brief profile of his first years in Australia:

> After leaving school in Italy, he joined the Military Service and was attached to the Cavalry Division for twelve months and was then transferred to a clerical branch in the Army, where he remained until the year 1921. He left Italy and arrived in Sydney on 15 May, 1922. Upon arrival in Sydney, Carmagnola proceeded to Ingham, Queensland, where he was employed on a sugar plantation for twelve months. He then left Queensland and went to Melbourne where he worked in a sawmill again returning to Ingham, Queensland in the year 1923, where he remained until 1926, he then went to Griffith, NSW and worked on a vineyard for a period of five months. He then returned to Sydney.[60]

Before going to Sydney from Griffith, Carmagnola stayed for a short while in Queanbeyan and Canberra where, according to his testimonial, "I received a letter from a friend, who told me that in Sydney people were ready to establish an Anti-Fascist League, but there was no organiser ... so I left right away for Sydney and we formed this League".[61] The League printed leaflets and in July 1927 distributed the first of three issues of the newspaper *Il Risveglio* (The Awakening) that aroused the anger of Consul-General Grossardi, who was successful in having the sheet banned by the Australian government.[62]

It is not known when Carmagnola and Bertazzon first met. Perhaps during Carmagnola's short stay in Melbourne in 1923, as documented by the above mentioned Security Service Report.

Carmagnola, in an interview with the author, said that it was at the time of the publication of *Il Risveglio* that he first received a letter from Bertazzon.[63] However, a note to the readers in the first issue of the paper is jointly signed, and a lengthy article on "The lies of Fascism" is signed by Bertazzon, indicating that by this time a working relationship and perhaps a friendship had been established between the two. In his article, Bertazzon advocated the struggle against Italian as well as international fascism (*non è solo il fascismo mussoliniano che dobbiamo combattere; in ogni angolo della terra dove vi sono oppressi e oppressori vi è fascismo*). Carmagnola, in his article "From the land of Maramaldo" [in the Italian lore eponymous of "ruthless", "villainous"], went further, encouraging physical violence against Italian supporters of fascism in Australia, even the murder of members of the diplomatic corps: "For us, outside Italy, there is only one way to fight, that could have some impact on the regime at home: that of showing our strength to official and private supporters of fascism abroad who are in reach of our blows. That is, we could contrast, make it difficult, or terminate, the life of fascist diplomats, impede their work and, to any crime committed in Italy against our people, respond abroad with an immediate act of reprisal against one of them. We too, if we want, have at our disposal means of defence and offence, it would be enough to use them in order to be feared and respected".[64] Although Carmagnola's determination to render the life of his political enemies difficult is beyond doubt, as demonstrated by the several assaults and beatings in which he was involved, it is doubtful whether he would have resorted to cold-blooded murder.

The third issue of *Il Risveglio*, published on 1 September 1927, eight days after the execution of Sacco and Vanzetti, dedicated its first page to the commemoration of the two martyrs with a banner headline proclaiming "Long live anarchy! And by the anarchists they will be avenged". It also printed a poem by Pietro Gori and listed the addresses of anarchist newspapers obtainable from other countries, among them

New York's *Adunata dei Refrattari*, Paris' *Il Monito*, Buenos Aires' *Culmine* and Geneva's *Il Risveglio*. Bertazzon's name was again next to Carmagnola's as co-editor, and he was the most generous among contributors to the newspaper with a donation of twenty shillings. He was also responsible for the collection and the forwarding of funds to the sons and daughters of political prisoners in Italy.

Undaunted by the closure of the newspaper, Carmagnola, who in the meantime had moved to Melbourne, founded in November 1927, together with Bertazzon and two other anarchists, Francesco Fantin and Valentino Ciotti, the Matteotti Club. Originally, it was located at 251 Spring Street, near the Treasury Building but, when its membership and popularity rose, moved to the Horticultural Society Hall in Victoria Street, opposite the Trades Hall. The Matteotti Club served as a meeting point for Italians in their fight against fascism. The name of Matteotti was deliberately chosen to attract to its premises all anti-fascists, be they socialist, republican, communist or of any other belief, although the core organisation was in the hands of its anarchist component. Again, to the chagrin of Consul-General Grossardi, the Club acted as a disseminator of anti-fascist propaganda, organised conferences, balls, commemorations of Matteotti, collected funds for several causes, subscribed to the anarchist press overseas and mailed propaganda to addressees in Italy. Its members, Carmagnola at the forefront, were responsible for several, violent clashes with fascist stalwarts. But this was not enough. Both Carmagnola and Bertazzon wanted to reach all Italians in Australia, and the best way was to publish a newspaper.

Having learned from previous experience with *Il Risveglio*, in January 1928 Isidoro Bertazzon made an application to the Commonwealth, through Melbourne's Barristers Maurice Blackburn & Co., seeking permission to publish a newspaper, twice monthly, in the Italian language and by subscription only. Its provisional name was *La Riscossa Libertaria* (The Libertarian Counterattack). In the meantime, following the suppression of *Il Risveglio* on 23 August 1927, Carmagnola and Bertazzon resorted to print and distribute anti-Fascist leaflets. Again, Grossardi wrote to Prime Minister Bruce, complaining against such literature, "stating that distribution of suppressed newspaper [had been] replaced by distribution of leaflets also printed in Italian containing the same praise for anarchy".[65] In February 1928, Inspector Roland Browne of Melbourne's Investigation Branch asked Bertazzon to come for an interview but was instead visited by Carmagnola, who declared that Bertazzon would be the editor of the newspaper and he its trustee. The purpose of the newspaper was to "supply information which the suppressed anti-fascist newspapers in Italy would otherwise have furnished". Inspector Browne concluded his negative report to his superior, Harold Edward Jones, Director of the Investigation Branch, Canberra, by commenting "to me it seems unfortunate that Australia should be bothered in the matter at all". Jones, writing to the Secretary of the Prime Minister's Department, stressed "Carmagnola is known to be fanatically anti-Fascist, while Bertazzon must assuredly be of the same political opinion". The advice that Jones gave was that "it is hardly advisable that Australia should encourage foreigners to air the political grievances of their respective native lands in this country ... I think it would be undesirable to give government approval to the introduction of a recognised form of anti-fascism or any other form of quasi-rebellious activity".[66] Permission to publish was denied.

In June 1928, socialist intellectual Omero Schiassi founded in Melbourne the Concentrazione Antifascista dell'Australasia (Anti-Fascist Concentration of Australasia). He enjoyed the support of several Australian left-wing intellectuals and staff of the University of Melbourne, where Schiassi was a Reader in Italian. Members of the Matteotti Club, that in the meantime had attracted the support of prominent leaders of the labour movement, among them W.J. Duggan, Federal President of the ACTU and the ALP and Labor Members Don

Cameron, Maurice Blackburn and W. Maloney, joined forces with the new anti-fascist body. The first initiative promoted by the Concentration was the commemoration of Matteotti's murder, which was held on 10 June 1928 at Melbourne's New Gaiety Theatre. Among the hundreds of people attending were the red-shirted members of the Matteotti Club. Following Schiassi's keynote speech, Duggan, Blackburn, R.S. Ross of the Socialist Party and J. Shelley of the Communist Party also spoke. Isidoro Bertazzon intervened on behalf of the Matteotti Club, speaking in English. The pamphlet commemorating the meeting commented "he was loudly applauded and spoke with considerable eloquence". He said "if he were speaking for weeks he could not convey in full the suffering of the people of Italy under Mussolini. Let them bear in mind that there were thousands of Matteottis being flung into prisons and exile... The members of the Matteotti Club were all in the Unions [many Italians were not]. They did not deserve to be called "damned Dagoes", and he asked that the workers of Australia recognise that many anti-fascists were here because to be in Italy was impossible".[67]

Bertazzon had not supinely accepted the Commonwealth's refusal to grant a permit to publish a newspaper in Italian. Having learned that there was no need to seek permission to publish single issues, provided they bore different mastheads, in August 1928 he embarked, to Grossardi's dismay and Canberra's powerlessness, on the project that would see nine of these sheets, opportunistically called "pamphlets" but in reality being single issue newspapers, printed and distributed throughout Australia. They bore the caption "Published by I. Bertazzon, for the Matteotti Committee, Victoria Street, Melbourne". The articles were well informed, as they heavily relied on material published by the anti-fascist press overseas, and their slant was decidedly propagandist. The first issue, *Il Calvario* (Calvary), an unusual religious reference for an anarchist publication, although the term is used in popular lore as synonym for suffering, came out on 23 August 1928, on the first anniversary of Sacco's and Vanzetti's execution, and contained their eulogy, anti-Fascist propaganda and reprints of articles from New York's *L'Adunata dei Refrattari*. The second issue, *L'Azione* (Action), followed in September 1928, on the occasion of the second anniversary of the attempt on Mussolini's life by the anarchist Gino Lucetti. It also published articles written by Bertazzon on "Italy under Fascist Terror" and on business in Italy. The third and fourth pamphlets, An *Appeal to the People of Australia* and *Sempre Avanti* (Always Forward) were printed in October and November 1928 respectively. The fifth newspaper, *La Riscossa*, in January 1929, reported on the opening on 1 December 1928 of the new Matteotti Club premises in Victoria Street and reprinted an article from the socialist *Avanti!*, printed underground in Paris, entitled "Fascism is drowning in slime and blood". In commenting on the opening of the new venue, the paper wrote "comrade Bertazzon, a most active member, explained to Australian members in the audience what fascism was and the Club's aims, and *venne calorosamente applaudito nella sua focosa, ma chiara esposizione antifascista in lingua inglese*.[68] On 10 June 1929 came out *G. Matteotti*, remembering again the sacrifice of the Italian Deputy and containing a column entitled "Subversive News", signed by Bertazzon.[69] The seventh issue, *Germinal*, came out in July 1929,[70] followed in August by *In Memoria*. The ninth and last single issue, *Il Risveglio*, was published on 19 October 1929.

The regular appearance of a broadsheet publishing venomous criticism against fascism, the Catholic Church, the Italian monarchy and, generally, against the established order of society, greatly annoyed Italian consular officials in Melbourne and Sydney. It troubled even more the Australian establishment. In the article entitled "Victory?" in *Il Risveglio*, Bertazzon charged former Prime Minister Stanley Bruce, "who copies Mussolini like an ape and who is the faithful servant of the British shipping magnates and industrialists" of "protecting and assisting reactionary men" and of having "a beastly fascist attitude".

Bertazzon claimed "that the Australian people are stupid as sheep and do not care very much for politics" and that politicians "ought really to be overthrown by means somewhat more effectual than the ballot paper" because, he asked rhetorically, "which equality can there be between those who order and those who are compelled to obey? ... Therefore", concluded Bertazzon, "governments must disappear".

In July 1929 the Melbourne Consulate sent a copy of *G. Matteotti* to the Criminal Investigation Branch, with translations of the articles that, in the words of its Director, H.E. Jones, were "repugnant to the Italian Consular officials". However, Jones commented that the sheet's "bellicose attitude to the Italian authorities is, to a certain degree, not within the scope of this Branch".[71] In August 1929, Mario Carosi, then Acting Consul-General, sent a copy of *Germinal* to Major L. Lloyd of Sydney's Branch. In his letter, Carosi pointed out that its editor, Bertazzon, with his endorsement of "the methods for suppressing oppression", was guilty of an "open instigation to crime". This "libel" should be prohibited because, in Carosi's opinion, had broken the law by not applying for permission to publish. He also ventured to give Mayor Lloyd unsolicited legal opinion by pointing out that "such activities are contemplated and severely dealt with by the Crimes Act". A few days later, Carosi sent a copy of *In Memoria* to Melbourne's CIB, stating that he took "a very serious view of the consequences which such pernicious literature may have amongst the Italian community and I am therefore compelled to repeat the request that steps be taken to end this abuse". Carosi continued his threatening letter by expressing his wish "that your Department will no longer stay its hand in launching a prosecution against the Melbourne publisher and printers and express the hope that the culprits will be given an exemplary punishment". He also tried to intimidate Inspector Ronald Browne by telling him that he was taking up the matter with Canberra.[72] Jones was of the opinion that "it would appear that both the Matteotti Club and Bertazzon are defying the laws of the Commonwealth by publishing a monthly newspaper in Italian".[73] However, he was reminded by Inspector Browne that "when Carmagnola was interviewed some months ago, he put forward the assertion that the publications were not, as a matter of fact, newspapers, and therefore were not subject either to the state law respecting registration, or the Commonwealth law respecting the publication of newspapers in a foreign language. Whether this contention is sound or not", quipped Browne, "it is not for me to say". Commenting on Bertazzon's issue of *Il Risveglio*, where he advocated that "governments must disappear", Browne wryly concluded that he "has on this occasion been more outspoken than usual with respect to Australian affairs", and concluded that "if the papers can be lawfully suppressed it would be worth while so doing".[74] Jones did not test the legality of Carmagnola's assertion; instead, on 4 December 1929 he wrote to his Prime Minister "such publications cannot, strictly speaking, be regarded as "newspapers in a foreign language". Despite this admission, he concluded his advice by contradictorily stating "it is most undesirable that an alien should be permitted to flout the law as Bertazzon has done. Secondly, some official protection from scurrilous publications should be afforded to an officially accredited representative of a Foreign Power".[75] However, no harm came to Isidoro Bertazzon for his bold publishing initiative. From 22 October 1929, following the Labor Party's victory at the federal elections, Jones' Prime Minister was no longer the Nationalist Stanley Melbourne Bruce, Mussolini's admirer, but Labor's James Henry Scullin. Despite his Catholicism, Scullin would be more eager to listen to the pleas of Italian anti-Fascists in Australia, including people from the Matteotti Club, although he had been made aware by his staff and by Fascist diplomats of its strong anarchist leanings.

Carmagnola moved fast, eventually realising his dream of producing a sheet that would reach nationwide the enemies of fascism in Australia. On 20 December 1929, the first number of the monthly newspaper *La Riscossa* was published, obviously without Commonwealth consent.

The editor of the new publication was not Bertazzon, but Carmagnola's friend Valentino Ciotti, an indication that the relationship between the two anarchist leaders had, as will be discussed later, soured during 1929. In fact, on 14 June 1930 Bertazzon began publishing fortnightly his own newspaper, *L'Avanguardia Libertaria*, also without government approval. On 10 February 1931, J. Strahan, Assistant Secretary of the Prime Minister's Department advised a baffled Jones that "an application for registration for transmission by post as a newspaper of a journal named "L'Avanguardia Libertaria" has been made to the Postmaster-General's Department by Mr. I. Bertazzon of Melbourne".[76] A few days later Jones replied, obviously confusing Bertazzon, who had never resided in Sydney, with Carmagnola. He wrote:

> Bertazzon is closely connected with the Matteotti Club in Melbourne, which is an anti-fascist organisation. He is also known to have been connected with the Communist Party when in Sydney, and he moved to Melbourne to endeavour to organise the anti-fascist Italian element there, as an Italian adjunct to the Communist Party of Australia. His actions had the support of the Central Executive in Sydney and it was strongly suspected that he had been aided in establishing his anti-fascist publications which were ultimately to assume undisguised communistic sympathies ... It is highly undesirable to permit foreigners to spread subversive propaganda among their own people, who are not in a position to judge for themselves.[77]

Yet, the mantra of communist subversion did not work. On 30 April 1931, Strahan wrote to Jones, advising him that approval had been granted for the publication of *La Riscossa* and *L'Avanguardia Libertaria*.[78] The only avenue left to Jones was to express to his subordinates his surprise at the Prime Minister's decision, and to ask them to report to him any "breach of the peace" on the part of the two anarchists.[79] Indeed, Carmagnola and Bertazzon continued to challenge the Australian as well as the Italian conservative order. In June 1930 thousands of copies of a leaflet titled *Patria* (Fatherland) were distributed in North Queensland and mailed to several addresses in Italy, to the chagrin of fascist officials. The leaflet claimed "we have nothing, nothing! We, the disinherited, have only our labour, and are compelled to sell it to our exploiters for a pittance ... why must we tolerate the insults of those who are persecuting us?" The Italian Consulate in Townsville, entrusted to find its culprits, was unsuccessful. Rome was informed that "there are in Halifax several co-nationals (approximately one thousand), among them there are many subversive elements and *fuoriusciti* (political refugees), and the identity [of the sender} is absolutely impossible to prove".[80]

However, Carmagnola's and Bertazzon's victory was short-lived. At the December 1931 elections, Scullin was defeated and the staunch Catholic sympathiser of Mussolini, the United Australia Party leader Joseph Aloysius Lyons, became Prime Minister. The conservative victory gave an opportunity to people objecting to the "subversive" nature of the two newspapers to seek their suppression. In March 1932 the Queensland government submitted a request to ban *La Riscossa*, preceded in February by a similar, predictable demand by Consul-General Grossardi. Jones reiterated that "this publication can be regarded as likely to cause a breach of the peace and I am strongly of the opinion that the permission granted in April 1931 be now withdrawn".[81]

Ironically, the Criminal Investigation Branch, although Melbourne's Italian Consulate made available a copy of the paper, had no other issues on which to base its assessment. Consequently, "in order to keep the paper under review", Inspector Browne wrote, "I have sent a small subscription to Queensland, 'as from an Italian', in order to receive further issues when published. Recent back numbers have also been asked for".[82] At that time *La Riscossa* was published in Ingham, Queensland, where in October 1931 Carmagnola had moved for work reasons. The first issue, a "circular" printed on 5 December, reported that "we have amongst us since several weeks comrade F. Carmagnola". The last issue printed in Melbourne had come out on 20 October 1931, while in Ingham only three numbers were published, respectively on 5 December 1931 and 15 January and 15 March 1932. *L'Avanguardia Libertaria* lasted a little longer, its last number being dated 15 November 1932. However, the life of both newspapers was doomed. John Greig Latham, Lyons' Attorney-General, advised the Prime Minister on 15 August 1932 that "permission to publish these papers should be withdrawn". On 18 November 1932, J.G. McLaren, Secretary of the Prime Minister's Department, advised Jones that consent to publish the two newspapers had been withdrawn "and that the publisher, Mr. I. Bertazzon, has been so informed".[83]

By the early 1930s, several factors contributed to the waning of anarchist activities in Australia, among them the demoralising effect of grassroots, persistent and hostile surveillance by Australian and Italian fascist authorities, ideological splits on how to fight fascism, the economic effects of the Great Depression, personality issues and internal dissent. Even without the prompting by fascist Consuls, the Criminal Investigation Branch kept watch on the activities of the Matteotti Club. Inspector Browne reported to Jones that its officers in June 1930 attended the Club's functions, "as in former years", and obtained at the Club the first issue *of L'Avanguardia Libertaria*, "a new publication, for which it appears I. Bertazzon is responsible". Despite scurrilous allegations by Grossardi, Browne made the comment that "the meeting, which was held at the Matteotti Club, was orderly, and apparently of a nature to which exception could not be taken, except perhaps by Italian Fascists, whose ideals of liberty may not be in accordance with those prevailing in this Commonwealth".[84] Occasionally, the Club was raided by police. In October 1930, during two searches, a loaded gun, a hunting knife and "subversive" literature were seized.[85] Bertazzon was singled out on account of his publications. In January 1929, H.E. Jones instructed Inspector Browne to have Bertazzon interviewed by Senior Detective Sainsbury concerning the publication of *Sempre Avanti* and *An Appeal to the People of Australia*, that Grossardi has sent to the Prime Minister, complaining that the latter contained "a bitter attack against fascism" and asking "to have it stopped". Jones ordered that Sainsbury's report "should be in the form of evidence for the purpose of prosecution, should such action be deemed advisable by the proper authorities". On 5 February 1929, the Senior Detective went to Bertazzon's home in Carlton and quizzed him on whether he or the Matteotti Club had sought permission to publish sheets in a foreign language. Bertazzon denied the Club's involvement and stated that "they are printed for me. I take the full responsibility. The first one was printed for the Matteotti Committee, and the same block has been used ever since". Browne's opinion was that Bertazzon believed that the issues were not a newspaper, that he had received legal advice as to his position and "will continue the publications whenever he has sufficient funds to do so".[86] Fascism's harassment was no less persistent, keeping him under quarterly surveillance. On 11 March 1930, Grossardi reported to Rome that "Bertazzon's claim that the anti-Fascist movement in Australia was harassed by local authorities is nor true ... but he is correct when he is referring to the constant surveillance carried out by this Royal Consulate ... my constant task is to monitor the activity of our subversives and to inform federal and state authorities of even the slightest infringement committed by them".[87]

Another situation that greatly contributed to the breakdown of the anarchist movement was the onslaught of the Great Depression. Carmagnola recollected in his florid language that "as in every family, when things start to go wrong, poverty enters the front door and love goes out of the window. Dissent began because some believed that they could run the Club better ... poverty was ever growing ... many anti-Fascists, advised by me, went to North Queensland, to go and cut cane, that was the only salvation ... the situation was disastrous, people who had a job were working at reduced time, in pitiful conditions, nobody could pay the Club's membership fee, nobody was spending any more, even the greatest beer drinker had stopped drinking".[88] Carmagnola and Isidoro Bertazzon would also try their luck in North Queensland.

Undoubtedly, one of the main causes for the demise of the Matteotti Club, the disappearance of anarchist propaganda and the decline of the anti-Fascist movement during the early 1930s was the internecine squabble in which the two undisputed leaders of the anti-Fascist movement in Australia, Francesco Carmagnola and Isidoro Bertazzon, became unexpectedly embroiled. Existing differences on the political line to pursue, personality issues and conflict on how better to use the Matteotti Club's dwindling financial resources became of public knowledge when, at the end of 1929, Bertazzon accused Carmagnola of having stolen from the Club's social fund the – for the time – considerable amount of one hundred pounds. The news was picked up in February 1930 by Sydney's Fascist paper *Il Corriere degli Italiani*, alleging that Carmagnola had bought with this money "a luxurious motor car".[89] In March 1930 the well informed Grossardi could wire Rome that "Carmagnola is the Secretary [of the Matteotti Club] and until a few weeks ago its President was the co-national Giuseppe Lesana. Following a large disappearance of funds, Lesana and Bertazzon had a serious quarrel with Carmagnola, whom they accused of embezzlement, and both resigned from the Club or were expelled. Thus, Carmagnola remained the unchallenged master of the Club, its members being seriously discontented ...[90] At the Matteotti Club's General Assembly, held on 17 August 1930, Isidoro Bertazzon, his brother Girolamo, Giuseppe Lesana and Giuseppe Da Conte were "expelled per *indegnità* (because unworthy)".[91] This was the sort of petty diatribe that might be expected to be found among little people in emigration, gradually becoming more detached from their origins.

The rift between the two anarchist leaders broke out in a mutually acrimonious campaign in the pages of *La Riscossa* and *L'Avanguardia Libertaria*. On 29 June 1930, *La Riscossa* published a declaration of support for Carmagnola by six members of the Club's Committee. Bertazzon, whose name was not made, was accused of mounting "a campaign of calumny and ignominious defamation" and of betraying the anti-fascist cause. In the following months, Carmagnola's paper published Letters to the Editor highly critical of Bertazzon. He was reproached for being ambitious, for pretending to be "an unacknowledged genius", for consorting with the fascists.[92] From December 1930, Carmagnola personally signed slanderous articles against his former comrade, charging him of "unbridled ambition", of being "worse than a fascist", "bilious", "a manic exhibitionist".[93]

Bertazzon was equally scathing from the columns of *L'Avanguardia Libertaria*. In November 1930, Carmagnola was indicted of "using everything and everybody in order to live in his repugnant brothel without having to work. His only ideal is his self interest". In the same article, Bertazzon stated that "it is almost one year since I accused the dictator of having dishonestly taken one hundred pounds form the social fund and, throughout this time, he has never denied my claim".[94] Carmagnola was also incriminated of consorting with fascist diehards by allowing one of them, Pietro Baffico, a squadrist alleged to have administered castor oil to anti-fascists and mistreated indigenous people while in Tripolitania, to come to the Matteotti Club and perform in a dancing exhibition.[95]

Their rift was never healed. Undoubtedly, Bertazzon and Carmagnola had a different character and personality. Many years later, in interviews given to the author, Carmagnola claimed that Bertazzon was resentful of him because he was widely known, "everybody was talking about me", while "he did not move from Melbourne, was always there ... In the evenings, often I could not go to his place, to chat, I had the Club, the newspaper ... he begrudged me, thinking

I wanted to become Prime Minister". According to Carmagnola, *Bertazzon si considerava importante, era di temperamento lunatico* (Bertazzon thought he was important, he was moody).[96] Impulsive by temperament, Carmagnola was always eager to look for a physical fight with the fascists, he preferred action to reflection. Bertazzon, on the other hand, was more inclined to pursue an intellectual course, to rely on propaganda rather than violence. This difference of character was also reflected in their different understandings of anarchism. Their dispute also exposed the narrow political horizon of the two leaders, who put their *faida di paese* (village feud) before the overarching strategy of fighting fascism.

In his newspaper, Bertazzon imputed to Carmagnola a lack of planning, of policy, manifested by his eagerness to act on the spur of the moment, without a long-term vision. Without mentioning him by name, Bertazzon believed that "alas, many, indeed most of our comrades seem to be hibernating, and come to life only when they discuss or approve something due to take place, perhaps, in the immediate future".[97] In a snipe against Carmagnola's obvious difficulty in writing fluently and with ideological rigour, Bertazzon made the point that "we do not entertain any particular grudge against *La Riscossa* that, poor thing, is never publishing articles of its own, but reprints articles [from other sheets], thus carrying out only a limited amount of propaganda".[98] Instead, from the first issue of *L'Avanguardia Libertaria*, Bertazzon underscored the importance of long-term planning. *Propaganda e preparazione* (propaganda and planning) was his catchcry. The task of the anarchist ought to be, he concluded in his editorial, "today, resistance and revolt, tomorrow, rebellion and struggle".[99] According to Carmagnola, Bertazzon favoured a rapprochement with the trade union movement, in order to obtain their support in fighting fascism, while Carmagnola unswervingly believed, with reason, that unionists were "racists of the first order" and *socialisti da caffelatte* (lukewarm socialists).[100] He scathingly condemned what to him looked like Bertazzon's treacherous inactivity: "It is not his fault if the great man

– who is always saying and writing that he will use the fascists for litter – when action is needed he is always staying in bed, acting like those [the Fascists] who say 'let's arm ourselves and you go and fight'. It is a matter of character".[101]

Bertazzon's editorials in *L'Avanguardia Libertaria* attest to his theoretical knowledge of anarchism and his impassioned appraisal of contemporary Australian and international political events. As well as the yearly commemorations of Sacco and Vanzetti, and the obituaries of anarchists who attempted Mussolini's life, among them Michele Schirru and Gino Lucetti, he commented on the defeat of Scullin's government (Il cambio della guardia, 1 February 1932), on May Day celebrations (1 May 1932), on the dismissal of NSW Premier Jack Lang (Politicantismo, 1 June 1932), on the suppression of *L'Avanguardia Libertaria* (Oscurantismo, 1 June 1932), on the execution by the regime of suspected *attentatori*, the anarchists Domenico Bovone and Angelo Sbardellotto (Sete di Sangue, 20 August 1932), on fascism's tenth anniversary (Dopo Dieci Anni, 1 October 1932). Like *La Riscossa*, also *L'Avanguardia Libertaria* reprinted articles written by prominent anarchists, among them Pietro Gori, Luigi Damiani, Sébastien Faure, Pyotr Kropotkin, Camillo Berneri, Errico Malatesta, Elisée Reclus and Luigi Galleani, the well-known Italian anarchist in the United States whose followers caused havoc with their dynamite bombings and assassination attempts during the "Red Scare" period of 1917-1920. When Galleani died in 1931, Bertazzon, who probably had met him in Seattle, sent his condolences to the family for the loss "of our comrade and teacher".[102] Bertazzon also published articles by people not belonging to the anarchist movement, among them Angelica Balabanoff and Emilio Lussu, illustrating his eagerness to muster support in the struggle against fascism also from the non-anarchist Left.

A regular contributor to *L'Avanguardia Libertaria* was Giacomo Pastega, born in 1900 at Possagno, in the province of Treviso, a miner by trade and Secretary of the Anti-Fascist League in Broken Hill. A vocal anarchist, his CPC file marking him as *attentatore*, Pastega's articles were always signed with his surname preceded by the name of a noted anarchist. For instance, Al limite estremo (To the Extreme Limit – 1 July 1930), dealing with British imperialism in India, was signed Ravachol Pastega, Nel Mondo della Lotta (In the World of Struggle – 15 September 1930), bore the name of Passanante, Il Domani (Tomorrow – 1 December 1930), that of Cipriani. His articles were highly charged, inciting violence. He claimed that "today action is needed" and "let us defend tomorrow's better world with fire and the iron, with poison and the powerful voice of dynamite, without pity, without mercy".[103] Despite Pastega's fire-and-brimstone articles, Bertazzon's ideological rift with Carmagnola was not on the issue of the use of dynamite or of assassination attempts. This fact was recognised by Carmagnola many years later, when he admitted that *le cose andavano molto male e c'era disaccordo fra gli antifascisti, per questioni di tendenza, per stupidaggini, o per questioni di nome, che uno voleva farsi vedere ed andare più in alto, queste cose capitano in politica* (things were going badly, there was disagreement among anti-fascists, on the political course of action, about foolish things, for personal reputation, someone wanted to look and be more important than others, these things do happen in politics).[104] Poverty and the rise and institution of the USSR as a major ideological menace were among the main factors causing the demise of the anarchist movement. Collections in favour of *L'Avanguardia Libertaria* were giving meagre results; from Broken Hill its supporters advised that "poverty here is reigning supreme", and that in Griffith there was "general unemployment", while in Sydney "the great economic crisis does not allow us to give more".[105] Even the Club Internazionale, founded after Bertazzon's expulsion from the Matteotti Club, in competition with the latter and with the purpose to gather Bertazzon's supporters, was compelled to close after seven months, following the loss of one thousand pounds. The Matteotti Club would linger until 15 December 1933, when it was officially closed.[106]

Bertazzon was well aware of the situation of widespread discouragement, economic stringency and breakdown in the unity of the movement. The editorial of the first issue of *L'Avanguardia Libertaria* reflected the sense of abject despair gripping the anarchist leader. In spite of it, he once again professed his indomitable faith in the principles that had guided his entire life. The newspaper was, he intimated "a brotherly tie among the scattered comrades in this vast country: a warning to the winners of the moment; an incitement to the lazy and the slumberers; a serene affirmation and an unshakeable faith which inspires us; and a newspaper which brings among the disbanded proletarian cells, lost in the harsh adversity of their exile, the message of revolt".[107] In order to galvanise his demoralised supporters, as well as to look for job opportunities for himself, between 1930 and 1932 Bertazzon was compelled to travel interstate. On 24 August 1930, his newspaper reported, with undisguised acrimony against Carmagnola, that Bertazzon had taken part in the "dignified" commemoration, "for the first time in Australia", of Sacco and Vanzetti at Melbourne's Gaiety Theatre, together with labour movement's stalwarts H. Payne, Sally Barker, Norman Romsey and Percy Laidler.[108] On 14 September he was in Griffith, where he gave three lectures, on "Il nostro antifascismo", "L"antifascismo in Australia" and "Dove andrà a finire il fascismo" to a crowded audience. One of the event organisers reported that "scattered over one hundred square miles, some alone, others with their wives and children [came] by every means of transport: bicycles, carriages, carts, trucks and autos, despite bad roads and rainy weather".[109]

In June 1931, Bertazzon returned to Tarrawanna, near Griffith, where he spoke, "keeping for three hours the large audience in admiring silence" and collected funds totalling only one pound, because "more could not be given, as almost everyone is unemployed from a long period".[110] The following month Bertazzon went to North Queensland. *L'Avanguardia Libertaria* reported that "for the last two months comrade Isidoro Bertazzon has been among us for work reasons". On 23 August he and Francesco Fantin commemorated Sacco and Vanzetti at Wooree, near Cairns, and collected five pounds for the children of jailed anarchists, that they sent for distribution to anarchist Carlo Frigerio in Geneva.[111] At the end of 1931, Bertazzon was still in North Queensland. On 22 November, he gave a lecture in Ayr on "Mali e Rimedi" (Ills and Remedies) of the then all-encompassing economic crisis.[112] In May 1932 Bertazzon again went back to Griffith, where he celebrated May Day, a day of "libertarian faith, of revolutionary promise and intent", and on 21 August he spoke at the fifth anniversary of the execution of Sacco and Vanzetti. This event was held at Melbourne's Matteotti Club, then no longer under the control of Carmagnola and his faithful.[113]

With the banning of *L'Avanguardia Libertaria*, the scattering throughout Australia of his comrades, his unsuccessful quest for a job and the collapse of organised anarchist activities, Bertazzon decided to move from Melbourne permanently and come and settle in Griffith, where previously he had struck up a number of friendships. On 12 June 1933, he mortgaged from a Robert Stuart Wilson the 32-acre orchard farm number 2187 at Beelbangera. Most probably, Wilson was a veteran from World War I who on 23 July 1923 had been assigned a farm in the Murrumbidgee Irrigation Area. Bertazzon paid six hundred pounds cash and took a loan of 773 pounds from the Rural Bank of New South Wales to complete the transaction.[114] The regime's spies promptly brought his new abode to Rome's attention. On 16 December 1933, Guido Leto, Head of the Political Police (Polpol) of the Ministry of the Interior was informed that *Bertazzon risiede a Griffith*.[115]

The property at 131 Station Street, Carlton, where Isidoro Bertazzon and his brother Girolamo had lived since the mid-1920s, was sold in the mid-1930s to a Miss Whitworth of North Fitzroy, who on her turn sold it in 1937 to Vincenzo and Caterina Storino.[116] Girolamo Bertazzon and his family moved to a farm at 487 Whitehorse Road, Balwyn, on the outskirts of Melbourne. On 23 December 1938, Isidoro Bertazzon's movements were belatedly communicated to the Prefect of Treviso by one of the ever present fascist *fiduciari*, who claimed that "Bertazzon is occasionally living in Melbourne and is often going to Griffith for work related matters".[117]

From the time Bertazzon landed in Melbourne in 1922 until he settled in Griffith, ten years had lapsed. For him, this was a period of intense political activity, publishing leaflets and single-issue newspapers, collaborating with *La Riscossa* and editing *L'Avanguardia Libertaria*, co-managing the Matteotti Club, taking part in rallies, marches and celebrations, delivering speeches, fundraising, subscribing to the overseas anarchist press, keeping correspondence with leading anarchist intellectuals in Italy and other European countries, and donating money, albeit in modest amounts, to worthwhile anarchist and anti-fascist causes. His name was found in the papers of Errico Malatesta, seized by Polpol even before the latter's death in Rome on 22 July 1932, and in an address book of Camillo Berneri, "confidentially" obtained, that is, stolen, in 1929, by the fascist Secret Service operating under the quizzical acronym of OVRA (probably staying for Opera Volontaria Repressione Antifascismo), when Berneri was living in exile in Bruxelles. Bertazzon was also a regular donor to Malatesta's activities, even during periods of economic stress. Polpol learned from Malatesta's papers that in 1925 Bertazzon had sent him two remittances of lire 130 and lire 56.50, and in 1926 another two remittances of lire 65 and lire 126 respectively.[118] Among European anarchists corresponding with Bertazzon were the already mentioned Pasquale Binazzi in La Spezia, and the Milanese Ugo Fedeli, to whom Bertazzon sent in 1932 the February and March copies of *L'Avanguardia Libertaria*, containing instalments of J. W. Fleming's *Storia del Movimento Anarchico in Australia*.[119]

As well as maintaining contacts with several anarchists abroad, throughout his life Bertazzon subscribed to quite a number of journals and newspapers. As already mentioned, during his stay in Seattle he received and distributed a considerable amount of anarchist press, including Galleani's *Cronaca Sovversiva* and Binazzi's *Il Libertario*. In 1923 he was subscribing to Palermo's *Vespro Anarchico*[120] and in 1928 Australian Customs seized the anarchist weekly *Il Monito* (The Admonition), that he was receiving from Paris.[121] Even in secluded Beelbangera, after 1933, Bertazzon continued to read "subversive" newspapers. He was on the list of subscribers to *Giustizia e Libertà* compiled by Polpol,[122] was receiving Communist literature from the Party's underground centre in Paris[123] and since 1929, although living in Melbourne, he was on the list of Italian emigrants in the United States who were "anarchist sympathisers, contributing funds to help their comrades and for propaganda purposes".[124]

Although there is no evidence linking Bertazzon to bombing attacks, despite the CPC marking him as *attentatore,* the same cannot be said for other anarchists in Australia. Paramount is the case for the contributor to *L'Avanguardia Libertaria*, as well as to Paris' *Lotta Anarchica*, San Francisco's *L'Emancipazione* and Melbourne's *La Riscossa*, the *attentatore* Giacomo Pastega. Broken Hill's Secretary of the Lega Antifascista, working in the local mines, Pastega stored under his house a box of gelignite sticks. According to a biographical profile drafted by Treviso's Prefect, in June 1927 he used them against the homes of people deemed to be members of or sympathising with the Fascist Party, in particular against an Alvise Oliviero, who had caused Pastega's arrest by the Italian Carabinieri when he was "involved in a terrorist action, including the throwing of grenades against Schio's factories". Sydney's Vice-Consul Mario Carosi reported that Oliviero was in fear of his life, was "armed" and his residence was under constant police protection.[125] In October 1927 Pastega and his cousin Angelo Cunial had been sentenced *in absentia* to a jail term of two-and-a-half years and 3,000 lire fine for slandering Mussolini in a letter sent to Possagno's *Podestà* (Mayor), hailing Malatesta and the anarchists involved in the bombing of Milan's Diana Theatre and calling the Italian dictator "a snake".[126] Unexpectedly, in February 1931 Pastega wrote another letter to Possagno's *Podestà*, abjuring his anarchism, which he described as "a moment of folly", seeking membership to the Fascist Party and declaring that he had decided to "return to the fatherland, till the fields and marry".[127] Following his unsuccessful plea, Pastega reverted to his usual anarchist self. He was not alone in his attempt to change sides for personal benefit, ill-placed patriotism or because he was disappointed at the resilience of the regime. During the 1930s scores of anti-fascists embraced fascism and, alternatively, many young fascists were attracted by communism, as well described in Davide Layolo's novel *I voltagabbana* (The Turncoats). In July 1932 Pastega sent a threatening letter to Guido Cristini, President of the Special Tribunal for the Defence of the State that had sentenced to death the anarchist Michele Schirru. In it, Pastega bombastically declared that "if you are going to use guns against us, we will use dynamite against you, if you will machine gun us, we will blow you up with nitroglycerine".[128] However, with the passing of time, romance took over Pastega's revolutionary yearnings. In April 1939 he became engaged to Veronica Esposito from Viggiano, from the southern province of Potenza, and later they married. Eventually, his anarchism sank into oblivion.[129]

For all his bluster, Pastega did not aim to kill. Other Italian anarchists in Australia, although having tumultuous pasts, were also averse to violence. Gaetano Panizzon, allegedly involved in the bombing of Milan's Diana Theatre, came to Melbourne in January 1922, soon after the event. His only overt act of "sedition" took place in 1926, when he returned for a brief period to his birthplace, Magré di Schio. Here, he organised a petition in favour of Sacco and Vanzetti, and sent it to the United States Embassy in Rome. For the remainder of his life in Australia he laid low, keeping, vouched Vicenza's Prefect, "a good moral conduct".[130] Another anarchist, Giacomo Argenti from Capoliveri (Isola d'Elba), at an early age had had a brush with the law in August 1897, when he was fined 15 lire for swimming "completely naked".[131] In 1908 he began subscribing to La Spezia's *Il Libertario* and in 1913 to Elba's *Il Martello*. His name apperared in Malatesta's address book and in 1914 he was corresponding with the anarchist Giovanni Solari in Boston, Massachussets. Having emigrated to San Francisco from September 1911 to June 1912, he returned to Capoliveri for health reasons. In 1918, Argenti was fined 50 lire for illegal possession of a dynamite stick, and in 1923 was sentenced for a jail term of three years for possession of three sticks of dynamite, but was amnestied on 5 November 1923. In his defence, he claimed that the explosive material had been placed in his room by his jilted lover. On 22 November 1925 Argenti sailed from Naples for Adelaide. While in Australia, he shunned political activities but got into trouble again with the fascist authorities in 1931 when, on the eve of his return to Italy, an anonymous denunciation from Melbourne alleged that he was planning to attempt Mussolini's life. On 22 December, Arturo Bocchini, Chief of Police, issued instructions to closely watch Argenti upon his arrival in Italy. It was a false alarm. Argenti had gone to Italy not to become an anarchist martyr, but to see whether he could find a job and, unable to resettle, had returned to Adelaide where he, in dire economic straits, found employment as a waterside worker. In May 1940, the "bully" and "impulsive" anarchist, as the Prefect of Livorno had described him, having abandoned since 1923 any political activity, humiliated himself by asking the Adelaide Vice-Consul whether he could forward to Mussolini a plea in favour of his son, who wanted to study singing in Italy. Since 29 April 1934 Argenti's son Gualberto had regularly attended Adelaide's Fascist Branch School. As was the case for many anarchists and anti-fascists, time, economic necessity and hopelessness had inexorably sapped Argenti's ideological fibre.[132]

An examination of CPC files on Italian anarchists in Australia, or presumed so (often anarchists were classified as communists, and vice-versa), held by Italian authorities confirms that they were not involved, either individually or in groups, in bombings aimed at provoking death and destruction. Australia scarcely had such a tradition, after all. Even Pastega's use of dynamite sticks in Broken Hill was made to intimidate, not to kill alleged fascists who, as Oliviero stated to Vice-Consul Carosi, "were not unduly worried" because, instead of exploding the device near his home, "if a serious attempt were planned, it would have been easy to throw the gelignite stick inside the house, as all front doors are never locked".[133] The use of bluster rather than bombs was confirmed by Carmagnola in an interview with the author, in which he maintained that "the anarchists were not ready to act in a violent way", although "we were ready to bomb if the fascists would have been serious", and that "we were in contact with anarchist bombers in the USA". In Australia, Carmagnola went on, "the anarchists were almost all individualist, not organisers" and could not tolerate swaggering comrades, as demonstrated by the fact that a certain "Fontana was expelled from the Anti-Fascist League. He was speaking in a violent way, to burn things down. He was expelled".[134]

The *de facto* eschewing terror and the natural drift into inaction by most Italian anarchists was an endorsement of Bertazzon's policy of alliances to fight international fascism, the state and the Church, outlined in the editorial Ai Compagni (To our Comrades) in the first issue of *L'Avanguardia Libertaria*. "We, Italians in Australia", he wrote, "are in many thousands, more or less violently torn from our dearest next-of-kin and work places and thrown into the vortex of a new life to seek our bread. Many hundreds of us have carried here the fire of passion, vowing to again cross the ocean at the first sign of resurgence, not because of the call of the fatherland, but because there ... we know we may most profitably resume our struggle ... But exile for us cannot only be a matter of hoping and waiting ... We cannot desert the place our faith is commanding us to defend".[135] However, the reality of the situation was that the endurance and the international successes of fascism, the Great Depression and the collapse of anti-fascist unity left anarchists to only hope and wait. In 1933, the Italian Consul-General in Sydney exulted at the demise of a vocal opposition to fascism. "The Italian communist and anti-fascist element", Marquis Agostino Ferrante claimed, "is totally isolated ... Today, I am happy to report that anti-fascism in the Italian settlements in Australia has disappeared, with the exception of some small enclaves in Queensland, such as Ingham and Innisfail".[136]

By 1933, Isidoro Bertazzon, *uno dei più pericolosi avversari del Regime ... sempre in prima fila in tutte le manifestazioni di carattere sovversivo (*one of the Regime's most dangerous enemies ... always to the forefront in all subversive rallies), as Consul-General Grossardi had characterised him[137] had withdrawn at Beelbangera. However, he maintained his rage and continued in his opposition to fascism even from the isolation of his outpost on the plains of Western New South Wales. In 1935, Sydney's Acting Consul-General Buoninsegni Vitali reported that "he is known as the leader of the local subversive movement and his home is always visited by local anti-fascists".[138] In 1937 he began correspondence with the anarchist "Pro-Spain" Committee in Paris and was behind (*l'istigatore*) some letters written by Griffith residents condemning Italy's aggression against Ethiopia.[139] In Griffith, members of the anti-fascist movement included Angelo Pastega, brother of the above-mentioned Giacomo. Angelo had emigrated to Adelaide in February 1914, in January 1921 married Luigia and on 8 July 1924 acquired Farm 1290 in Griffith, a 12.5-acre fruit orchard near the one that Bertazzon would purchase in 1933.[140] Reports in his CPC file describe him as a communist who had sent letters to Possagno's parish priest defaming the state and religion. In 1934, Consul-General Agostino Ferrante commented that in Griffith he was "known for his anti-fascist feelings" and "is associating with subversive people", while in 1937 Acting Consul-General Marocco reported that Angelo Pastega "is considered as one of the anti-fascist leaders, although he is not carrying out significant political activity".[141] Another Italian anarchist farmer in Griffith was Domenico Cunial, owner of Farm 1875, a relative of the above-mentioned Angelo Cunial, who in 1930 also had moved from Broken Hill to Griffith, and in 1937 went to Innisfail, Queensland. In 1937, Domenico was joined by his young relative Andrea, a farmer from Possagno, who arrived in Sydney on 15 November on board the *MV Romolo*.[142]

Indeed, after fascism's aggression against Ethiopia and its intervention in the Spanish Civil War, the anarchist diaspora prevented any significant activity. Anarchists marked as "dangerous" in the CPC, like Umberto Maggiani from La Spezia, corresponding from Australia with anarchist fellow citizen Pasquale Binazzi and having previously been sentenced to five years' *confino* (forced residence elsewhere) but fugitive in Australia, or Giuseppe Farina, *attentatore*, being in disgrace because caught singing *Bandiera Rossa* (Red Flag) while intoxicated, were still kept under close watch by the regime's spies.[143] At times, fascist authorities misrepresented the allegiance of known anarchists such as Francesco Carmagnola, who was marked in the CPC as a communist, or as Valentino Ciotti and Mario Tardiani, generally classified as "anti-fascist". This confusion was in part due to the dismal political education shown by police informers, Prefects and Polpol analysts, generally not privy to the ideological nuances of the Left. It also reflected on the lack of doctrinal rigour on the part of the *sovversivi,* who often claimed to be at the same time anti-fascist, anarchist and communist. In an interview with the author, Carmagnola reiterated that he never *mi sono messo col Partito Comunista* (I never joined the Communist Party), albeit admitting that "having printed *Il Risveglio* with the communists' help put the anarchists in trouble".[144] By 1933, any significant, public act of anarchist militancy in Australia, in Italy and in most places, except Spain, had practically ended.

Facing a desperate situation in the face of fascism's increasing international popularity and of the Great Depression, it would have been easy to give up the struggle. Not for Isidoro Bertazzon. In the last issue of *L'Avanguardia Libertaria* of 15 November 1932, he published an article titled L'Anarchismo, signed "Indomitable Wanderer" but probably written by him, where he outlined what could be considered his political testament. "There are comrades who believe that the time of political agitation has ended ... that any collective action has no purpose ... who baulk (*tentennano*) ... We modestly believe that we need to keep alive in the masses the will to redeem themselves and to regain their freedom ... We remain anarchists even if it were true that anarchy will not triumph tomorrow ... To the disbelieving, the disheartened, the defeated and the traitors (*venduti*) we say: go away, We continue fighting (*restiamo sulla breccia*), confident that the masses will rebel and resume the struggle."

During 1933 Isidoro Bertazzon withdrew to Beelbangera with his unwedded partner Bruna Franceschini, whom he had probably met at one of Matteotti Club's meetings or dancing nights. Bruna was born on 30 October 1910 in Fredericktown, Pennsylvania, the daughter of Giovanni Franceschini and Rosa De Rosa. Both parents were from the village of San Foca, in the province of Pordenone, where they married on 17 February 1906. On 21 November 1907 Giovanni, with US$30 in his pocket, sailed from Naples for the United States on board the *SS Re D'Italia*, "to leave the poverty of the village behind and make a new start".[145] The ship's manifest recorded that Giovanni Franceschini was 25 years of age, a labourer, was born at San Quirino (a village some four kilometers south of San Foca), was five feet and seven inches tall, with brown eyes and hair, and was going to join his "cousin Franceschini Angelo [at] Fredericktown". On the same ship, as shown by the passengers' manifest, were also Angelo's wife, Dina Fioretto, aged 27, and their sons Massimiliano, aged 3, and Fioravante, aged 2. They too were born at San Quirino. Dina's mother, Carolina Fioretto, was living at San Foca. Dina declared that she had only US $25 in her possession, less than the US$50 required by US Immigration authorities. The manifest registered that upon arrival at Ellis Island, both Dina and the children were admitted at the Station's hospital for an undisclosed illness, and later discharged.

Giovanni Franceschini's wife Rosa and their daughter Mary, born on 27 November 1906, followed him one year later. Giovanni was an anarchist, having embraced this faith in San Foca, where he witnessed "social injustice", and "kept these ideals throughout his life, implementing them in a most altruistic and unassuming manner".[146] Like many Italian migrants holding anarchist beliefs, he was fortunate to slip through the net of American screening at Ellis Island. Before arriving at New York, the Master of the *SS Re d'Italia* had to sign an affidavit swearing that no passenger on the ship was "an idiot or imbecile or a feeble minded person, or a prostitute", or "an anarchist". Understandably, Master Cignoni was very lax in assessing Giovanni Franceschini's political beliefs if, at question 21 of the passengers' manifest, asking "Whether an Anarchist", he wrote "no". In Fredericktown the Franceschinis bore four children, Bruna, Gori, born on 16 January 1912, Boris, born on 20 September 1914 and Teresa, born on 22 December 1918. Gori was named after Pietro Gori, and Boris after some Russian activist, perhaps Boris Souvarine. In Fredericktown, Giovanni was employed in the coalmines and had very close anarchist friends.

The Franceschinis planned to move to California, where they also had friends, but around 1920 returned to Italy, to comfort Giovanni's distraught mother and other family members after, in late 1915, three of Giovanni's sisters and one brother were killed by a land mine in a field near where they were living. They made repeated attempts to return to the USA but were not able to obtain a visa as there had been a quota system introduced. Feeling unsafe in San Foca due to his political beliefs – in 1941 he declared that "he left Italy about the time that the Fascist Party were obtaining power there, and that he is, in his political beliefs, opposed to the policy of that Party"[147] – Giovanni Franceschini emigrated to Australia on the *MV Caprera*, arriving in Melbourne on 29 June 1925. His wife Rosa and their children joined him, after arriving on board the *MV Caprera* on 16 August 1929.[148] The family settled in Glenmaggie, near Heyfield, in Victoria, where Giovanni worked for wages on a farm. His anarchist beliefs did not attract the attention of fascist or Australian authorities. On the contrary, in 1941 Melbourne's Investigation Branch vouched that Giovanni Franceschini "has been the subject of a number of favourable reports by this office to the Department of the Interior. He is of good character and loyal". Obviously, the Australian authorities were not aware of the fact that Giovanni Franceschini, while in the United States, had kept contact with and received literature from Luigi Galleani.[149] In April of that year Giovanni applied for the Attorney-General's consent to purchase a property, apparently disused for two years, at Narre Warren, near Dandenong, Victoria, to manage, together with his son Gori, as a vegetable and poultry farm. Consent was granted, on grounds that there was "no evidence of the existence of a strong feeling against the acquisition ... by naturalised persons of enemy origin".[150] All Franceschini children were staunch anarchists. Boris was for some time President of the Casa d'Italia, an anti-fascist organisation set up in Melbourne at the end of the 1930s. During the war, he worked on his father's farm at Narre Warren, then later as a woodcutter, a concreter, finally settling into the marble business. Even during the harsh years of the Depression, the Franceschinis contributed financially to the anarchist cause. For instance, in August 1932 Giovanni donated the – for the time – not insignificant amount of one pound, fourteen shillings and sixpence to *L'Avanguardia Libertaria*, and in February 1931 Boris gave one pound towards *La Riscossa*.[151] Given the small size of the Italian community in Melbourne at the end of the 1920s, it was natural for the Franceschini's to seek friendships and to socialise within the anti-fascist and anarchist environment offered by the Matteotti Club. After the Second World War Boris Franceschini maintained contacts with Italian comrades, especially during the difficult years of the "strategy of tension" in the 1970s, when anarchists were wrongly charged of having committed terrorist crimes, in particular the bombing of Milan's Banca dell'Agricoltura in Piazza Fontana. Boris was a regular contributor to Milan's *Editrice A*, Ancona's *L'Internazionale*, Livorno's *Umanità Nuova*, Reggio Emilia's Centro Studi Camillo Berneri until his death in Melbourne on 26 August 1986. His brother Gori had died a few months earlier, on 8 April 1986.

While living in Melbourne with his brother Girolamo and his family, Isidoro Bertazzon carried out an active social life. As already mentioned, Francesco Carmagnola used to dine at the Bertazzons before their split. Photographs held by Carlton's Italian Historical Society attest to the lively atmosphere at their home in Station Street, with gatherings, parties, and music enjoyed from a gramophone built by one of their comrades, Mr De Santis. Girolamo's son, Luigi, sculpted a bust of his sister Chiara, and Chiara, wearing an Italian regional costume, was portrayed marrying Osvaldo Rigutto after celebrating Carnevale at the Matteotti Club. This atmosphere of camaraderie was predominant also at Beelbangera, where Bruna Franceschini used to host almost daily Italian friends from neighbouring farms and from Griffith, as well as visiting anarchist comrades. Bruna was a very outgoing and strong-willed woman with a great sense of humour and fun. Although little is known of their daily life between 1933 and 1938, a wealth of information is available from the diaries that Bruna kept in 1939 and 1940. Incidentally, in 1934 fascist informers had also found it difficult to monitor Bertazzon's life and activities. The Prefect of Treviso, who regularly had Bertazzon's mother's house in Pieve di Soligo raided, in search of information on the *sovversivo*, wrote to the CPC that "despite further investigations, it was not possible to find out

Bertazzon's address overseas, as he continues not to give news about himself to relatives and friends".[152]

Conditions in what was a recent settlement in the New South Wales outback were harsh. Extreme high temperatures in summer sapped Bruna's energy. On 11 January 1939 she wrote that "it is very hot. I am getting desperate. Only one inch of water in the tank". Heat and hard work contributed to her frequent headaches, tiredness and depression. The entry on 15 February 1939 read "am sick of working for nothing", that of 13 May 1939 "did more gardening. It seems to be an endless job", on 2 April 1939 "severe headache at night", on 26 January 1940 "getting headaches all the time", on 15 March 1940 "a most awful bilious attack, worse on record", and on 14 January 1940 "don't know what the devil is wrong with me. I have such a hopeless feeling". Indeed, work was exhausting, picking grapes, peaches, oranges and peas, minding the chickens and the vegetable garden, making wine, going to the market to sell the produce. On the other hand, the diaries document Bruna's and Isidoro's (Isy, as she called him) busy social life. They visited or were visited almost daily by their local Italian and Australian farming friends, the Toniolos, Pietrobellis, Rossettos, Giudicis, Sorrentinos, Faveros, Turrins and Crockers, just to mention a few. Bruna was very close to Mrs Zili. Cooking, knitting, reading, going to picnics, dances and to the pictures were also frequent pastimes, as well as some infrequent trips to Melbourne, to visit family and friends. Undoubtedly, the most rewarding aspect of life for Bruna was to live there with Isidoro. On 16 April 1940 she entered in her diary: "Quite happy just with Isy".

The diaries do not make mention of Isidoro's political meetings at the farm with his anarchist comrades, although they record, albeit in a generic fashion, Bruna's, and presumably Isidoro's, increasing concern for and feelings towards the worsening international situation. On 28 January 1939 she wrote "Bad news from Spain", and on 4 September "It seems so ironical this war, which is the will of some people and it is on us like a tidal wave, something which we cannot stop. One feels so miserable and helpless". The entry at the end of the year read "So ended 1939. One lives and hopes". Yet, it was with Italy's joining the world conflict that her anguish increased. On 11 June 1940 she wrote "Italy entered the war. How horrible, will all this ever end?" and, two days later, "This war is getting me down. Will we ever be able to feel happy again and will this war ever end? Jen Crocker came here, all we think and talk about is war, war, war". Her entries on the subject became more frequent. 17 June: "Quite upset about war news"; 18 June: "News bit better, still hoping for the salvation of the world"; 30 June: "Good news about Marshal Balbo's death, hope Mussolini follows"; 5 July: "Wish the war was ended"; 11 July: "Wish the war would end"; 11 August: "This war is awful"; 25 August: "Will this war ever finish? Makes me ill to think of it"; 3 September: "One year of war, when will it end? It seems terrible to think it may last for years yet"; 10 September: "News from the war bad. Will it ever finish?". Bruna's last entry in her diary, written on 20 September, one day before her death, is almost a political testament, outlining her wish for a better future: "Hope war will be finished and hope we will be happier about all international affairs".

The war affected Bruna and Isidoro directly. Bruna, being born in Fredericktown, was an American citizen, a country then having declared its neutrality. Isidoro had never sought to take up the Certificate of Naturalisation and still was an Italian subject. On 6 August 1940, according to her diary, Bruna had to go to Griffith's Police Station, "to get questioned". On 26 August the police went to Bertazzon's farm, evidently for the same reason. At the beginning of that month, enquiries had been made in Melbourne about his whereabouts. Police interviewed, without much success, Luigi Bertazzon and the previous and current owners of the house in Station Street, Carlton, Miss Whitworth and Caterina Storino. They also questioned a naturalised Italian who, as the police report stated, "for obvious reasons desires to remain anonymous". The man obviously knew Bertazzon, and gave an unsympathetic account of him. Bertazzon, he stated, "had been associated with two men also Italians named Sacco and Vanzetta [sic] ... He is an anarchist ... although he received only a scanty education in Italy he has improved his knowledge since he left that country and he is now regarded as a highly educated man". This anonymous informant also considered Bertazzon to be "a menace to the community ... and as he was always well supplied with money he is of the opinion that he had another source of supply apart from his earnings". In exchange for this information, the interviewing police officer recorded that the informant was "desirous to ascertain whether this man [Bertazzon] has been placed in a concentration camp".[153]

Most probably Bertazzon, like many other diehard anarchist antifascists, among them Francesco Fantin and Valentino Ciotti, would have been interned, were it not for his and Bruna's sudden and tragic death. According to Bruna's diary, on 19 September 1940 their old friend Harry Barcan had arrived from Melbourne to visit them. Barcan, a Londoner from Russian Jewish background, had come to Australia in his early '20s and was managing a bookshop in Elsternwick. Holding very left-wing political views, he had met Bertazzon at the Matteotti Club. Two days after his arrival, on the morning of 21 September, while all three were returning to Beelbangera from Griffith, the Chevrolet truck driven by Bertazzon was struck at a level crossing by an incoming goods train travelling from Temora to Griffith. They were killed instantly. At the inquest, held on 10 October 1940, the locomotive driver declared in his sworn affidavit that "I saw the driver of the lorry first, he accelerated when he saw me, in my opinion to beat the train over. When his vehicle fouled the line, the engine struck him ... The driver of the lorry made no effort to deviate from his course".[154]

On 9 July 1937, Bertazzon had executed his Will in the chambers of Cater & Blumer Solicitors, Griffith, leaving his estate to Bruna and, in case of her death, to her father Giovanni Franceschini. As Bruna was also the nominated Executor of the Will, after their death the estate was administered by Sydney's Public Trustee. In 1943, the Public Trustee advised that all assets in the estate had been sold and "absorbed in the payment of a dividend on claims against the deceased's estate". Upon going through Isidoro's and Bruna's personal papers, the Trustee's local agent found that, in his words, "they were concerned in subversive activities". The documents were given for appropriate action to Griffith Police. They were never returned to the family.[155] Neither Giovanni Franceschini nor other family members benefited from the disposal of the estate. Bruna's sister, Teresa, recovered after the accident Bruna's "wedding" ring and her wristwatch. Both items had to be purchased from the Public Trustee.[156]

Isidoro Bertazzon's tragic death ended a life lived with a staunch belief in the realisation of a libertarian society, of a classless society, a society free from tyranny and oppression. In 1918 Vladimir Ilyich Lenin contemptuously stated that "the majority of Anarchists think and write about the future without understanding the present".[157] To some extent, the Bolshevik leader's aphorism characterises the life and activities carried out by Isidoro Bertazzon and by his Italian anarchist comrades in Australia. They had to go through, from an early age, exploitation by capitalists in Schio and Piovene, hunger and alienation in their birthplace, emigration, work in an alien and hostile land and, perhaps most hurting, the lack of solidarity from their fellow workers. Throughout their life they were hunted like animals by fascism's cronies, even in the furthest corners of the world, even in places with unpronounceable names like Beelbangera. They never constituted a real threat to the "established order". As Giovanni Giolitti, five times the Prime Minister of Italy between 1892 and 1921, believed, according to one of his Prefects, irredentists were more irresponsible and damaging to the public interest than were anarchists.[158]

In fact, the anarchists represented little but themselves. Anarchism, except in Spain, was never a coherent philosophical position or a political movement. Most anarchists in Australia were against violence. Those who did take action were often loners and their attacks were disorganised attempts to punish the lackeys of fascism, rather than to subvert the capitalist status quo. They were ready to take up the torch on behalf of the oppressed, claiming to act on behalf of the working class but the gap between Italian anarchists and Australian workers widened because, in the opinion of the trade unions, the former were individualist, foreigners, sometime "scabs" and always "dagos". Their deeds did not weaken the state but antagonised the police and the government. Importantly, the working class began to have another way to express its aspirations. Even in Australia, especially during the 1930s, many anarchists turned to the labour movement and trade unions. Social democracy offered workers personal dignity, a sense of identity and a full place in society. They no longer felt isolated and at war with society. The lawful and constitutional route proved to be a more effective way of winning political and social rights and bringing about economic improvement.

Endnotes

1. Gianfranco Cresciani, '"Socialismo per la generazione presente". Rifugiati politici italiani e movimento socialista australiano', in: *Italian Historical Society Journal*, Vol. 20, 2012, pp. 1-24.
2. Moreno Marchi, *Emigrazione anarchica italiana in Australia, Libertarian Workers for a Self-Managed Society*, Melbourne 1988, pp. 8-9.
3. Amilcare Cipriani, in: Franco Andreucci and Tommaso Detti (Eds), *Il movimento operaio italiano. Dizionario biografico*, Editori Riuniti, Roma 1976, Vol. 2, pp. 48-51.
4. For a general history of Anarchism, see: George Woodcock, *Anarchism. A History of Libertarian Ideas and Movements*, Penguin Books, Harmondsworth, Middlesex, U.K. 1962. Also: James Joll, *The Anarchists*, Eyre & Spottiswoode, London 1964.
5. For more information on the CPC, see: Gianfranco Cresciani, 'Refractory Migrants. Fascist Surveillance on Italians in Australia, 1922-1943', in:

Altreitalie, Vol. 28, January-June 2004, pp.6-47.
6. Luigi Meneghello, *Libera Nos a Malo*, Mondadori, Milano 1986.
7. Lucio Avagliano, 'Un imprenditore e una fabbrica fuori del comune: Alessandro Rossi e il lanificio di Schio', in: Giorgio Mori (Ed.), *L'industrializzazione in Italia (1861-1900)*, Il Mulino, Bologna 1977, pp. 255-267.
8. Ezio Simini, 'Espulsione di operai e dinamiche sociodemografiche in un distretto industriale: l'emigrazione da Schio a fine Ottocento', in: Emilio Franzina (Ed.), *Un Altro Veneto. Saggi e studi di storia dell'emigrazione nei secoli XIX e XX*, Francisci Editore, Abano Terme (Padova) 1983, pp.49-66. Also, Emilio Franzina, *La grande emigrazione*, Marsilio Editori, Venezia 1976, pp.187-228.
9. Pietro Tresso, in: Franco Andreucci and Tommaso Detti, op. cit., vol. 5, pp.100-105.
10. Emilio Castellani, in: Franco Andreucci and Tommaso Detti, op. cit., vol. 1, pp. 532-534.
11. http://en.wikipedia.org/wiki/Luigi_Galleani, accessed 25 July 2012. Also, Luigi Galleani in: Franco Andreucci and Tommaso Detti, op. cit., vol. 2, pp. 418-424. On the Italian anarchist movement in Paterson, see: Salvatore Salerno, 'I delitti della razza bianca. Il discorso razziale degli anarchici italiani come reato', in: Jennifer Guglielmo and Salvatore Salerno (Eds.), *Gli italiani sono bianchi? Come l'America ha costruito la razza*, Il Saggiatore, Milano 2006, pp. 136-149.
12. Archivio Centrale dello Stato, Rome, Ministero dell'Interno, Direzione Generale di Pubblica Sicurezza, Casellario Politico Centrale (hereafter ACS-CPC). Busta 1408, codice identificativo C13321, Collet, Angelo Antonio. In 1940, the Public Trustee Office of NSW stated that while Girolamo Bertazzon was residing in Balwyn, Mount Albert, Victoria, Angelo still was in Pieve di Soligo, and Pietro was "last heard of as living in Paris, France". Of the Bertazzon's sisters, Luigia had married Ernesto Rossetto from Pieve di Soligo, Anna married Olivo Belle from the same village and Giuseppina was the wife of Luigi Spina, also from Pieve di Soligo (National Archives of Australia, Canberra, Series A1401, Control symbol EPI302, Item barcode 4271961, Isadore Alessandro Bertazzon deceased, The Public Trustee Office to The Controller of Enemy Property, 8 October 1940).

13. ACS-CPC, Bertazzon, Isidoro, busta 551, Prefetto of Treviso, biographical note dated 27 May 1929.
14. http://ellisisland.org/search/shipmanifest.asp?MID=16896506760889400416&FNM=ISIDORO&LNM=BERTAZZON&PLNM, accessed on 3 August 2012. See also: Thomas Guglielmo, ' "Nessuna barriera del colore". Italiani, razza e potere negli Stati Uniti', in: Jennifer Guglielmo and Salvatore Salerno (Eds.), *Gli italiani sono bianchi?* op. cit., p.50.
15. In the *MV Liguria*'s ship manifest, Bertazzon gave his father's name as his living next-of-kin, while his 1917 CPC file attests that Luigi was already dead.
16. http://en.wikipedia.org/wiki/Industrial_Workers_of_the_World, and http://ita.anarchopedia.org/Storia_dell'anarchismo_negli_Stati_Uniti, accessed 2 August 2012.
17. http://radsearem.wordpress.com/2010/03/05/march-5-1917-the-wobblies-on-trial/, accessed 30 June 2012.
18. James Green, 'La "Red Scare": la spinta alla deportazione degli stranieri sovversivi negli Stati Uniti (1917-1920), in: http://www.acoma.it/pdfvolumi/volume11/11green.pdf, accessed 15 June 2012.
19. Ibid.
20. Vincenzo Zaccagnini, Deferred Hearing, 7 December 1917, in: ACS-CPC, Bertazzon, Isidoro, busta 551.
21. Titino Dentino, Deferred Hearing, 6 December 1917, in: ACS-CPC, Bertazzon, Isidoro, busta 551. Also: National Archives of Australia, Canberra, Item A367, control symbol C1822G, "La Riscossa Libertaria" Isidore Bertazzon, Jones to Prime Minister's Department, 1 March 1928.
22. Ibid. Also, Annibale Scialdo, Deferred Hearing, 3 December 1917, in: ACS-CPC, Bertazzon, Isidoro, busta 551.
23. Costantino D'Ascenco, Deferred Hearing, 7 December 1917, in: ACS-CPC, Bertazzon, Isidoro, busta 551.
24. Battista Querio, Deferred Hearing, 7 December 1917, in: ACS-CPC, Bertazzon, Isidoro, busta 551.
25. Pietro Sandretti, Deferred Hearing, 7 December 1917, in: ACS-CPC, Bertazzon, Isidoro, busta 551.
26. Annibale Scialdo, Deferred Hearing, 3 December 1917, in: ACS-CPC, Bertazzon, Isidoro, busta 551.

27. ACS-CPC, Bertazzon, Isidoro, busta 551, Ministero dell'Interno to Italian Consulate-General, New York, 7 September 1917. Also, *Seattle Daily Times*, 27 November 1917.
28. Vincenzo Zaccagnini, Deferred Hearing, 7 December 1917, in: ACS-CPC, Bertazzon, Isidoro, busta 551.
29. ACS-CPC, Massullo Bartolomeo, busta 3143.
30. *Seattle Daily Times*, 27 November 1917.
31. Ibid.
32. ACS-CPC, Bertazzon, Isidoro, busta 551, Tritoni, Italian Consul-General, New York, to Ministero dell'Interno, 13 May 1918.
33. Achille Ricci, Deferred Hearing, 7 December 1917, in: ACS-CPC, Bertazzon, Isidoro, busta 551. Also, Giovanni Cavierno, Statement, 30 November 1917, in: ACS-CPC, Bertazzon, Isidoro, busta 551. Also, ACS-CPC, Bertazzon, Isidoro, busta 551, Tritoni, Italian Consul-General, New York, to Ministero dell'Interno, 13 May 1918.
34. Giovanni Cavierno, Deferred Hearing, 7 December 1917, in: ACS-CPC, Bertazzon, Isidoro, busta 551.
35. Titino Dentino, Deferred Hearing, 6 December 1917, in: ACS-CPC, Bertazzon, Isidoro, busta 551.
36. Vincenzo Zaccagnini, Deferred Hearing, 7 December 1917, in: ACS-CPC, Bertazzon, Isidoro, busta 551.
37. Giuseppe Bertolotti, Deferred Hearing, 10 December 1917, in: ACS-CPC, Bertazzon, Isidoro, busta 551.
38. Nicola Farro, Deferred Hearing, 13 December 1917, in: ACS-CPC, Bertazzon, Isidoro, busta 551.
39. Giovanni Morgando, Deferred Hearing, 8 December 1917, in: ACS-CPC, Bertazzon, Isidoro, busta 551.
40. Federico Catalini, Deferred Hearing, 1 December 1917, in: ACS-CPC, Bertazzon, Isidoro, busta 551.
41. Costantino D'Ascenco, Deferred Hearing, 7 December 1917, in: ACS-CPC, Bertazzon, Isidoro, busta 551.
42. Vittorio Zaccagnini, Statement, 28 November 1917, in: ACS-CPC, Bertazzon, Isidoro, busta 551.
43. *Seattle Daily Times*, 27 and 29 November 1917.

44. ACS-CPC, Bertazzon, Isidoro, busta 551, Tritoni to Ministero dell'Interno, 4 June and 13 May 1918.
45. *New York Times*, 12 February 1919.
46. Leonardo Bettini, *Bibliografia dell'anarchismo*, Vol. 1, Part 2, CP Editrice, Firenze 1976, p. 294n.
47. http://en.wikipedia.org/wiki/Emma_Goldman, accessed 8 August 2012. For a resume on this period, see: Robert K. Murray, 'L'Arca dei Bolscevichi', in: Anna Maria Martellone (Ed.), *La <questione> dell'immigrazione negli Stati Uniti, Il Mulino*, Bologna 1980, pp. 265-278. James Joll in his *The Anarchists* (p. 190) writes that "Emma Goldman and Alexander Berkman arrived in Russia as honoured guests and, although they had already had doubts about some of the activities of the Bolsheviks, they were as anxious to be impressed by the revolution as Kropotkin had been. However, they were increasingly worried and disappointed, and soon began to be an object of suspicion to the secret police".
48. National Archives of Australia, Canberra, Series A1, Control symbol 1918/15166, Exclusion of anarchists from USA (Deportation of anarchists from the USA), Home and Territoriers to Attorney-General's, 8 November 1918. Also: National Archives of Australia, Canberra, Series A456, Control symbol W26/241/46, Unrest in Queensland –Bolshevism, 'Sinn Fein' [Complaint re entry of 'Bolshevik anarchists' into Australia], G.W.T. Perry to Acting Prime Minister, 24 April 1919.
49. ACS-CPC, Bertazzon, Isidoro, busta 551, Tritoni, Italian Consul-General, New York, to Ministero dell'Interno, 26 February, 13 May and 10 July 1918.
50. ACS-CPC, Bertazzon, Isidoro, busta 551, Italian Consulate-General, New York, to Ministero dell'Interno, 8 Junne and 6 August 1920; Ministero dell'Interno to Italian Consulate-General, New York, 8 September 1920. Also: Rebecca Pixler, Assistant Archivist, King County Archives, Seattle, to Author, email dated 21 July 2012. Also: Zack Wilske, Historian, USCIS History Office, Records Division, ESD, to author, email dated 1 November 2012.
51. ACS-CPC, Bertazzon, Isidoro, busta 551, Prefetto of Treviso, biographical note dated 27 May 1929.
52. ACS-CPC, Bertazzon, Isidoro, busta 551, Prefetto of Treviso, biographical note dated 27 May 1929; Bollettino delle Ricerche, 11 August 1927, No.

4932. In 1929, Arturo Bocchini, Chief of Police, issued instructions to the Italian Consul in Melbourne to *intensificare misure attenta vigilanza persona noto anarchico Bertazzon Isidoro provvedendo telegrafiche segnalazioni ogni utile emergenza et eventuali spostamenti* (Ibid., Bocchini to Melbourne Consul, 18 December 1929).

53. ACS-CPC, Panizzon, Gaetano, busta 3699, fascic. 56631. Also, David Faber, 'The Italian Anarchist Press in Australia between the wars', in: *Italian Historical Society Journal*, Vol. 17, Melbourne 2009, p. 7n. Also: National Archives of Australia, Canberra, Item A12217, Control symbol L5822, Gaetano and Margherita Panizzon – Purchase of property North Geelong Vic. Also: National Archives of Australia, Melbourne, Series B741, Control symbol V/8005, Gaetano Panizzon and wife Margherita Panizzon.

54. National Archives of Australia – Passenger arrivals index, 1921-1939, barcode 30151512.

55. Nick Storino, 'My Carlton Years: Time of Austerity. 1937-1947', in: *Italian Historical Society Journal*, Vol. 19, Melbourne 2011, p. 7.

56. ACS-CPC, Bertazzon, Isidoro, busta 551, Grossardi to Ministero dell'Interno, Roma, 27 September 1927.

57. Ibid.

58. On this, see: Gianfranco Cresciani, *Fascism, Anti-Fascism and Italians in Australia. 1922-1945*, Australian National University Press, Canberra 1980, pp. 12-15.

59. On this, see: Gianfranco Cresciani, 'The Proletarian Migrants: Fascism and Italian Anarchists in Australia', in: *The Australian Quarterly*, Vol. 51, No. 1, March 1979, pp. 4-19.

60. National Archives of Australia, Canberra, CRS A373, item 3744, Security Service, Correspondence File, Single Number Series: [Anti-Fascists in Internment Camps], 1942-43, Report dated 29 October 1942.

61. Francesco Carmagnola, interview with Author, 18 September 1971.

62. Gianfranco Cresciani, *Fascism, Anti-Fascism and Italians in Australia. 1922-1945*, op. cit., pp. 101-102.

63. Francesco Carmagnola, interview with Author, 23 June 1978.

64. *Il Risveglio*, 1 July 1927.

65. National Archives of Australia, Canberra, Series A367, Control symbol

C1822G, "La Riscossa Libertaria" (Isidore Bartazzon) (sic), Investigation Branch Sydney to Investigation Branch, Canberra, handwritten note, 16 December 1927.

66. Ibid., Browne to Jones, 15 February 1928; Jones to Prime Minister's Department, 1 March 1928.
67. Fascism Exposed! To the Australian People and All Political Representatives, bilingual pamphlet printed by the Executive Committee of the Anti-Fascist Concentration of Australasia, Fraser & Jenkinson, Melbourne 1928. See also: Gianfranco Cresciani, *Fascism, Anti-Fascism and Italians in Australia. 1922-1945*, op. cit., pp. 230-231.
68. Copy of this issue obtained by the Author from the New York Public Library.
69. Copy of this issue is in: National Archives of Australia, Canberra, Series A367, Control symbol C1822F, "G. Matteotti".
70. Copy of this issue obtained by the Author from the Internationaal Instituut voor Sociale Geschiedenis, Amsterdam.
71. National Archives of Australia, Canberra, Series A367, Control symbol C1822F, "G. Matteotti", Browne to Jones, 19 July 1929; Jones to Secretary, Prime Minister's Department, 25 July 1929.
72. National Archives of Australia, Canberra, Series A367, Control symbol C1822E, "Germinal" and "In Memoria" – Italian Pamphlet, Carosi to Lloyd, 29 August 1929; Carosi to Browne, 18 September 1929.
73. Ibid., Jones to Secretary, Prime Minister's Department, 11 September 1929.
74. National Archives of Australia, Canberra, Series A367, Control symbol C1822O, Italian Publications – Information asked for by 6th Nov 1929 – In Memoria, La Riscossa, G. Matteotti, Germinal, Browne to Jones, 1 and 25 November 1929.
75. Ibid, Jones to Prime Minister's Department, 4 December 1929.
76. National Archives of Australia, Canberra, Series A367, Control symbol C1822R, "L'Avanguardia Libertaria" "La Riscossa", Strahan to Jones, 10 February 1931.
77. Ibid., Jones to Secretary, Prime Minister's Department, 17 February 1931.
78. Ibid., Strahan to Jones, 30 April 1931.

79. Ibid., Jones to Commonwealth Investigation Branch, Melbourne, 6 May 1931.
80. Archivio Centrale dello Stato, Ministero dell'Interno, Direzione Generale di Pubblica Sicurezza, Serie III-45, Anno 1930-31, busta 388, Categ. J4-1, Movimento sovversivo antifascista – Australia, Ministero degli Affari Esteri to Ministero dell'Interno, Telespresso, 30 July 1930.
81. Ibid., J. G. McLaren, Secretary, Department of External Affairs to Jones, 21 March 1932; Grossardi to J. E. Fenton, Postmaster-General, 8 February 1932; Jones to Secretary, Department of External Affairs, 29 April 1932.
82. Ibid., Browne to Jones, 18 April 1932.
83. Ibid., McLaren to Jones, 18 November 1932.
84. Ibid., Browne to Jones, 24 June 1930.
85. *La Riscossa*, 1 November 1930.
86. National Archives of Australia, Melbourne, Series B741, item V/6002, Alleged Prohibited Publication by Matteotti Committee, Secretary, Prime Minister's Department to Secretary, Attorney-General's Department, 10 December 1928; Jones to Browne, 17 January 1929; Senior Detective Herbert Sainsbury, Report, 7 February 1929; Browne to Jones, 8 February 1929.
87. Archivio Centrale dello Stato, Ministero dell'Interno, Direzione Generale di Pubblica Sicurezza, Serie III-45, Anno 1930-31, busta 388, Categ. J4-1, Movimento sovversivo antifascista – Australia, Grossardi to Ministero dell'Interno, 11 March 1930. See also: Gianfranco Cresciani, 'Refractory Migrants. Fascist Surveillance on Italians in Australia', op. cit.
88. Francesco Carmagnola, interview with Author, 18 September 1971.
89. *La Riscossa*, 9 August 1930.
90. Archivio Centrale dello Stato, Ministero dell'Interno, Direzione Generale di Pubblica Sicurezza, Serie III-45, Anno 1930-31, busta 388, Categ. J4-1, Movimento sovversivo antifascista – Australia, Grossardi to Ministero dell'Interno, 11 March 1930.
91. *La Riscossa*, 1 September 1930.
92. Ibid., 16 October 1930.
93. Ibid., 1 December 1930, 27 February 1931, 29 April 1931, 10 June 1931.
94. *L'Avanguardia Libertaria*, 1 and 15 November 1930.

95. Ibid., 22 April 1931 and 14 May 1931.
96. Francesco Carmagnola, interviews with Author, 18 September 1971 and 23 June 1978.
97. *L'Avanguardia Libertaria*, 15 August 1930.
98. Ibid., 14 May 1931.
99. Ibid., 14 June 1930.
100. Francesco Carmagnola, interview with Author, 23 June 1978.
101. *La Riscossa*, 1 December 1930.
102. *L'Avanguardia Libertaria*, 1 January 1932.
103. Ibid., 15 November and 1 December 1930.
104. Francesco Carmagnola, interviews with Author, 18 September 1971.
105. *L'Avanguardia Libertaria*, 31 January 1931.
106. *La Riscossa*, 10 June 1931; *Il Giornale Italiano*, 13 December 1933.
107. *L'Avanguardia Libertaria*, 14 June 1930.
108. Ibid., 1 September 1930.
109. Ibid., 1 October 1930.
110. Ibid., 8 July 1931.
111. Ibid., 11 September 1931.
112. Ibid., 1 January 1932.
113. Ibid., 1 June and 20 August 1932.
114. Mirrool No. 1 Irrigation Area, Irrigation Farm Lease Register, Farm 2187, Particulars of Holding, Isidoro Alessandro Bertazzon (Courtesy Robyn Manakis).
115. ACS-CPC, Bertazzon, Isidoro, busta 551, Elenco di connazionali maggiormente noti per le loro idee comuniste, 16 December 1933.
116. National Archives of Australia, Melbourne, Series B741, item V/4580, barcode 38190, Isidore Bertazzon "La Riscossa Libertaria", Victoria Police, CIB, Detective Const. Newton to Sub-Inspector Birch, 8 August 1940; Nick Storino, 'My Carlton Years: Time of Austerity. 1937-1947', in: *Italian Historical Society Journal*, Vol. 19, Melbourne 2011, p. 7.
117. ACS-CPC, Bertazzon, Isidoro, busta 551, Prefect of Treviso to CPC, 12 February 1939.

118. Ibid., Malatesta papers; Nominativi avuti confidenzialmente da un taccuino di indirizzi di Camillo Berneri.

119. Internationaal Instituut voor Sociale Geschiedenis, Amsterdam, Ugo Fedeli Papers, Inventory Number 553, Movimento Anarchico Australia, 1932. In the issue of 31 January 1931 of L'Avanguardia Libertaria, Bertazzon jokingly quipped that OVRA was the acronym for Opera Vendicatrice della Riscossa Antifascista (Organisation for Anti-Fascist Counterattack and Vengeance).

120. ACS-CPC, Bertazzon, Isidoro, busta 551, Prefetto of Treviso, biographical note dated 27 May 1929.

121. National Archives of Australia, Series MP707/1, item V4764, CIB Melbourne to Collector of Customs, 29 March 1928. Also: David Faber, 'The Italian Anarchist Press in Australia between the Wars', in: *Italian Historical Society Journal*, Vol. 17, 2009, p. 9.

122. ACS-CPC, Bertazzon, Isidoro, busta 551, Elenco di abbonati al libello antifascista Giustizia e Libertà.

123. Ibid., DGPS, Sezione Prima (Polpol) to CPC, Paris, 25 April 1933.

124. Ibid., 18 June 1929.

125. ACS, Ministero dell'Interno, Direzione Generale di Pubblica Sicurezza, Casellario Politico Centrale, busta 3772, fascic. 28052, Pastega Giacomo, Prefettura di Treviso, Cenno biografico, 31 January 1928; also, Ibid., Carosi to Grossardi, 28 June 1927. Also: National Archives of Australia, Canberra, Series A1, Control symbol 1930/3737, Giacomo Pastega – Naturalisation Certificate. Also: National Archives of Australia, Canberra, Series A261, Control symbol 1939/1457, Applicant – Pastega Giacomo; Nominee – Pastega Veronica; nationality Italian.

126. ACS, Ministero dell'Interno, Direzione Generale di Pubblica Sicurezza, Casellario Politico Centrale, busta1558, fascic. 17724, Cunial Angelo, Treviso's Prefect to Ministero dell'Interno, 23 December 1927.

127. ACS, Ministero dell'Interno, Direzione Generale di Pubblica Sicurezza, Casellario Politico Centrale, busta 3772, fascic. 28052, Pastega Giacomo, Pastega to Possagno's Podestà, 21 February 1931.

128. Ibid, Pastega to Tribunale Speciale per la Difesa dello Stato, 5 July 1932.

129. Ibid., Mammalella to Ministero dell'Interno, 26 April 1939.

130. ACS, Ministero dell'Interno, Direzione Generale di Pubblica Sicurezza,

Casellario Politico Centrale, busta 3699, fascic. 56631, Panizzon, Gaetano, Prefect of Vicenza to Grossardi, 27 May 1930.

131. ACS, Ministero dell'Interno, Direzione Generale di Pubblica Sicurezza, Casellario Politico Centrale, busta 184, fascic. 14013, Argenti Giacomo, Prefect of Livorno to Ministero dell'Interno, 15 December 1909.

132. Ibid.

133. ACS, Ministero dell'Interno, Direzione Generale di Pubblica Sicurezza, Casellario Politico Centrale, busta 3772, fascic. 28052, Pastega Giacomo, Carosi to Grossardi, 28 June 1927.

134. Francesco Carmagnola, interview with the Author, 23 June 1978.

135. *L'Avanguardia Libertaria*, 14 June 1930.

136. Archivio Centrale dello Stato, Ministero dell'Interno, Direzione Generale di Pubblica Sicurezza, Serie III-48, Sezione 1a, Anno 1933, busta 25, Categ. K1-B, Movimento comunista – Australia, Ministero degli Affari Esteri to Ministero dell'Interno, 4 March 1933.

137. ACS-CPC, Bertazzon, Isidoro, busta 551, Ministero degli Affari Esteri to Ministero dell'Interno, 19 November 1929.

138. Ibid., Luigi Buoninsegni Vitali to Ministero dell'Interno, 30 July 1935.

139. Ibid., Ernesto Arrighi to Ministero dell'Interno, 27 September 1937; Carmine Senise to Ministero degli Affari Esteri, 29 June 1937; Paolo Vita-Finzi to Ministero dell'Interno, 4 February 1937. See also: Paolo Vita Finzi, *Giorni lontani. Appunti e ricordi*, Il Mulino, Bologna 1989, p. 365.

140. National Archives of Australia, Canberra, Series A1, item 1924/22922, Pastiga Anglo [correct spelling Angelo Pastega].

141. ACS-CPC, busta 3772, fascic. 68201, Pastega Angelo, Ferrante to Ministero dell'Interno, 8 May 1934; Marocco to Ministero dell'Interno, 13 May 1937.

142. National Archives of Australia, Canberra, Series A12508, Control symbol 31/1473, Cunial Andrea Angelo. On Angelo Cunial, see: National Archives of Australia, Melbourne, Series MP1103/1, Control symbol Q8224, Prisoner of War/Internee: Cunial Angelo. Also: ACS, Ministero dell'Interno, Direzione Generale di Pubblica Sicurezza, Casellario Politico Centrale, busta 1558, fascic. 17724, Cunial Angelo.

143. ACS-CPC, busta 2917, fascic. 87471, Maggiani Umberto; busta 1960,

fascic. 122984, Farina Emilio.
144. Francesco Carmagnola, interview with Author, 23 June 1978.
145. Robyn Manakis, email to Author, 18 September 2012.
146. Ibid.
147. National Archives of Australia, Canberra, Series A12217, Control symbol L3109, Giovanni Franceschini, K. Cargill Rankin Solicitor to the Secretary, Attorney-General's Department, 16 April 1941.
148. National Archives of Australia, Canberra, Series B6531, Control symbol NATURALISED/1946-1947/ITALIAN/FRANCESCHINI BORIS.
149. National Archives of Australia, Canberra, Series A12217, Control symbol L3109, Giovanni Franceschini – purchase of property North Narre Warren near Dandenong Vic., Inspector Browne to Director, CIB Canberra, 2 June 1941. See also Gori Franceschini's obituary in *L'Internazionale*, May 1986, p. 4. This anarchist paper was founded in 1901 by Errico Malatesta.
150. Ibid.
151. See: *L'Avanguardia Libertaria*, 20 August 1932; *La Riscossa*, 10 February 1931.
152. ACS-CPC, Bertazzon, Isidoro, busta 551, Vaccari to CPC, 12 October 1934.
153. National Archives of Australia, Melbourne, Series B741, Control symbol V/4580, Isidore Bertazzon "La Riscossa Libertaria", Sargeant E. C. Ewen to Special C. I. Branch, Melbourne, 4 August 1940.
154. State Archives of New South Wales, Sydney, Item 1503 of 1940, Container 19/3648, Isidoro Bertazzon Inquest, October 1940. See also: National Archives of Australia, Sydney, Series C123, Control symbol 7738, Franceschini Bruna [Italian – born in USA] [Box 230].
155. National Archives of Australia, Canberra, Series A1401, Control symbol EPI302, Item barcode 4271961, Isadore Alessandro Bertazzon deceased, The Public Trustee Office to The Controller of Enemy Property, 8 October 1940; Ibid., 29 September 1943.
156. Jill Bortolotto, email to the Author, 12 September 2012.
157. James Joll, *The Anarchists*, op. cit., p. 174.
158. A. Nasalli Rocca, *Memorie di un Prefetto*, Casa Editrice Mediterranea, Roma 1946, p.235, cit. in: RJB Bosworth, Venice, manuscript, chapter 3.

Conclusion

The essays published in this book, on a wide range of topics and on issues barely researched in the past, attest to existence of many areas, yet to be studied, of the history of an Italian Australia and of diplomatic, cultural, political and economic exchanges between Italy and Australia. Relations between the two countries were asymmetrical because their national interests diverged, Italy historically looking towards Europe, while Australia's traditional ties were with the United Kingdom and, later, the USA and Asia. Despite the prevailing, spurious mythology of multiculturalism, people who emigrated to Australia from the many Italies, taking with them their vastly different values, found it difficult to be accepted as equal partners by a monocultural Anglo-Saxon society.

It is commonly accepted, almost as a matter of faith, that Italian migrants have "done well" in this country, have settled, have "integrated" after a long period of actual discrimination and unconscionable pressure to "assimilate". Data from the Australian Bureau of Statistics question the validity of the claim that, on the whole, Italian migrants did as well as mainstream Australians, although their economic situation Down Under was preferable to that of their friends and next-of-kin whom they left behind in their Italian villages. One of the reasons for this inequality could be found in the uneven power relationship between society at large and Italian minority groups. What were the reasons why people from disparate Italian regions did not act as "no longer exiled, but protagonists", as advocated by Carlo Levi, author of the book *Christ Stopped at Eboli* and founder of the Federation of Italian Migrants and their Families (FILEF)? Why did the plea, in June 1978, by the Chairman of the NSW Ethnic Affairs Commission, Paolo Totaro, to 'participate', mostly fall on deaf ears? It could be inferred that migrants and their community organisations were not eager, nor united, to wrestle from society what in the final analysis was due to them: equal rights, as well as responsibilities. This is not surprising, because being 'Italian', then as now, is not a set thing, nor a thing that is agreed between 'Italians'. Class and gender discrimination, domineering family ties, 'ethnic' patron-client bonds, isolation in self-imposed Little Italies, local and regional feuds and a poor standard of education, just to mention a few, were barriers to participation. Moreover, gloating over Mafia's and 'Ndrangheta's criminal deeds – a sad reality of Italy's contemporary history – by Australian commercial radio and television stations, and the stereotyping of Southern Italians in the press and in advertising, heightened the uncomfortable perception of being "the other", felt by migrants and their families.

Those who came to Australia during the 1950s and 1960s, before the so-called Italian economic miracle, were predominantly peasants from the South and from the Friuli and Veneto regions. They left a pre-industrial society, only to land in a country undergoing a rapid but uneven and derivative process of industrialisation. Their concept of *patria* often encompassed only their *paese* and the land around it that could be seen from the top of its *campanile* (hence the term *campanilismo)*. The rhythm of their life was regulated by the meagre daily meal of *pizza* (in the South) or *polenta* (in Friuli and the Veneto), the *prete* and his *processioni,* and an atavist distrust for the *padroni,* the State and its local representatives, the *Prefetto* and the *Carabinieri*. Political participation, the vocal assertion of their rights and collective unionism were not an experience they had shared in their geographically and socially limited world. Rather, exploitation, subservience and repression were the norm. Therefore, it is not surprising that they eschewed militancy, exposure and confrontation. When they did take a stand, as was the case for Bertazzon and his anarchist comrades, they were kept under surveillance, harassed, arrested and persecuted, be it in Italy, the United States or Australia.

Another reason for the failure of a more assertive attitude on the part of migrants lies in the fact that during the 1970s Italian mass emigration to Australia practically ceased. The young, militant people who had witnessed and taken part in the 1968 student revolt, some of them landing in Sydney and Melbourne during the 1970s, were too few to form a critical mass able to 'move' the bulk of Italian emigrants and to challenge the policies, behaviour and power of the ruling classes. Such radicalism as there was in Italy ran out after 1978 and would soon lead to the know-nothingism of *Berlusconismo*. Paradoxically, the success of the Italian economic miracle had drained Australia of educated, articulate and militant migrants who could carry forward the struggle for structural change.

As documented in the essays of this book, also diplomatic, economic and cultural relations between Italy and Australia were affected by this asymmetrical stance. They were conditioned by distance, ideology and national interest. Only the issue of migration brought the two nations, temporarily, to meaningfully speak to each other, at a time when Italy wanted to shed its surplus population and Australia desperately needed manpower. Yet, despite volumes written on the history of Italian emigration to Australia, only the surface has been scratched, and much more research needs to be done.

For instance, it would be interesting to study the files of the Migration Office at the Rome Embassy and those of the local ASIO station head, to ascertain the process of selection – and rejection – of prospective emigrants. What was the knowledge base of Australian bureaucrats, operating in a complex foreign world? It is known that Communists and members of the Mafia were targeted for exclusion. However, how successful was this process? Was it based only on political and ideological grounds, or was it also an attempt at social engineering? How successful was this screening process and how reliable was information supplied by the Italian *Carabinieri?* Not very accurate, to judge from the fact that many card-carrying Communists slipped through the net, among them Agostino Agresta, a member of the Italian Communist Party (PCI) since its foundation in 1921, and Mario Abbiezzi, a member since 1926. After all, it would have been a herculean task, beyond the resources and the will of Italian politicians, to screen all PCI members, numbering 1.5 million during the Cold War.

To date, research has not been carried out on the few Italian associations that were assertive in pursuing migrants' rights to education, welfare, political representation, employment and cultural and linguistic maintenance. One of these bodies, FILEF, some of its members being PCI cadres, was heavily infiltrated by ASIO agents. Its history is still access restricted in the files of this intelligence organisation. The bogey of a Communist fifth column was still alive during the 1970s, as evidenced by the fact that the May 1977 issue of *Quadrant* published a scaremongering article entitled, "Italian Communism at Home and Abroad: The New Class". Migrants' relations within the trade union movement, business enterprises, the public service, the universities, welfare organisations, political parties, the media and social clubs, are all largely untapped areas of research.

People who emigrated from the Italies failed to pull Australia's national culture in a direction more inclusive of their values and aspirations. The country was and to some extent still is crassly paying lip service to their 'contribution' of food and folklore. It seems, as Richard Bosworth is saying in the preface of this book, that Italians, be they migrants or not, "on some world hierarchy of significance ... did not [and do not] really matter" to Australians.

This book aims to put the emphasis on past lights and shadows in Italo-Australian relations, to document them and to stimulate others to research other aspects of this history of emigration, exchanges, aspirations and setbacks. Only in doing so, will the history of an Italian Australia matter.

Biographical Notes

Dr Karen Agutter is an historian of migration, particularly issues of migrant identity and host society reception, in Australia, Canada, and Great Britain. Her focus areas include the migrant experience at times of conflict and stress (e.g. World War One) and in regional areas including Broken Hill and the West Australian goldfields. Karen has been involved in a variety of interdisciplinary collaborative research projects on topics including migrant belongings and migrant ageing. Her current research is looking at the migrant experience in the post-World War Two migrant hostels as part of the ARC funded *Hostel Stories* project at the University of Adelaide.

Professor Richard J. B. Bosworth is an Australian historian and author, and a leading expert on Fascist Italy. He received his bachelor›s and master›s degrees from the University of Sydney before going on to doctoral study at St John's College, Cambridge. He taught at the University of Sydney and was Winthrop Professor of History at the University of Western Australia until his retirement in 2011. He is also a Senior Research Fellow at Jesus College, Oxford and held a professorship at the University of Reading from 2007 to 2012. He is a fellow of the Academy of the Social Sciences in Australia and of the Australian Academy of the Humanities.

Gianfranco Cresciani was born in Trieste, Italy and emigrated to Australia in 1962. He worked for Electric Power Transmission Pty Ltd, the Ethnic Affairs Commission and the Ministry for the Arts of the NSW government. In 1989 and 1994 he was a member of the Australian Delegation re-negotiating with the Italian government the Italo-Australian Cultural Agreement and obtained a Doctor of Letters, *honoris causa,* from the University of New South Wales in 2005. In 2004 the Italian government awarded him the honour of *Cavaliere*

Ufficiale dell'Ordine al Merito. Member of the Scientific Committee of the journal *Altreitalie*, published by the Centro Altreitalie, Turin, Italy. He has researched the history of Italian migration to Australia since 1971, and is the author of many books, articles, exhibitions, radio and television programs and web sites in Australia and Italy.

Dr. Catherine Dewhirst is Senior Lecturer in History at the University of Southern Queensland, Toowoomba. She has published on Italian migration history in the *Journal of Australian Studies*, *Parergon*, *Spunti e Ricerche* and *Studi Emigrazione*, with forthcoming articles in *Queensland History Journal* and *The Journal of Imperial and Commonwealth History*. She has co-edited a special *Spunti e Ricerche* edition of '150 Years of Italians in Queensland' and is current working on her book, *Diaspora Italy: Migrants of the Imperial Project, 1880-1920*, to be published by Ashgate.

Dr. Bruno Mascitelli is an Associate Professor in International Studies at the Swinburne University of Technology, Melbourne, Australia. Prior to joining Swinburne University, Bruno was employed by the Australian Consulate General in Milan for almost 18 years. He has published eleven books in areas including *Expatriate Voting in Italy* (2008, 2010, 2012, 2013), *The History of the Italian Newspaper in Australia: Il Globo* (2009) and *An introduction to the Italian Economy* (2010).

Gerardo Papalia is a specialist in the study of the history and culture of the Italian diaspora in Australia. He has studied and conducted research in both Australia and Italy. He is currently a Research Associate in Italian Studies at Monash University in Melbourne. His publications cover a wide range of disciplines including the history of relations between Italy and Australia, Italian and Australian cinema and diaspora literature.

Index

Aliens Act, 89, 92-93, 97, 101, 129
Alitalia, 28, 58, 61, 70, 197
Altro Polo, 54, 57, 59, 61, 64, 67, 71, 73, 76
Anarchism (Italian), 211-275
Andreotti G., 23, 47
Angeletti S., 21, 60, 64-66, 68-69
Anglo-Italian Treaty, 81, 83-84, 95, 105, 171, 182
Anzilotti E., 149-153, 155, 166
Asia (Asian and Asian century), xii, 3, 15, 23, 26, 76-77, 90, 148, 200, 203, 285
Austrade (Australian Trade Commission), 192-193
Australian Consulate (Milan), 22, 192-193
Australian Embassy (Rome), 20-21, 30, 43, 191-192
Australian Labor Party (ALP), 15-16, 23, 27, 57, 135-136, 155-156, 163-164, 167, 172, 178, 242, 246
Australian Legation (Rome), 19, 43

Baccarini A., 42, 188-189
Baracchi P., 42, 180
Belgiorno-Nettis F., 44, 61, 70
Belgium, 63
Berlusconi S., xii, 287

Bertazzon I. A., xii, 211-274
Boer War, 13
Bonegilla (Immigration reception centre), 19
Bossi U., 40
Bosworth R., iii, ix, 6, 8, 54, 57-58, 60, 64-67, 72, 74-76, 212, 288
Britain (Great), x, xiii, 3-4, 7, 9-10, 13, 17, 23, 26, 83-84, 86-89, 93, 100-101, 115-116, 119-120, 146-147, 149-151, 155, 161-162, 166, 170-172
Bruce S. M., 148, 151, 155, 163-166, 170, 242, 244, 246

Calwell A., 16-17
Canada, 6-7, 32, 56, 69, 115, 120, 141, 200-201, 220, 226, 235
Carr B., 48, 69, 103
Carr E. H., 103
Casellario Politico Centrale (CPC), 214-215, 219, 224, 228, 235-237, 255, 259, 262-264, 268
Cassamarca Foundation in Australia, 50
Catholicism (Australian), 14, 28, 63
Christian Democratic Party (DC), 2, 14
Chifley B., 15-17
China, 23, 33, 47, 149, 162, 178-179, 201-202

Cipriani A., 211, 255
COASIT (*Comitato Assistenza agli Italiani*), 20, 22, 50, 181
Cold War, 2-3, 14, 22, 288
Commonwealth, 10, 40, 44, 65-66, 84, 87, 89, 91, 95, 100, 116, 127, 129, 148, 151, 153-154, 166-167, 170-171, 186, 241, 243, 245-246, 249
Communist Party of Australia (CPA), 57, 243, 247, 259
Corriere della Sera, 63, 71
Corte P., 3
Cossiga F., 47, 52
Costello P., 26
Cresciani G. Xii, 9, 11, 39, 48-49, 54-57, 60-62, 65-66, 72, 74, 76, 85-86, 91-92, 122, 145, 189-190, 211, 289
Cronaca Sovversiva, 218, 223-225, 228, 230-231, 259
Curtin J., 10, 154-155

Da Rin E., 21, 69, 71
Dante Alighieri, 3, 11
De Gasperi A., 14, 17, 73
Del Drago A., 11
Democratic Labour Party, 27
De Nardis F., 45-46
Department of Foreign Affairs and Trade (DFAT), 25, 29, 32, 177, 192, 196, 199
Dini L., 48, 52

Downer A.,52

Electric Power Transmission Co., 55, 58, 198
Eles E., xiii, 117-121, 124, 126-135, 137-142
ENI, 197
Ethiopia (Italian-Ethiopian war), xiii, 68, 86, 146-147, 149-152, 155, 157-158, 163, 166-167, 171, 263, 264
European Union (EU) European Economic Community, 23, 25, 178, 186, 204, 212
Evatt Dr., 14-15

Fascism (fascist), xi, 8-9, 42, 55-57, 59-60, 67, 145, 190, 212, 215, 239-241, 244, 246, 249-250, 253-254, 256, 260, 262-265, 272-273
Ferrante M.A., 97, 100, 103, 263
FIAT, 197-198
FILEF, (Federation of Italian Migrant Workers and Families), 57, 285, 288
France (French), x, 9, 25-26, 33, 68, 83, 120, 167, 178, 185-186, 200-201, 203, 211-212, 218
Fraser L., 51
Fraser M., x, 51, 60, 75
Genova (Genoa-Migration processing office), 20
Germany, 8-10, 13, 25-26, 33, 68,

83, 116, 118, 121, 147, 157, 159, 167-168, 178, 185-186, 199, 201, 203
Gobbo J., 20
Goldman E., 221, 224, 234
Gorton J., 23
Grandi D., 163
Grassby A., 27
Greece (Greek), 68
Grollo (Rino and Bruno), 50-51
Grossardi A., 148, 150, 159, 238-239, 241-243, 248-251, 263

Hickey B., 44-45
Howard J., (Howard government), 26

Il Giornale Italiano, 190
Il Globo, 22, 24, 28, 75, 181, 194
Il Libertario, 224-225, 232-233, 259, 261
Il Risveglio, 54, 239-242, 244, 246, 264
Italian Chamber of Commerce, 84, 186-188, 191, 207-209
Italian Community, 17-18, 20, 22, 24, 29, 31-32, 59, 64, 71, 76, 101, 120-121, 128, 139, 141, 180, 190, 203-204, 222, 245, 267
Italian expatriate voting, 32-33, 76
Italian Socialists (socialists), 8, 56, 214, 238, 241-244, 253

IVECO, 197-198

Jupp J., 27-28

Keating P., x, 26

La Fiamma, 22, 28
La Questione Sociale, 218
Lang J. (faction), 154-156, 164-165, 254
Lazzarini P., 27, 155, 165
League of Nations, 8-9, 86, 146-148, 150-151, 153, 165, 170,
Letters from Rome, 157, 169
Lowy Institute, x, 20, 33
Lyons J., 95, 98, 103, 105, 147, 151, 154, 161, 167, 170-171, 248

Malatesta E., 211, 213, 218, 254, 258, 260-261
Marshall Plan, 14
Marx K. (Marxism), 56, 75, 211
Massullo B., 223-226, 228, 230
May Frederick (Foundation), xii, 39, 49, 53-54, 59-61, 64-6, 70-4, 76
McGuire P., 19-21, 43, 191
Melocco Brothers P. & A., 190
Menzies R., 4, 9-10, 17
Messina ("Milan of the south"), 20, 58, 117

Messina earthquake, 58, 117
Morgando G., 228-229, 231,
Moro A., 23-25, 43
Mussolini Benito, xiii, 8-9, 40.43, 56,67, 145-146, 148, 161, 189, 238, 240, 243-244, 246, 248, 254, 260-261, 270

NATO, 14
Nazism, ix, 158, 212
Northern League, 40
NSW government, 49, 62, 68, 70-71

OECD, 177
O'Grady D., 44

Ottawa Agreement, 182
OVRA (Italian fascists secret service), 258

Papal visits to Australia, 52
Parmalat, 197
Partito Comunista Italiano (PCI), 2, 14, 16, 23, 264, 287-288
Pesman R., 6, 54, 58, 61, 66, 73
Piano R., 46
Pirelli, 57, 197-198
POW (Prisoner of war), 12,
Prysmian, 198

Qantas, 29

Randazzo N., 24-25, 122, 194
Rizzo G., 53-55, 58-59, 61, 64, 67-68, 71-74, 76
Romano S., 47, 60-1, 64, 69, 71
Rosoli G., 48, 63
Rossi M., 189
Rudd K., (Rudd government), 178

Sacco & Vanzetti, 238, 240, 244, 254, 256-257, 260, 271
Salteri C. & R., 54
Santamaria B., 27
Saragat G., 20, 22, 52, 192
Schiassi O., 42, 242-243
Sister (twin) city arrangements, 30, 49
SMEs (small medium enterprises), 199
Snowy Mountains Hydro-Electric Scheme, 18
Spender J., 47
Steele R., iii, 21, 29-33, 47, 181-182, 192
Stirling A., 20-21
Sydney Morning Herald, 44, 125, 170

The Australian, 24-25
The Bulletin, 121, 156-163, 168-170
The Economist, xii
The Labour Daily, 151, 156, 159-163, 168-169

Totaro P., iii, 197, 285
Trambaiolo S., 53-54, 72-73
Transfield, 44, 54, 61-62, 198
Tresca C., 221
Trieste, 20, 57, 235, 289

UN (United Nations), 15, 30
USA, 69, 201, 218, 221, 224, 262, 266, 285
USSR (former Soviet Union), 14-15, 47, 69, 234, 255

Vaccari G., 50, 70, 181
Vatican (The), 2, 28, 44
Vita-Finzi P., 149-150, 153, 155-167, 169-170
Vitali B., 151-152, 155, 263
Vitetti L., 103-104

Whitlam G., x, 23-24, 27, 43-44, 59-60, 63, 75
White Australia Policy, 6, 23, 81, 90, 148
Wobblies, 221-222
Wool, 20, 40, 157, 159, 161-162, 168-170, 179, 182, 191, 194, 196, 200
Woolcott R., 24
World Trade Organization, 177

Zampatti C., 47

www.ingramcontent.com/pod-product-compliance
Lightning Source LLC
Chambersburg PA
CBHW032018230426
43671CB00005B/129